Key Stage Three
Science
Foundation Level

KS3 Science can be pretty challenging, but don't hang up your lab coat just yet — this brilliant CGP book will help you get to grips with everything you need.

It's packed with crystal-clear notes and diagrams covering all the most important topics, so it's perfect if you're working at a foundation level. We've also included plenty of practice questions and mixed-topic tests to help you check how you're getting on.

There's even a final practice exam that'll *really* put your Science knowledge to the test!

How to access your free Online Edition

This book includes a free Online Edition to read on your PC, Mac or tablet. You'll just need to go to **cgpbooks.co.uk/extras** and enter this code:

0144 9553 8188 066A

By the way, this code only works for one person. If somebody else has used this book before you, they might have already claimed the Online Edition.

Complete
Revision & Practice
<u>Everything</u> you need for the whole course!

Contents

Published by CGP

From original material by Richard Parsons and Paddy Gannon.

Editors:
Alex Billings, Emma Clayton, Sharon Keeley-Holden, Duncan Lindsay and Ethan Starmer-Jones.

Contributors:
Josephine Horlock and Lucy Muncaster.

ISBN: 978 1 78908 067 4

With thanks to Jamie Sinclair, Hayley Thompson and Karen Wells for the proofreading.
With thanks to Ana Pungartnik for the copyright research.

Printed by Elanders Ltd, Newcastle upon Tyne.
Clipart from Corel®
Illustrations by: Sandy Gardner Artist, email sandy@sandygardner.co.uk

The Microscope

A microscope is used to look at objects that are <u>too small</u> for you to see normally.
The microscope <u>magnifies</u> the objects (makes them <u>look bigger</u>) so that you can <u>see them</u>.

Learn the Different Parts of a Microscope

This is a microscope:

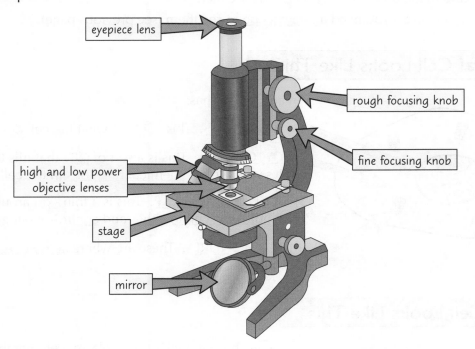

eyepiece lens

rough focusing knob

fine focusing knob

high and low power objective lenses

stage

mirror

Follow These Easy Steps to Using a Microscope

1) Place your microscope near a <u>lamp</u> or a <u>window</u>.
2) Move the mirror so light shines up through the <u>hole</u> in the stage.
3) Get your <u>slide</u> — it should have the object you want to look at <u>stuck to it</u>.
4) Clip your slide to the <u>stage</u>.
5) Select the <u>lowest</u> powered <u>objective lens</u> (the <u>shortest</u> one).

6) <u>Turn</u> the <u>rough focusing knob</u> to move the <u>objective lens</u> down. Stop when the lens is just above the slide.
7) <u>Look down</u> the <u>eyepiece lens</u>.
8) You want to see a <u>clear image</u> of whatever's on the slide. Turn the <u>fine focusing knob</u> until this happens.

9) If you need to make the image bigger, use a <u>higher powered objective lens</u> (a longer one).
10) Now refocus the microscope (repeat steps 6 to 8).

Microscopes are great for looking at cells

A microscope lets you see all the <u>tiny building blocks</u> (called <u>cells</u>) that make up living things. Choosing the correct equipment and using it safely is a key part of being a scientist.

Cells

This page is all about what living things are <u>made of</u>. And that includes <u>you</u>.

Living Things are Made of Cells

1) Another word for a <u>living thing</u> is an <u>ORGANISM</u>.
2) <u>All organisms</u> are made up of <u>tiny building blocks</u> called <u>cells</u>.
3) Cells are <u>really small</u>. So you need a <u>microscope</u> to see them (see previous page).

An Animal Cell Looks Like This...

An <u>animal cell</u> has:

1) A <u>NUCLEUS</u>. This <u>controls</u> what the cell <u>does</u>.
2) <u>CYTOPLASM</u>. This is a sort of <u>jelly</u> that fills the cell. It's where most <u>chemical reactions</u> in the cell happen.
3) A <u>CELL MEMBRANE</u>. This is a thin <u>skin</u> around the cell. It <u>holds the cell together</u> and <u>controls</u> what goes <u>in and out</u>.
4) <u>MITOCHONDRIA</u>. These are where <u>aerobic respiration</u> happens. See page 4.

A Plant Cell Looks Like This...

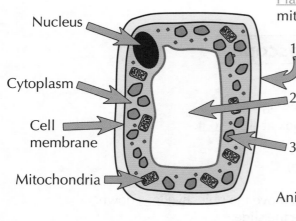

Nucleus
Cytoplasm
Cell membrane
Mitochondria

<u>Plant cells</u> have a nucleus, cytoplasm, cell membrane and mitochondria — just like animal cells. But plant cells <u>also have</u>:

1) A <u>CELL WALL</u>. This is a stiff <u>outer layer</u> around the cell membrane. It <u>supports</u> the cell.
2) A <u>VACUOLE</u>. This is filled with <u>cell sap</u>. Cell sap is a liquid containing sugar and salts.
3) <u>CHLOROPLASTS</u>. These are where <u>photosynthesis</u> happens. See page 31.

Animal cells <u>DO NOT</u> have a cell wall, a vacuole or chloroplasts.

Some Living Things Only Have One Cell

1) <u>Animals</u> and <u>plants</u> are made up of <u>lots of cells</u>. They're <u>multicellular</u> organisms.
2) But many living things <u>only have one cell</u>. These are called <u>UNICELLULAR organisms</u>.

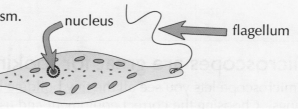

multicellular organism

- A <u>Euglena</u> is a <u>type</u> of unicellular organism. This is a Euglena.
- A Euglena lives in <u>water</u>.
- It has a '<u>tail</u>' called a <u>flagellum</u>. This helps it to <u>swim</u>.

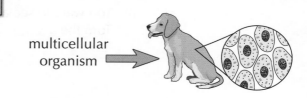

nucleus

flagellum

Cell Organisation and Diffusion

The great thing about cells is that they're always organised.

Cells are **Organised**

In organisms with lots of cells, the cells are organised (sorted) into groups. Here's how:

1) A group of similar cells work together to make a tissue.
2) A group of different tissues work together to make an organ.
3) A group of organs work together to make an organ system.
4) A multicellular organism is usually made up of several organ systems.

Here's an example from a plant.

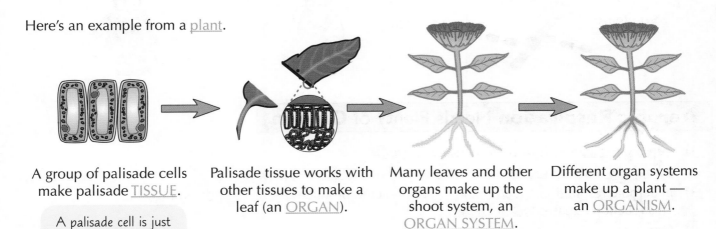

A group of palisade cells make palisade TISSUE.

A palisade cell is just a type of plant cell.

Palisade tissue works with other tissues to make a leaf (an ORGAN).

Many leaves and other organs make up the shoot system, an ORGAN SYSTEM.

Different organ systems make up a plant — an ORGANISM.

Stuff **Moves Into** and **Out of** Cells by **Diffusion**

1) Substances move into or out of cells by a process called diffusion.
2) Diffusion is where stuff moves from where there's lots of it to where there's less of it. Just like glucose in this diagram...

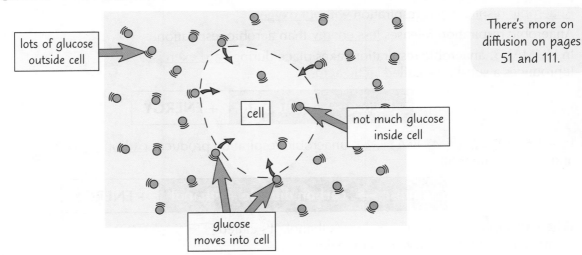

lots of glucose outside cell

cell

not much glucose inside cell

glucose moves into cell

There's more on diffusion on pages 51 and 111.

Cells are the building blocks of organisms

Remember: cells → tissues → organs → organ systems → organisms. You need to get your head around diffusion too — it comes up all the time in KS3 science, so it's worth getting to grips with now.

Respiration

Respiration is important. Without it you wouldn't have energy to do stuff, like learning KS3 science...

Respiration is a Chemical Reaction

1) In a chemical reaction one or more 'old' substances get changed into new ones.
   The old substances are called reactants. The new substances are called products. See page 71.
2) Respiration is a chemical reaction. It happens in every cell.
3) Respiration changes glucose (a sugar) into new substances. This releases energy.
4) The energy released by respiration is used for just about everything. For example:

building
proteins

using your
muscles

keeping
warm

Aerobic Respiration Needs Plenty of Oxygen

1) Aerobic respiration is respiration using oxygen.
2) It happens in the mitochondria of animal and plant cells (see page 2).
3) In aerobic respiration, glucose and oxygen react to produce carbon dioxide and water.
   This reaction releases lots of energy.
4) Here's a word equation to show what happens:

> The white arrow in the word equation shows that glucose and oxygen change into carbon dioxide and water.

| glucose + oxygen ➡ carbon dioxide + water | + ENERGY |

These are the reactants.   These are the products.

Anaerobic Respiration Takes Place Without Oxygen

1) Anaerobic respiration is respiration without oxygen.
2) Anaerobic respiration releases less energy than aerobic respiration.
3) In HUMANS, anaerobic respiration takes place during hard exercise.
   It produces a substance called lactic acid.

| glucose ➡ lactic acid | + ENERGY |

4) In MICROORGANISMS like YEAST, anaerobic respiration produces carbon dioxide and ethanol (alcohol):

| glucose ➡ carbon dioxide + ethanol | + ENERGY |

5) When anaerobic respiration produces ethanol, it's called FERMENTATION.
   Fermentation is the process used to make beer.

There are two types of respiration — learn the difference

It can be tricky to get your head around respiration, but it just means turning glucose into energy. Make sure you've learnt those equations — cover the book and write them down.

Warm-Up and Practice Questions

Take a deep breath then ease yourself in gently with these warm-up questions. Then have a go at the practice questions. All the answers are somewhere in this section, so there are no excuses.

Warm-Up Questions

1) What is a microscope used for?

2) True or false? Most of the chemical reactions in a cell take place in the cytoplasm.

3) Name two structures that are found in both plant and animal cells.

4) What is the difference between a tissue and an organ?

5) What is the name of the process where a substance moves from an area where there is lots of it to an area where there's less of it?

6) What is released in every respiration reaction?

7) True or false? Anaerobic respiration involves oxygen.

Practice Questions

1   The diagram below shows a plant cell.

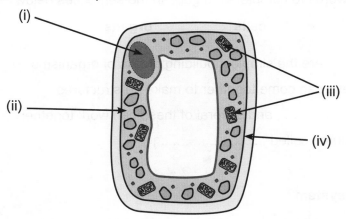

(a) Name the cell parts labelled **(i)-(iv)** on the diagram. Use the words from the box.

cell membrane	nucleus	cytoplasm	mitochondria

(4 marks)

(b) What is the cell wall used for? Tick **one** box.

☐ It gives support to the plant cell.

☐ It controls what the plant cell does.

☐ It contains cell sap.

(1 mark)

(c) Some organisms are made up of only one cell.
What word describes organisms that have only one cell?

(1 mark)

Practice Questions

2   Respiration is a very important life process for all organisms.

   (a)   In which part of animal and plant cells does **aerobic** respiration take place?
         Tick **one** box.

   ☐ nucleus   ☐ vacuole

   ☐ mitochondria   ☐ cytoplasm

(1 mark)

   (b)   Sometimes respiration does not involve oxygen.

         (i)   Which sort of respiration does **not** involve oxygen?

(1 mark)

         (ii)   Complete the word equation for this process when it occurs in **humans**.

                glucose → _____ + energy

(1 mark)

         (iii) Give **one** example of an activity that might cause a human to start respiring
                in this way.

(1 mark)

3   (a)   Use the following words to complete the gaps in the sentences below.

         tissues   **cells**   **organs**

         .... are the simplest building blocks of organisms.

         Several of these can come together to make up structures

         called .... , and several of these can work together

         to make structures called ....

(3 marks)

   (b)   What is an **organ system**?

(1 mark)

4   Alana's class are investigating the cells in onion skin using light microscopes.
     Alana collects a microscope from the teacher and places it near a window.

   (a)   Alana puts a piece of onion skin on a slide. She then clips the slide to the stage.
         Alana wants to get a clear image of the onion cells. Some of the steps she should
         take are shown below. Put the steps Alana should take in the correct order.

         •   look down the eyepiece lens
         •   adjust the fine focusing knob
         •   select the lowest powered objective lens
         •   adjust the rough focusing knob until the lens is just above the slide

(3 marks)

   (b)   Alana would like to make the image of the onion cells bigger.
         Describe how she can do this.

(2 marks)

Revision Summary for Section One

Welcome to your very first Revision Summary. It's full of questions that will help you find out what you actually know — and, more importantly, what you don't. Here's what you have to do...

- Go through the whole lot of these Revision Summary questions and try to answer them.
- Look up the answers to any you can't do and try to really learn them
  (hint: the answers are all somewhere in Section One).
- Try all the questions again to see if you can answer more than you could before.
- Keep going till you get them all right.

1) What part of a microscope do you clip your slide onto? ☑
2) What do the focusing knobs on a microscope do? ☑
3) What is an organism? ☑
4) What piece of equipment would you use to look at a cell? ☑
5) Name two structures that are only found in plant cells. Say what they both do. ☑
6) True or false? Plants are multicellular organisms. ☑
7) What is a unicellular organism? ☑
8) Explain the meaning of: a) tissue   b) organ c) organ system. ☑
9) What is diffusion? ☑
10) Give an example of a substance that moves into or out of cells by diffusion. ☑
11) What's the name of the chemical reaction that goes on in every cell and releases energy? ☑
12) What is the energy released by this reaction used for? Give three examples. ☑
13) What is aerobic respiration? ☑
14) What are the products of aerobic respiration? ☑
15) What is anaerobic respiration? ☑
16) What are the products of anaerobic respiration in yeast? ☑
17) What is fermentation? What can fermentation be used to make? ☑

Nutrition

Nutrition is <u>what you eat</u> — and what you eat is really <u>important</u> for your <u>health</u>.

A **Balanced Diet** Contains All These Things

A <u>balanced diet</u> will have the right amount of the <u>five nutrients</u> below:

Nutrient	What it's found in	What it's needed for
Carbohydrates	Bread, potatoes, cereals	You need <u>lots</u> of carbohydrate if you're <u>active</u> or <u>growing</u>. Energy
Proteins	Meat, eggs, fish	You need proteins to <u>grow</u> and to <u>repair</u> damage.
Lipids (fats and oils)	Butter, cooking oil, cream	You use lipids for energy if your body <u>runs out</u> of <u>carbohydrates</u>. Energy
Vitamins e.g. Vitamin A, Vitamin C	Vegetables, fruit, cereals	Vitamins keep many <u>important</u> <u>processes</u> happening in your body.
Minerals e.g. calcium, iron	For example: • <u>calcium</u> is found in milk, • <u>iron</u> is found in meat.	<u>Minerals</u> are needed for lots of things. For example: • <u>calcium</u> is needed for strong <u>bones</u> and <u>teeth</u>, • <u>iron</u> is needed for healthy <u>blood</u>.

A <u>balanced diet</u> will also have enough <u>fibre</u> and <u>water</u>:

	What it's found in	What it's needed for
Fibre	Vegetables, fruit, cereals	Fibre helps food <u>move</u> through your <u>digestive system</u>.
Water	Drinks, watery foods like soup	All the <u>chemical reactions</u> in your body happen in water.

More on Nutrition

Your body needs energy all the time. You get energy from carbohydrates and fats in your diet.

Different People Have Different **Energy Needs**

1) The heavier you are, the more energy you will need.
2) Also, the more active you are, the more energy you will need.

You Can **Work Out** Your **Daily Basic Energy Requirement**

1) Your daily basic energy requirement (BER) is the energy you need every day just to stay alive.

2) You calculate BER like this:

Daily BER (kJ/day) = 5.4 × 24 hours × body mass (kg)

A kJ is a unit of energy.

Example: Work out the daily BER for a 60 kg person.
Answer: Daily BER = 5.4 × 24 × 60 = 7776 kJ/day.

You Need **Extra Energy** for Your **Activities**

For example:

Walking for half an hour uses 400 kJ of energy.

Running for half an hour uses 1500 kJ of energy.

The total amount of energy you need in a day = daily BER + extra energy for activities.

An **Unbalanced Diet** Can Cause **Health Problems**

Obesity

1) If you take in more energy than you use up, you will put on weight.
2) Over time you could become obese (very overweight).
3) Obesity can lead to health problems such as heart disease.

Starvation

1) Some people don't get enough food to eat — this is starvation.
2) Starvation can cause slow growth in children and irregular periods in women.

Deficiency Diseases

1) Some people don't get enough vitamins or minerals — this can cause deficiency diseases.
2) For example, not getting enough vitamin C can cause scurvy.
    This is a deficiency disease that causes problems with the skin and gums.

Digestion

Digestion is all about breaking food down so we can use the nutrients it contains.
But it's not easy — lots of different organs have to work together to get the job done.

There are **Two Steps** to **Digestion**

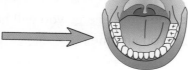

1) MECHANICAL digestion, e.g. chewing with teeth:

2) CHEMICAL digestion — this uses enzymes.
Enzymes are biological catalysts — this means they speed up chemical reactions in the body.

Your **Digestive System** is Where **Digestion Happens**

There are seven bits of the digestive system you need to learn:

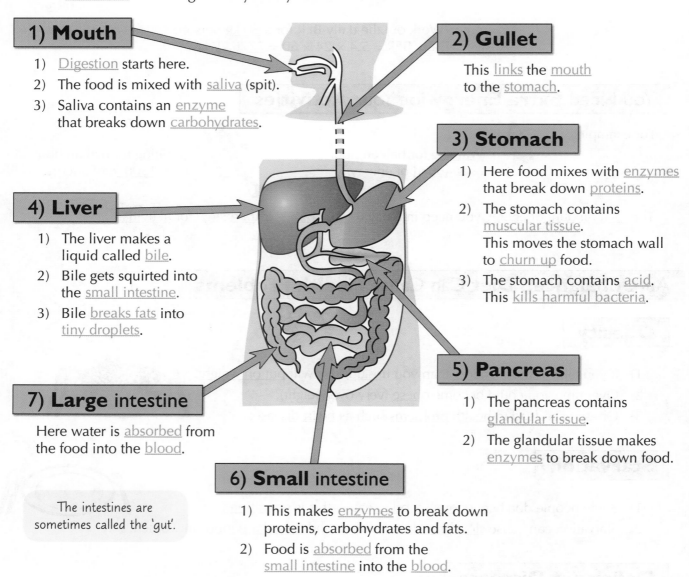

1) **Mouth**

1) Digestion starts here.
2) The food is mixed with saliva (spit).
3) Saliva contains an enzyme that breaks down carbohydrates.

2) **Gullet**

This links the mouth to the stomach.

3) **Stomach**

1) Here food mixes with enzymes that break down proteins.
2) The stomach contains muscular tissue. This moves the stomach wall to churn up food.
3) The stomach contains acid. This kills harmful bacteria.

4) **Liver**

1) The liver makes a liquid called bile.
2) Bile gets squirted into the small intestine.
3) Bile breaks fats into tiny droplets.

5) **Pancreas**

1) The pancreas contains glandular tissue.
2) The glandular tissue makes enzymes to break down food.

7) **Large** intestine

Here water is absorbed from the food into the blood.

The intestines are sometimes called the 'gut'.

6) **Small** intestine

1) This makes enzymes to break down proteins, carbohydrates and fats.
2) Food is absorbed from the small intestine into the blood.

We break down food using our digestive system

The digestive system is made up of several different organs all working together — so it's a great example of an organ system. Look back at page 3 if you need a reminder about organ systems.

More on Digestion

Well <u>would you believe it</u>? There's more to learn about digestion.

Food Molecules Get Absorbed in the Small Intestine

1) <u>Big</u> food molecules <u>can't</u> fit through the <u>small intestine wall</u>.

2) So enzymes <u>break up</u> the <u>big molecules</u> into <u>smaller molecules</u>.

3) The small molecules <u>pass through</u> the small intestine wall into the <u>blood</u>.

4) They then travel round the body in the <u>blood</u> to <u>body cells</u>, where they are used.

Absorbed means 'taken in'.

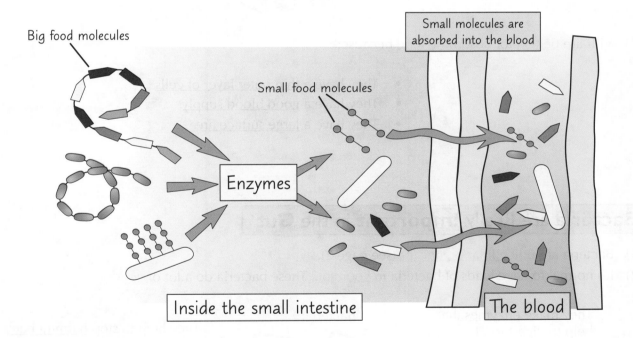

You need to absorb all of these facts

Phew, two pages on digestion down, one more to go. Make sure you're happy with everything on the last two pages before moving on. Check you understand both diagrams, and that you know the <u>name</u> and <u>function</u> of all <u>seven</u> bits of the <u>digestive system</u>. To test yourself, cover up these pages and draw the diagrams showing how food is digested. Include as much detail as you can remember, and keep trying until you can do it all from memory.

More on Digestion

More on digestion — don't worry, it's the last page on it, I promise. (Apart from the questions, anyway...)

The **Small Intestine** is Covered with **Millions** of **Villi**

1) The small intestine is lined with tiny <u>finger-like projections</u> (bits that stick out).
2) These are called <u>VILLI</u>.

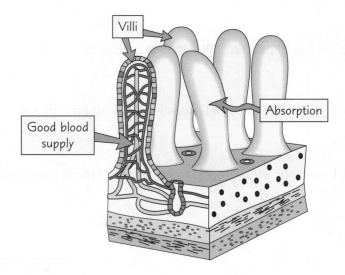

Villi

Good blood supply

Absorption

3) Villi are <u>perfect</u> for <u>absorbing food</u> because:

- They have a <u>thin outer layer of cells</u>.
- They have a <u>good blood supply</u>.
- They have a <u>large surface area</u>.

Bacteria are Really **Important** in the **Gut**

1) Bacteria are <u>unicellular organisms</u> (see page 2).
2) It's normal to have loads of bacteria in <u>your gut</u>. These bacteria do a lot of <u>good</u>:

They make <u>enzymes</u> that help to digest food.

<u>Bacteria</u>:

They help to stop <u>harmful bacteria</u> growing in your intestines. Harmful bacteria can make you <u>ill</u>.

They make <u>useful vitamins</u>.

Villi may look funny, but they do an important job

Villi are brilliant absorbers of food. Make sure you know the <u>three</u> things that make villi so great at doing this — their <u>large surface area</u>, their <u>blood supply</u> and their <u>thin outer layer of cells</u>.

Warm-Up and Practice Questions

When you've digested all that information, have a crack at these questions to test what you know.

Warm-Up Questions

1) Name one nutrient that the body gets energy from.

2) Name one type of food that contains fibre.

3) What does BER stand for?

4) What health risk is caused by taking in more energy than you use up?

5) Name one type of digestion.

6) Which part of the body does digestion start in?

7) What do enzymes do to large molecules of food?

8) True or false? Bacteria make useful vitamins in the gut.

Practice Question

1 The diagram shows some of the organs of the human digestive system.

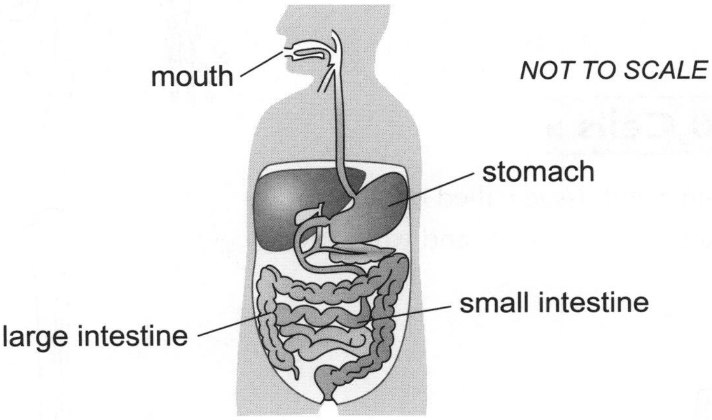

mouth

NOT TO SCALE

stomach

small intestine

large intestine

(a) Draw a line pointing to the gullet and label it **G**.

(1 mark)

(b) The small intestine contains villi, which are used to absorb food.
Which of the following statements about villi are **true**? Tick **two** boxes.

[ ] They have a small surface area.　　[ ] They have a thin outer layer of cells.

[ ] They have a good blood supply.　　[ ] They make enzymes to digest food.

(2 marks)

(c) What is the name of the organ that produces bile? Tick **one** box.

[ ] pancreas　　　[ ] large intestine　　　[ ] liver

(1 mark)

(d) Why does the stomach contain acid?

(1 mark)

The Skeleton

Your skeleton is really important. For one thing, it lets you stand up.

The **Skeleton** Has **Four Main Jobs**

All the bones in your body make up your skeleton.
The skeleton's jobs are:

1) **Protection**

1) Bone is tough, so it can protect organs.
2) For example, the skull protects the brain.

2) **Support**

1) Bones are rigid (they can't bend).
2) This means they can support the rest of
   the body — which lets us stand up.

3) Making **Blood Cells**

1) Many bones contain a soft tissue called bone marrow.
2) Bone marrow makes red blood cells and white blood cells.

4) **Movement**

1) Muscles are attached to bones.
2) The action of muscles lets the skeleton move.

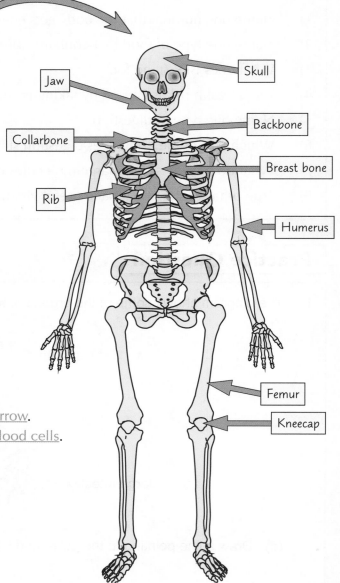

Skull

Jaw

Backbone

Collarbone

Breast bone

Rib

Humerus

Femur

Kneecap

A body without bones? Ever seen a tent without poles?

Lots of bone-tinglingly exciting facts to learn here. You don't need to learn the names of all
those bones — the main thing here is to learn what it is that the skeleton actually does.
The skeleton has four main jobs. Cover up the page and jot them all down.

Muscles

If you want to be able to walk or pick something up, you need more than just a skeleton. That's where muscles come in. Muscles and the skeleton work together so that you can move around.

Muscles Move Bones

1) Muscles are attached to bones with tough bands called tendons.
2) When a muscle contracts (tightens) it pulls the bone it's attached to.
3) This applies a force to the bone, which can be measured.
4) It also makes the bone move.

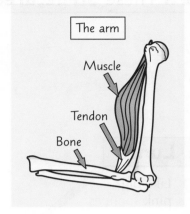

The arm

Muscle

Tendon

Bone

Antagonistic Muscles Work in Pairs

1) Antagonistic muscles are pairs of muscles that work against each other.
2) When one muscle in the pair contracts, the other one relaxes.
3) For example, the biceps and triceps muscles in the arm:

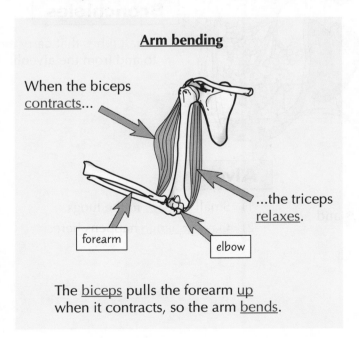

Arm bending

When the biceps contracts...

...the triceps relaxes.

forearm

elbow

The biceps pulls the forearm up when it contracts, so the arm bends.

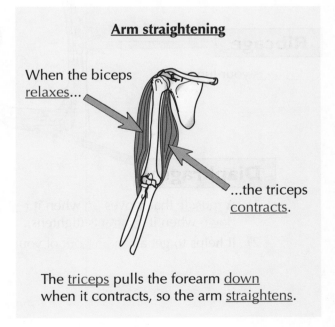

Arm straightening

When the biceps relaxes...

...the triceps contracts.

The triceps pulls the forearm down when it contracts, so the arm straightens.

REVISION TIP

When you show off your muscles, you can claim it's revision

Antagonistic muscles come in pairs. You can't have one without the other. And they just can't get along — whatever one is doing, the other is doing the opposite.

Gas Exchange

Yep, there's another organ system for you to learn. This time it's all about how we get <u>air</u> into our lungs when we breathe. Introducing the <u>gas exchange system</u>...

Learn These Structures in the Gas Exchange System

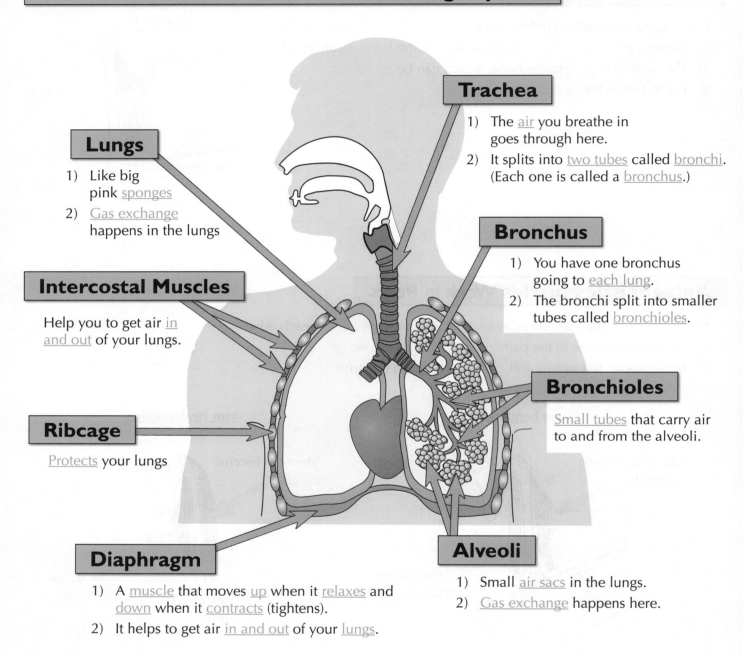

Trachea

1) The <u>air</u> you breathe in goes through here.
2) It splits into <u>two tubes</u> called <u>bronchi</u>. (Each one is called a <u>bronchus</u>.)

Lungs

1) Like big pink <u>sponges</u>
2) <u>Gas exchange</u> happens in the lungs

Bronchus

1) You have one bronchus going to <u>each lung</u>.
2) The bronchi split into smaller tubes called <u>bronchioles</u>.

Intercostal Muscles

Help you to get air <u>in and out</u> of your lungs.

Bronchioles

<u>Small tubes</u> that carry air to and from the alveoli.

Ribcage

<u>Protects</u> your lungs

Diaphragm

1) A <u>muscle</u> that moves <u>up</u> when it <u>relaxes</u> and <u>down</u> when it <u>contracts</u> (tightens).
2) It helps to get air <u>in and out</u> of your <u>lungs</u>.

Alveoli

1) Small <u>air sacs</u> in the lungs.
2) <u>Gas exchange</u> happens here.

Each bronchus splits into bronchioles

Take care if you're ever asked to label a gas exchange diagram. The bronchus, bronchioles and alveoli are quite close together (as are the intercostal muscles and the ribcage). So it can be easy to accidentally label the wrong bit — especially if you're in a hurry.

More on Gas Exchange

Once you've breathed air into your lungs, you need to get oxygen from that air into your blood. You also need to get rid of the carbon dioxide that's in your blood. This is gas exchange.

Gas Exchange Happens in the Lungs

1) Your body needs oxygen for respiration (see page 4).
   It also needs to get rid of carbon dioxide (a waste product of respiration).
2) Oxygen is found in the air.
3) Air is breathed into the lungs.
4) Oxygen moves from the air into the blood in the lungs.
5) Carbon dioxide moves out of the blood. It is then breathed out.
6) This is gas exchange.
7) The lungs are well adapted for gas exchange:

   • They're moist.

   • They have a good blood supply.

   • The alveoli (air sacs) give the lungs a big inside surface area.

O_2 is oxygen and CO_2 is carbon dioxide.

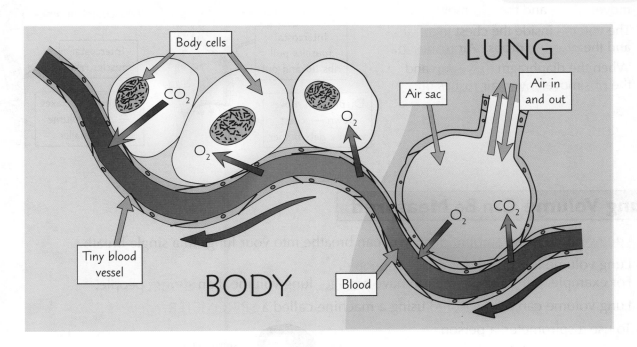

Oxygen in, carbon dioxide out — that's gas exchange

There are a couple of detailed diagrams on the last two pages. Make sure you learn them — sooner or later you'll be expected to know all the parts of the gas exchange system and what they do.

Breathing

Breathing is how the air gets in and out of your lungs. It's definitely a useful skill.

The **Process** of **Breathing**

The Bell Jar demonstration shows us what's going on when you breathe:

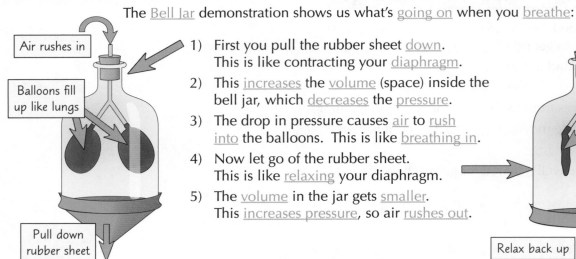

1) First you pull the rubber sheet down. This is like contracting your diaphragm.

2) This increases the volume (space) inside the bell jar, which decreases the pressure.

3) The drop in pressure causes air to rush into the balloons. This is like breathing in.

4) Now let go of the rubber sheet. This is like relaxing your diaphragm.

5) The volume in the jar gets smaller. This increases pressure, so air rushes out.

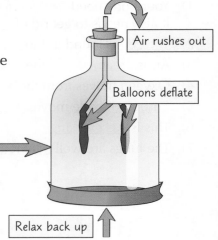

Air rushes in
Balloons fill up like lungs
Pull down rubber sheet

Air rushes out
Balloons deflate
Relax back up

Inhaling and **Exhaling** is **Breathing In** and **Out**

1) The space inside your chest is like a bell jar.

2) When you breathe in, the diaphragm moves down and the ribs move up.

3) The volume inside the chest increases and the pressure drops. Air rushes in.

4) When the diaphragm moves up and the ribs move down, air rushes out.

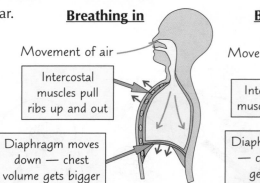

Breathing in

Movement of air

Intercostal muscles pull ribs up and out

Diaphragm moves down — chest volume gets bigger

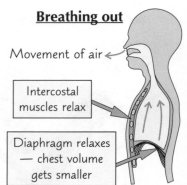

Breathing out

Movement of air

Intercostal muscles relax

Diaphragm relaxes — chest volume gets smaller

Lung Volume Can Be **Measured**

1) Lung volume is the amount of air you can breathe into your lungs in a single breath.

2) Lung volume is different for different people. For example, taller people tend to have a bigger lung volume than shorter people.

3) Lung volume can be measured using a machine called a SPIROMETER.

4) To use a spirometer, a person breathes into the machine (through a tube) for a few minutes.

5) The volume of air that is breathed in and out is measured.

6) A graph (called a spirogram) is drawn.

spirometer

spirogram

Exercise, Asthma and Smoking

Exercise, asthma and smoking can all affect your gas exchange system (see p.16) and your breathing.

Exercise

1) You breathe faster and more deeply when you exercise.
2) This is so you can get more oxygen to your muscles.
3) If you exercise regularly these two things happen:

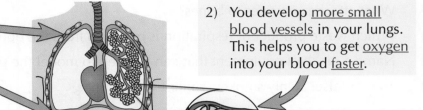

1) The muscles you use to breathe get stronger. This helps you to get more air into your lungs.

2) You develop more small blood vessels in your lungs. This helps you to get oxygen into your blood faster.

air sacs

small blood vessels

Asthma

1) People with asthma have lungs that are too sensitive to certain things (e.g. pet hair, dust, smoke...).
2) If a person with asthma breathes these things in, it affects the bronchioles (tubes in the lungs). This can cause an asthma attack. This is what happens:

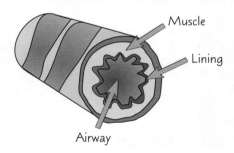

A bronchiole BEFORE asthma attack

Muscle

Lining

Airway

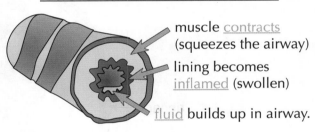

A bronchiole DURING asthma attack

muscle contracts (squeezes the airway)

lining becomes inflamed (swollen)

fluid builds up in airway.

These changes make it hard to breathe.

Smoking

Cigarette smoke contains tar. Tar is really bad for you:

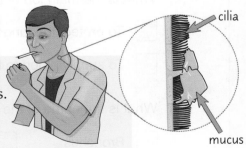

cilia

mucus

1) Tar covers the cilia (little hairs) in your airways.
2) Cilia normally move mucus (thick sticky stuff) out of your airways. The damaged cilia can't do this properly.
3) The mucus sticks in your airways.
4) This makes you cough more — it's called smoker's cough.
5) The damage can eventually lead to lung diseases, which make it difficult to breathe.
6) Tar also contains chemicals that cause cancer.

REVISION TASK

This page is just breathtaking

So there you have it, three different things that have an impact on the gas exchange system. Now try covering up the page to see how much you can write about each one.

Warm-Up and Practice Questions

That's it for bones, muscles and the gas exchange system. Time to test how much of the last few pages has made it inside your skull by having a go at these questions...

Warm-Up Questions

1) Name one property of bone that makes it suitable for protecting delicate organs.

2) Which part of a bone makes blood cells?

3) What attaches muscles to bones?

4) Which waste product of respiration is removed from the body via the gas exchange system?

5) Name a piece of equipment that can be used to model the process of breathing.

6) True or false? Only smokers suffer from asthma.

Practice Question

1 The diagram below shows the structures in the gas exchange system.
One of the lungs is drawn in cross-section to show the air sacs.

(a) What is the main job of the ribcage? Tick **one** box.

☐ To protect the lungs.

☐ To supply blood to the lungs.

(1 mark)

(b) What is the name of the structure labelled **A**? Tick **one** box.

☐ Bronchus ☐ Intercostal muscle ☐ Trachea

(1 mark)

(c) Complete the sentences using some of the words below.

blood **lungs** **back** **down** **up**

When you breathe in, the diaphragm contracts and moves ....

The pressure inside the chest decreases, causing air to rush into the ....

(2 marks)

Section Two — Humans as Organisms

Practice Questions

2 The human skeleton is attached to muscles, which allow us to move.

(a) Write down **one** main job of the human skeleton, other than movement.

(1 mark)

(b) Tick the correct box to show whether each sentence about muscles is **true** or **false**.

		True	False
(i)	When a muscle contracts, it applies a force to the bone it is attached to.	☐	☐
(ii)	Bones can move without muscles.	☐	☐
(iii)	Antagonistic muscles work in pairs.	☐	☐

(3 marks)

3 Cigarette smoke contains tar which can damage your airways.

(a) Name **one** health problem that smoking can cause.

(1 mark)

(b) Explain why the tar in cigarette smoke causes smokers to cough more.

(3 marks)

4 Exercise can affect the gas exchange system.

(a) Which of the following changes can be caused by exercising regularly?
Tick **two** boxes.

☐ The muscles used to breathe get stronger.

☐ The amount of fluid in the airways decreases.

☐ More small blood vessels are developed.

☐ The bronchioles increase in size.

☐ Less carbon dioxide is breathed in.

(2 marks)

(b) Rashida wants to investigate how exercising regularly affects lung volume.
She plans to measure the lung volume of two of her friends:

• Justin is 38 and 188 cm tall. He goes jogging 5 times a week.
• Chris is 30 and 175 cm tall. He does not exercise regularly.

(i) What is meant by 'lung volume'?

(1 mark)

(ii) How could Rashida measure the lung volume of Justin and Chris?

(1 mark)

(iii) Suggest why this might **not** be a fair test of how regular exercise affects lung volume.

(1 mark)

Human Reproduction

Like all mammals, we have male parts and female parts that allow us to reproduce (make babies).

The **Male Reproductive** System

1) We need sex cells to be able to reproduce. Sex cells are also called 'gametes'.
2) The male sex cells are called sperm.
3) Sperm are made in the testes after puberty.
4) Sperm leave the penis during sexual intercourse.

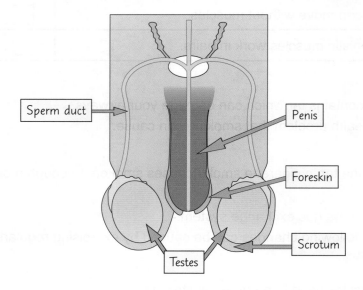

Sperm duct

Penis

Foreskin

Scrotum

Testes

The **Female Reproductive** System

1) The female sex cells are called eggs.
2) Eggs are made in the ovaries.
3) After puberty, an egg is released from an ovary into a Fallopian tube every 28 days.
4) This is part of the menstrual cycle (see page 24 for more).

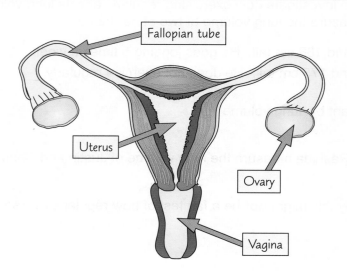

Fallopian tube

The uterus can also be called the womb.

Uterus

Ovary

Vagina

More on Human Reproduction

It takes <u>both</u> the male and female reproductive systems for humans to <u>reproduce</u>. This process is called <u>sexual intercourse</u>. No giggling now...

An **Egg** May be **Fertilised** After **Sexual Intercourse**

1) <u>Sperm</u> are released into the <u>vagina</u> during <u>sexual intercourse</u>.

2) They then travel to a <u>fallopian tube</u>, where they might meet an <u>egg</u>.

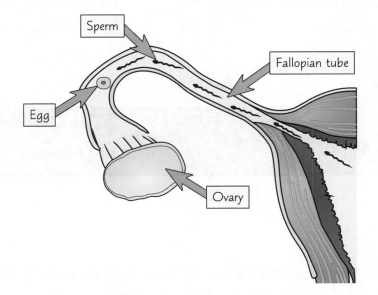

3) The <u>nucleus</u> of a <u>sperm cell</u> and the <u>nucleus</u> of an <u>egg cell</u> may then <u>combine</u>. This is <u>FERTILISATION</u>.

4) The fertilised egg <u>divides</u> to become a <u>ball of cells</u>. This ball of cells is called an <u>EMBRYO</u>.

5) The embryo develops into a baby in the <u>UTERUS</u>.

6) If an egg is <u>not fertilised</u>, it will <u>break down</u> and pass out of the vagina during a <u>period</u> (see next page).

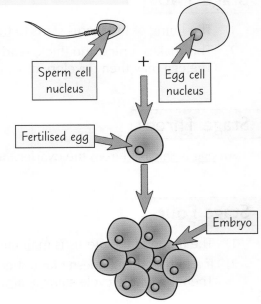

Fertilisation requires both a sperm cell and an egg cell

Make sure you know all the stuff about human reproduction that has been covered so far. Try <u>covering up the last two pages</u> and <u>making a mind map</u> of all the key points.

The Menstrual Cycle

From the age of puberty, women undergo a monthly sequence of events called the menstrual cycle.

The **Menstrual Cycle** Takes **28 Days**

1) In the menstrual cycle the body prepares the uterus in case it receives a fertilised egg.
2) The diagram below shows the four main stages of the menstrual cycle:

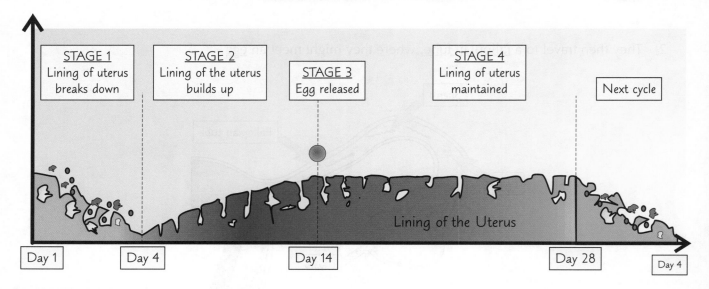

STAGE 1
Lining of uterus breaks down

STAGE 2
Lining of the uterus builds up

STAGE 3
Egg released

STAGE 4
Lining of uterus maintained

Next cycle

Lining of the Uterus

Day 1   Day 4   Day 14   Day 28   Day 4

Stage One

1) BLEEDING STARTS. The lining of the uterus breaks down and passes out of the vagina.
2) This is called "having a PERIOD". It usually lasts 3 to 4 days.

Stage Two

1) The lining of the uterus starts to build up again.
2) This makes it nice and thick, ready for a fertilised egg to land there. The egg may then develop into a baby — see next page.

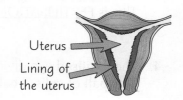

Uterus

Lining of the uterus

Stage Three

An egg is released from the ovaries. It may now be fertilised.

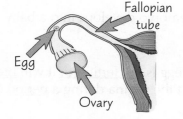

Fallopian tube

Egg

Ovary

Stage Four

1) The lining of the uterus is maintained (kept thick).
2) If a fertilised egg doesn't land there, the lining will break down and pass out of the vagina. Then the whole cycle starts again.

The end of the cycle depends on whether the egg's fertilised...

There are quite a few details to learn here. Make sure you know exactly what happens in all four stages of the menstrual cycle. You also need to know when each stage happens.

Having a Baby

A sperm fertilises an egg, the gestation period passes, a baby is born. Sounds easy enough.

Gestation Lasts For 39 Weeks

1) The time between the egg being fertilised and the baby being born is called GESTATION.
2) Once a fertilised egg has developed into an embryo (see page 23), it implants (sticks itself) into the uterus lining.
3) The embryo then starts to grow...

At 1 Month

The embryo is 6 mm long.
It has a brain, heart, eyes, ears and legs.

At 9 Weeks

The body is about 25 mm long.
It is completely formed —
it's now called a FOETUS.

At 3 Months

The foetus is 54 mm long.
It looks much more like a baby.

At 5 Months

It's now about 160 mm long.
It kicks its legs.

At 7 Months

The foetus is 370 mm long.
It would probably survive
if it were born now.

At 39 weeks

The baby is about 520 mm long.
It's ready to be BORN.

Health and Pregnancy

Good health is when both your body and your mind are fine and dandy. It's important to make sure you look after your health if you're pregnant, as your health affects the baby's health.

Health is More Than Just Not Being Ill

1) Good health means having:

- A healthy body that's all working properly with no diseases.
- A healthy mind so you can cope with the ups and downs of life.

2) Taking drugs can affect your health.

A Pregnant Woman's Lifestyle is Important

1) A placenta is an organ that attaches the foetus to the uterus lining.
2) The placenta lets the foetus get things it needs from its mother's blood. For example, food and oxygen.

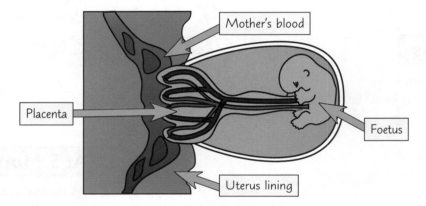

3) But harmful chemicals can also get from the mother's blood to the foetus through the placenta.
4) Harmful chemicals get into the mother's blood if she:

smokes   drinks alcohol   takes other drugs

5) These chemicals can harm the foetus. For example, if a pregnant woman smokes:

- there's more chance her baby will be born before it's properly developed — so it might be quite small.
- the baby may have problems breathing.

The mother's lifestyle can have a huge impact on a foetus

Having a healthy lifestyle is very important, especially when you're pregnant. And remember, being healthy doesn't just mean looking after your body — it means looking after your mental health too.

Drugs

Recreational drugs can have serious, <u>bad effects</u> on your health.

Drugs

1) A drug is anything that <u>affects the way</u> the body works. For example, a drug may increase heart rate.
2) Drugs can affect <u>LIFE PROCESSES</u>. For example, drugs that affect the <u>brain</u> are likely to affect <u>movement</u> and <u>sensitivity</u>.
3) <u>RECREATIONAL DRUGS</u> are drugs used for enjoyment, rather than as medicine. They can be <u>legal</u> (like alcohol) or <u>illegal</u> (like ecstasy).

The 7 Life Processes
Movement — moving parts of the body.
Reproduction — producing offspring.
Sensitivity — responding and reacting.
Nutrition — getting food to stay alive.
Excretion — getting rid of waste.
Respiration — turning food into energy.
Growth — getting to adult size.

A handy way of remembering the seven life processes is '<u>MRS NERG</u>'. (Read the first letter of each process)

Solvents

1) Solvents are found in things like <u>paints</u> and <u>glues</u>.
2) Sniffing solvents can make you <u>see</u> and <u>hear</u> things that are <u>not really there</u>. <u>Misusing</u> solvents like this can affect your <u>behaviour</u>.
3) Solvents also <u>damage</u> the <u>lungs</u>, <u>brain</u> and <u>kidneys</u>.

Alcohol

1) Alcohol is found in <u>beers</u>, <u>wines</u> and <u>spirits</u>.
2) It <u>decreases brain activity</u>. This means you <u>react</u> to things <u>more slowly</u>.
3) It can damage the <u>brain</u> and <u>liver</u>.
4) It <u>impairs judgement</u> — so you might end up doing silly things.

Illegal Drugs

1) There are many <u>illegal</u> recreational drugs. For example, <u>ecstasy</u>, <u>heroin</u> and <u>LSD</u>.
2) Many illegal drugs are <u>very addictive</u>. This means the user feels like they <u>NEED</u> to have them.
3) They affect <u>behaviour</u>.
4) They can have very <u>bad effects</u> on a person's <u>body</u>. For example, <u>ecstasy</u> can lead to <u>dehydration</u> (not enough water in the body), which can cause <u>DEATH</u>.

Drugs aren't harmless fun — they're a slippery slope

It's important that you know the different effects that drugs can have on your health. Make sure that you know how different types of <u>recreational drugs</u> can affect <u>behaviour</u>, <u>health</u> and <u>life processes</u>. You can use 'MRS NERG' to remember the seven life processes.

Warm-Up and Practice Questions

Well, that's almost it for this section. Just a few questions to go and you're done.

Warm-Up Questions

1) What are the male sex cells called?

2) In which stage of the menstrual cycle (1, 2, 3 or 4) does bleeding start?

3) You need a healthy body to have good health. What else do you need to have good health?

4) Name one thing that is supplied to a foetus through the mother's blood in the uterus.

5) Give one possible harmful effect on the baby if a woman smokes during pregnancy.

6) True or false? A recreational drug is a drug that is used for enjoyment rather than as medicine.

7) Name one organ that you can damage by using solvents.

Practice Questions

1   The diagram below shows the human female reproductive system.

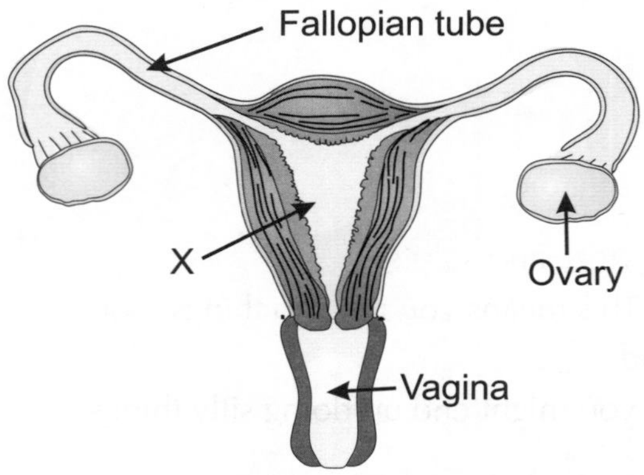

(a) What is released from an ovary roughly every 28 days? Tick **one** box.

☐ an egg   ☐ an embryo

(1 mark)

(b) Name part **X** in the figure above.

(1 mark)

(c) Which of the following is the correct definition of **fertilisation**? Tick **one** box.

☐ When sperm are released into the vagina.

☐ When the nuclei of the egg and sperm join.

(1 mark)

(d) After how many weeks of pregnancy is a human baby considered ready to be born? Tick **one** box.

☐ 19   ☐ 24   ☐ 39

(1 mark)

Section Two — Humans as Organisms

Practice Questions

2   (a)   Five parts of the human male reproductive system are named in the table below.
Using the diagram, write the letter for each part next to its name.

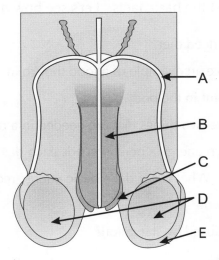

name of organ	letter
sperm duct	
foreskin	
penis	
scrotum	
testes	

(5 marks)

  (b)   Sperm is released by the male during sexual intercourse.
Where in the male reproductive system are sperm made?

(1 mark)

3   Drugs can affect life processes. Alcohol is one type of legal drug.

  (a)   Name **one** other type of legal drug.

(1 mark)

  (b)   State **three** life processes.

(3 marks)

  (c)   Write down **two** organs in the body that can be damaged by drinking alcohol.

(2 marks)

  (d)   Why does drinking alcohol slow down a person's reactions?

(1 mark)

Section Two — Humans as Organisms

Revision Summary for Section Two

Well, there's certainly some stuff in Section Two — all you ever wanted to know about human beings, and a good deal more besides. Now what you've got to do is make sure you learn it all.
Remember, you have to keep coming back to these questions time and time again, to see how many of them you can do. All they do is test the basic facts. Let's see how much you've learnt so far...

1) Name all five nutrients in a balanced diet.
2) For each of the five nutrients, give an example of a food they're in.
3) Say why each nutrient is important in the body.
4) Apart from the five nutrients, give two things that are needed in a balanced diet.
5) What two things affect how much energy a person needs each day?
6)* Sonia has a body mass of 70 kg. What is her daily basic energy requirement (BER)?
7) What is obesity? How is it caused?
8) What health problems can be caused by starvation?
9) What causes deficiency diseases?
10) Name seven main bits of the digestive system.
11) Say what each of these seven bits does.
12) What are villi? What is their job?
13) Give three reasons why bacteria are important in the gut.
14) What are the four jobs of the skeleton?
15) What makes bones move?
16) What are antagonistic muscles?
17) What is a bronchus? What are alveoli?
18) Name six other structures in the gas exchange system.
19) What gases are exchanged in the lungs? Where does each gas move from and to?
20) Give three ways in which the lungs are well-adapted for gas exchange.
21) What happens to the diaphragm when you breathe in?
22) What happens to the chest volume when you breathe in? How is this different to when you breathe out?
23) Give three things that happen to a bronchiole during an asthma attack.
24) Give two ways in which smoking affects the gas exchange system.
25) What are the female sex cells called? Where are they made?
26) What is happening when a woman has a period?
27) What starts on day 4 of the menstrual cycle? What happens at day 14?
28) Describe what an embryo looks like at: 1 month, 9 weeks, 3 months, 5 months, 7 months, 39 weeks.
29) What is a 'recreational' drug?
30) Name one recreational drug. Explain how it affects behaviour.

Section Two — Humans as Organisms

*Answer on page 189.

Plant Nutrition

Plants make their own food — it's a nice trick if you can do it.

Photosynthesis Makes Food From Sunlight

1) Photosynthesis is a chemical process. It takes place in every green plant.
2) Photosynthesis produces food — in the form of glucose (a carbohydrate).
3) Photosynthesis happens mainly in the leaves.

Four Things are Needed for Photosynthesis...

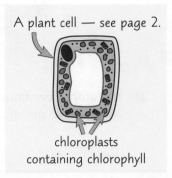

A plant cell — see page 2.

chloroplasts
containing chlorophyll

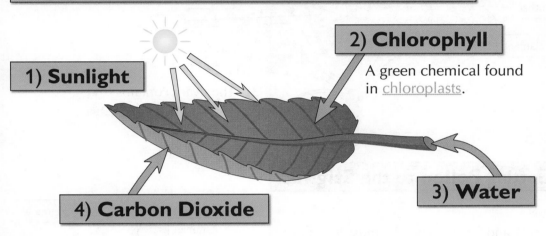

1) Sunlight

2) Chlorophyll

A green chemical found in chloroplasts.

3) Water

4) Carbon Dioxide

1) Chlorophyll absorbs sunlight.
2) Photosynthesis uses the energy from sunlight to turn carbon dioxide and water into glucose. Oxygen is also made.
3) You can write this word equation to show what happens:

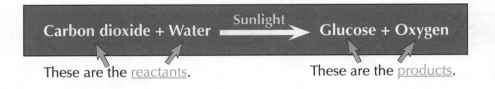

Carbon dioxide + Water $\xrightarrow{\text{Sunlight}}$ Glucose + Oxygen

These are the reactants.

These are the products.

There's more on reactants and products on page 71.

Leaves are Great at Photosynthesis

1) Leaves are broad. This gives them a big surface area for absorbing light.
2) Leaves have lots of chloroplasts. These are mainly at the top of the leaf, where there's most light.
3) The bottom of the leaf has lots of tiny holes called stomata. These let carbon dioxide move into the leaf from the air. They also let oxygen move out.

Plants Also Need Things from the Soil

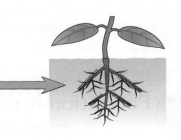

1) Plants need minerals from the soil to keep healthy.
2) Plants absorb minerals through their roots.
3) Plants also absorb water from the soil through their roots.

Plant Reproduction

Just like humans, plants reproduce (make babies). This page is all about how plant reproduction starts.

The **Flower** Contains the **Reproductive Organs**

1) **Stamens**

1) The male parts of the flower.
2) The stamens are made of the anther and the filament.

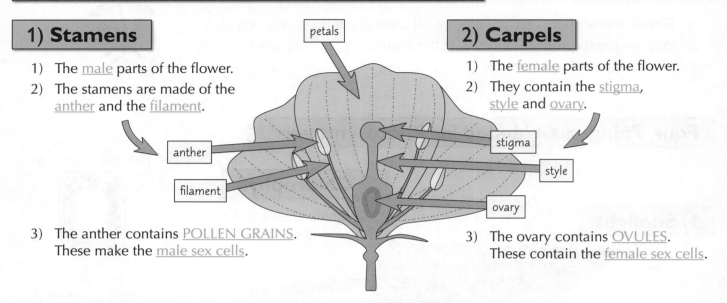

3) The anther contains POLLEN GRAINS. These make the male sex cells.

2) **Carpels**

1) The female parts of the flower.
2) They contain the stigma, style and ovary.

3) The ovary contains OVULES. These contain the female sex cells.

"Pollination" is Getting **Pollen** to the **Stigma**

1) Plants grow from seeds.
2) To make a seed, the male and female sex cells must "meet up".
3) To do this, the pollen grains must get from a stamen to a stigma. This is POLLINATION.
4) Pollen can get from the stamen of one plant to the stigma of a DIFFERENT plant in different ways. For example...

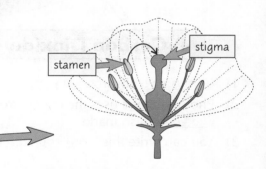

1) **Insect** Pollination

1) Insects visit flowers to get food.
2) While they are there, the pollen sticks to them.
3) When they travel to other flowers, they carry the pollen with them.
4) Insect-pollinated flowers have a sticky stigma to pull the pollen off the insects.
5) They also have bright petals to attract insects.

2) **Wind** Pollination

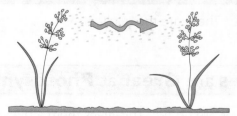

1) The anthers of wind-pollinated plants dangle outside the flower.
2) This means pollen gets blown off the anthers when the wind blows.
3) Other flowers have a feathery stigma to 'catch' the pollen as it blows past.

Pollination is the first step in plant reproduction

It's easy to remember that the stamens are the male parts of the flower. Just think sta**men**.

Fertilisation and Seeds

Here's what happens _after_ a flower is <u>pollinated</u>. Make sure you've learnt the words on page 32.

Fertilisation is the **Joining** of **Sex Cells**

1) <u>Pollen</u> lands on a <u>stigma</u> with help from <u>insects</u> or the <u>wind</u>.
2) A <u>pollen tube</u> then grows out of a <u>pollen grain</u> into the <u>ovary</u>.
3) The <u>nucleus</u> from a <u>male sex cell</u> inside the pollen grain <u>moves down</u> the tube.
4) It <u>joins</u> with the <u>nucleus</u> of a <u>female sex cell</u> inside an <u>ovule</u>. This is <u>FERTILISATION</u>.

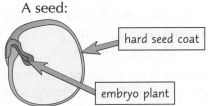

stigma
pollen grain
pollen tube
female nucleus inside ovule
male nucleus travelling to ovary

Seeds are **Formed** From **Ovules**

1) After fertilisation, the <u>ovule</u> develops into a <u>seed</u>.
2) Each seed contains an <u>embryo plant</u>.
3) The <u>ovary</u> develops into a <u>fruit</u> around the seed.

A seed:

hard seed coat

embryo plant

Seed Dispersal is **Scattering** Seeds

Seeds need to be <u>dispersed</u> (scattered) from the parent plant before they can grow. Here are four <u>different methods</u> of seed dispersal...

1) **Wind** dispersal

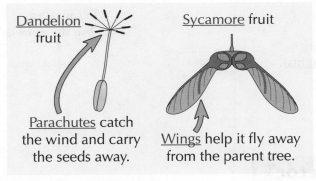

<u>Dandelion</u> fruit

<u>Parachutes</u> catch the wind and carry the seeds away.

<u>Sycamore</u> fruit

<u>Wings</u> help it fly away from the parent tree.

2) **Animal** dispersal

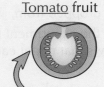

<u>Tomato</u> fruit

1) Fruit gets <u>eaten</u>.
2) Seeds come out in the animals' <u>poo</u>, away from the parent plant.

<u>Burdock</u> fruit

1) <u>Hooks</u> stick to animals' coats.
2) Animals <u>carry</u> the fruit <u>away</u>.

3) **Explosions**

<u>Peas</u>

The pods <u>dry out</u> and <u>flick</u> the seeds out.

4) **Drop and Roll**

<u>Horse Chestnut</u> fruit.

1) The heavy fruit <u>falls</u> down from the tree.
2) It <u>splits</u> when it hits the ground and the seeds <u>roll</u> out.

Plants come up with all sorts of ways to disperse their seeds

After <u>pollination</u> and <u>fertilisation</u>, next comes <u>seed development</u>. Then you've got the business of <u>dispersal</u>. Eventually, the seeds will <u>grow</u> into <u>new plants</u> far away from their parents.

Investigating Seed Dispersal

At last, a little bit of science in action. Roll up your sleeves and let's get started.

You Can **Investigate** Seed **Dispersal** by **Dropping Seeds**

You can investigate how well different seeds disperse.
It's easiest to investigate wind and drop and roll dispersal.

Here's what you have to do.

1) Get a few different types of fruit (which contain seeds).
   For example, sycamore fruit and horse chestnut fruit.
2) Decide on a fixed height to drop the fruit from.
3) Drop the fruit one at a time from this height,
   directly above a set point on the ground.
4) Measure how far along the ground the seeds
   have travelled from the set point.
5) Record this distance in a table.
6) Do this experiment three times for each type of seed.
   Then find the average distance each type disperses.

Seed Type	Distance Dispersed (cm)		
Sycamore	20	25	24
Horse Chestnut			

Make Sure it's a **Fair Test**

You need to keep these things the same each time you do the experiment:

- the person dropping the fruit,
- the height the fruit are dropped from,
- the place you're doing the experiment (stay away
  from doors and windows that might cause draughts).

> This is called
> "controlling the variables".

Use a **Fan** to Investigate the "**Wind Factor**"

You can investigate how much the wind affects seed dispersal using an electric fan.
Here's how:

1) Set up the fan a fixed distance from the person dropping the fruit.
2) Switch the fan on — it needs to be set to the same speed for every
   fruit you drop. This makes sure the experiment will be a fair test.
3) Drop the fruit as before and measure how far along the ground the seeds travel.

Come on now, fair's fair

Knowing how to control variables to make a test fair is an important part of being a scientist.

Warm-Up and Practice Questions

Photosynthesis and plant reproduction are really important. You're bound to get asked about them at some point or another, so make sure you can answer all these questions without looking back.

Warm-Up Questions

1) State two things that are needed for photosynthesis.

2) Describe one way in which leaves are adapted for photosynthesis.

3) True or false? Carpels are the female parts of a flower.

4) What part of the flower develops into the seed after fertilisation?

Practice Questions

1   Jen found a packet of seeds in her garage. The packet wasn't labelled, so Jen decided to plant the seeds to see what kind of plants grew from them.

   (a)   Circle the things below that are needed for the seeds to grow into healthy plants.

| carbon dioxide | insects | sunlight | water | wind |

(3 marks)

   (b)   The flowers of the plants that grew from the seeds have bright yellow petals. Why might the plants need bright yellow petals? Tick **one** box.

☐ To make more chloroplasts.   ☐ To absorb more sunlight.   ☐ To attract insects for pollination.

(1 mark)

   (c)   After the plants had flowered, Jen noticed some seed heads covered in little tiny hooks on the plants. Describe how the hooks would help the plant to disperse its seeds.

(1 mark)

2   The leaves of plants absorb light for photosynthesis.

   (a)   Write the word equation for photosynthesis using the words below.

      oxygen   **carbon dioxide**   **water**   **glucose**

(2 marks)

   (b)   Rob planted some marigold plants in his garden. He planted some under a tree and some in full sunlight.

      The plants in full sunlight grew much better than those under the tree. Suggest why the plants grew better in full sunlight.

(2 marks)

   (c)   Rob also planted some marigold plants in his greenhouse. Half the marigolds were planted in mineral-rich compost bought in a shop. The other half were planted in ordinary soil from the garden. Suggest which group of marigolds were healthier. Explain your answer.

(2 marks)

Section Three — Plants and Ecosystems

Practice Questions

3   Elspeth is investigating how well different seeds are dispersed by wind.
She sets up a fan and a ruler, as shown below. She then drops a sycamore fruit
and a horse chestnut fruit in front of it and measures how far along the ground
each of them travels. She does this three times for each fruit.

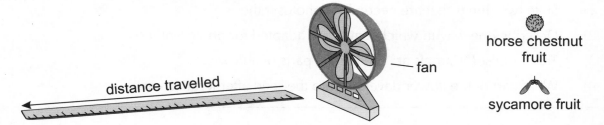

distance travelled

fan

horse chestnut
fruit

sycamore fruit

(a) Give **one** thing Elspeth needs to keep the same each time she repeats the
experiment to make sure it is a fair test.

(1 mark)

(b) Which fruit would you expect to travel the furthest?
Explain your answer.

(2 marks)

(c) Give **one** way that seeds are dispersed from plants, other than wind dispersal.

(1 mark)

4   (a) Chris and Jim are talking about fertilisation in plants.

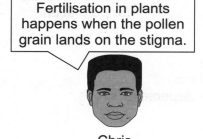

Fertilisation in plants
happens when the pollen
grain lands on the stigma.

Fertilisation is when the nuclei
from the ovule and male sex
cell actually join together.

Chris

Jim

Who is correct, Chris or Jim?

(1 mark)

(b) Describe how the nucleus from the male sex cell reaches an egg cell after
pollination has occurred. Include the following words or phrases in your answer:

pollen grain   **ovary**   **pollen tube**

(3 marks)

(c) After fertilisation has taken place, what does the ovary begin to develop into?

(1 mark)

(d) Suggest why seeds are surrounded by a hard seed coat.

(1 mark)

Section Three — Plants and Ecosystems

Dependence on Other Organisms

Organisms depend on (need) other organisms for their survival.

Organisms in an Ecosystem are Interdependent

1) An ecosystem is all the living organisms in one area, plus their environment.
2) The organisms in an ecosystem are interdependent.
3) This means that they need each other to survive.

Almost All Living Things Depend on Plants

Plants Capture the Sun's Energy

1) Almost all energy on Earth comes from the Sun.
2) Plants use some of the Sun's energy to make food during photosynthesis (see page 31).
3) Plants use the food to build molecules (like proteins) which become part of the plants' cells.
4) These molecules store the Sun's energy.
5) The energy gets passed on from plants to animals when animals eat the plants.
6) Animals can't carry out photosynthesis. But they do all need energy to stay alive.
   So animals need plants to capture the Sun's energy for them.

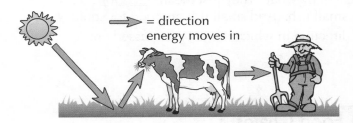

→ = direction energy moves in

Plants Give Out Oxygen and Take in Carbon Dioxide

1) When plants and animals respire (see p.4) they TAKE IN oxygen and GIVE OUT carbon dioxide.
2) But during photosynthesis, plants GIVE OUT oxygen and TAKE IN carbon dioxide.
3) Without plants there wouldn't be enough oxygen in the air for respiration.
4) Also, there would be too much carbon dioxide in the air.

Many Plants Depend on Insects to Reproduce

1) We grow crops for food — for example, we grow apple trees to make apples.
2) Many crop plants need insects to pollinate them.
3) If they don't get pollinated, they won't be able to make fruit and seeds for us to eat.
4) So we need insects to pollinate our crops and give us food.

Section Three — Plants and Ecosystems

Food Chains

Organisms mainly depend on each other for <u>food</u>.

Food Chains Show **What** is **Eaten** by **What**

1) This is an example of a <u>food chain</u>:

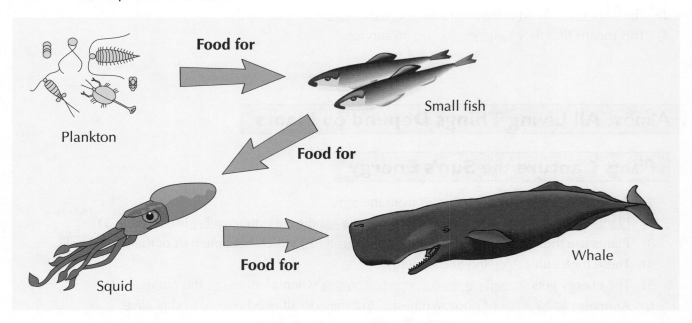

2) The <u>arrows</u> show what is eaten by what. They just mean "<u>food for</u>".
   Here, plankton is <u>food for</u> small fish. And small fish are <u>food for</u> squid.

3) The arrows also show the direction in which <u>energy</u> gets passed on.

Poison Builds Up in Food Chains

1) Poison can sometimes get into a food chain and <u>harm</u> the organisms involved.
2) Animals <u>at the top</u> of the food chain are likely to be the <u>worst affected</u>.
3) This is because the poison <u>builds up</u> as it's passed along the food chain.

Food chains show what's highest in the pecking order

Food chains are simple, so you've no excuse not to <u>learn</u> them. They show you <u>what eats what</u>, right up to the <u>top</u>. In the exam, if you're asked to draw a food chain, make sure you have the arrows pointing the <u>correct way</u> — you don't want to say a leaf eats a snail.

Food Webs

You saw simple <u>food chains</u> on the last page — now it's time to look at the more complicated <u>food webs</u>. In a food web, lots of the animals and plants are <u>linked</u> together in <u>multiple ways</u>.

Food Webs are Lots of Food Chains Joined Together

1) The arrows in a food web still mean "<u>food for</u>".
2) So in this food web, <u>tadpoles</u> are food for <u>water beetles</u> AND <u>minnows</u>:

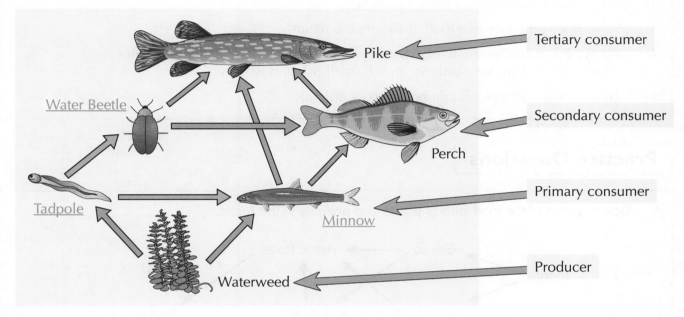

Learn these <u>words</u>:

> PRODUCER — all <u>plants</u> are <u>producers</u>. They store energy from the Sun.
> CONSUMER — all <u>animals</u> are <u>consumers</u>. They eat other living things.
> PRIMARY CONSUMER — an animal that eats <u>producers</u> (plants).
> SECONDARY CONSUMER — an animal that eats primary consumers.
> TERTIARY CONSUMER — an animal that eats secondary consumers.

A Change in One Organism Can Affect Other Organisms

<u>Example</u> — What happens if the minnows are removed?
1) The number of <u>tadpoles</u> might <u>increase</u> because there are no minnows to eat them.
2) The perch might get hungry and start eating more water beetles.
   So the number of <u>water beetles</u> might <u>decrease</u>.

Learn about food webs — but don't get tangled up

Once you've got this page learnt, you can practise this typical food web question:
"If the number of pike decreased, give one reason why the number of tadpoles might decrease." You can find the answer to this question on page 190.

Warm-Up and Practice Questions

It's easy to think you've learnt everything in the section until you try to answer the Warm-Up Questions. If you get stuck, look back and write out what you got wrong until it sticks in your head.

Warm-Up Questions

1) True or false? The organisms in an ecosystem are interdependent.

2) Why do animals rely on plants for energy?

3) What does an arrow in a food chain or web mean?

4) Plankton is eaten by small fish. Squid eat small fish and are eaten by whales.
   Draw a food chain for plankton, squid, small fish and whales.

5) True or false? Producers can be plants or animals.

Practice Questions

1   Below is part of the food web of plants and animals in the Arctic.

(a) Which of the following is a primary consumer in the food web above? Tick **one** box.

   ☐ Plants   ☐ Geese   ☐ Red foxes

(1 mark)

(b) Suggest what may happen to the number of lemmings if the number of plants suddenly decreased. Explain your answer.

(2 marks)

(c) Suggest why there would be more jaegers if the number of owls decreased.

(2 marks)

(d) Explain why red foxes would be the worst affected if a toxic material was taken up by the plants.

(2 marks)

(e) Jaegers and arctic foxes eat both lemmings and geese.
   Explain why the number of geese might decrease if the number of lemmings suddenly decreased.

(1 mark)

Revision Summary for Section Three

The end of another section. At least plants make a change from all that tricky human biology. No pictures of your insides here, just lots of lovely plant diagrams to learn.

Make sure you know the answers to all of these questions before you turn the page.

1) What four things are needed for photosynthesis to happen? ☑

2) What are the products of photosynthesis? ☑

3) Name two things that plants need from the soil. ☑

4) Name the male parts of the flower. Name the female parts of the flower. ☑

5) What is pollination? ☑

6) Describe two ways plants can be pollinated. ☑

7) What is a pollen tube needed for? ☑

8) What is fertilisation? ☑

9) What does an ovule develop into after fertilisation? ☑

10) What is seed dispersal? ☑

11) Give four methods of seed dispersal.
   Give an example of a fruit that disperses seeds in each of these ways. ☑

12) Johnny has three different types of seed. He wants to investigate how far
   each seed disperses when dropped. Describe how Johnny can do this. ☑

13) Describe how Johnny could investigate the effect of wind on seed dispersal. ☑

14) What is an ecosystem? ☑

15) Where does almost all the Earth's energy come from? ☑

16) What do plants do with this energy? How do they store it? ☑

17) Plants affect the level of oxygen in the air. Why is this important?
   What else do plants change about the air? ☑

18) What do crops rely on insects for? How does this affect us humans? ☑

19) What is a food chain? What is a food web? ☑

20) What happens to poison as it's passed along a food chain? ☑

21) What do each of the terms below mean?
   a) producer   b) consumer   c) primary consumer
   d) secondary consumer   e) tertiary consumer ☑

DNA and Inheritance

This page is all about the teeny tiny things inside your cells that control what features you have.

Chromosomes, DNA and Genes

1) Most of the cells in your body have a nucleus.
2) The nucleus contains CHROMOSOMES. Chromosomes are long lengths of DNA.
3) DNA is a long list of chemical instructions on how to build an organism.
4) Chromosomes carry GENES. A gene is a short length of DNA.
5) Different genes control different CHARACTERISTICS (features).

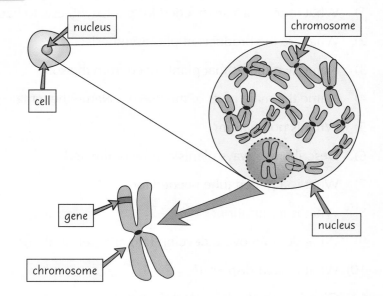

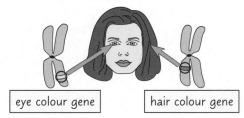

eye colour gene   hair colour gene

Genes Are Passed Down From Our Parents

1) During reproduction (see p.23) genes from the mother and father get mixed together.
2) So a baby has an equal mix of its parents' genes.
3) When genes get passed on like this it's called HEREDITY.
4) Remember genes control characteristics. So a baby will have a mixture of its parents' characteristics.
5) A characteristic passed on in this way is called a 'hereditary' characteristic.

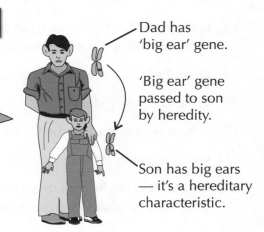

Dad has 'big ear' gene.

'Big ear' gene passed to son by heredity.

Son has big ears — it's a hereditary characteristic.

Scientists Worked Out The Structure of DNA

1) Crick and Watson were the first scientists to build a model of DNA.
2) They used data from other scientists called Wilkins and Franklin.
3) This data helped them to understand that a DNA molecule is a spiral made of two chains twisted together.

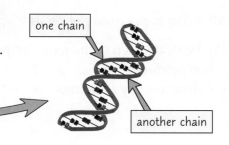

one chain

another chain

REVISION TASK

Some important details to learn on this page

There are three main headings and thirteen numbered points to learn here, not to mention a few important diagrams too. Sit down and challenge yourself to repeat the main details. If you struggle with any bits, reread the page, then cover it back up and try again.

Variation

This page is all about differences between organisms — both big, obvious differences, like those between a tree and a cow, and less obvious differences, like people having different blood groups.

Different **Species** Have Different **Genes**

1) VARIATION is the differences between living things.
2) There's variation between different species. This is because they have very different genes.
3) There's also some variation within a species.

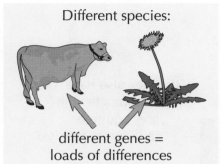

Different species:

different genes = loads of differences

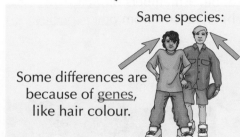

Same species:

Some differences are because of genes, like hair colour.

Some differences are because of our environment (this includes things like the conditions we live in and things that have happened to us in our life). For example, hair style.

Any difference is known as a characteristic feature.

Continuous and **Discontinuous** Variation

Variation within a species is either continuous or discontinuous.

Continuous Variation — the feature can be **any value**

1) Examples of this are things like height and weight — these features can be any value within a range.
2) For example, humans can be any height within a range (usually between 150 and 200 cm for adults), not just tall or short.
3) Here is an example of a graph showing continuous variation:

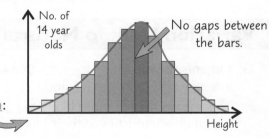

No. of 14 year olds

No gaps between the bars.

Height

Discontinuous Variation — the feature can only take **certain values**

1) An example of this is a person's blood group. There are only four separate blood groups. Everyone fits into one of these groups — no one is in between.

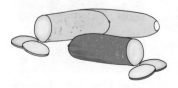

2) Another example is the colour of a courgette. A courgette is either yellow, light green or dark green — there's no range of values.

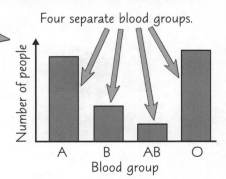

Four separate blood groups.

Number of people

A   B   AB   O

Blood group

You need to be able to explain variation in terms of genes

Don't let the fancy word "variation" put you off. It's really not as complicated as it sounds. It just means "differences" (between any living things). You can have variation (differences) between different species, and you can also have variation (differences) within one species.

Natural Selection and Survival

Characteristics that make organisms good at surviving are likely to become more common over time.
The process by which this happens is called natural selection.

Organisms Need to **Compete**

1) Organisms need certain resources so they can survive and reproduce. For example, food and water.
2) Often there aren't enough of these resources to go around,
   so organisms need to compete ('fight') for them.
3) They have to compete with: a) other members of their own species,
                                                b) organisms from other species.

EXAMPLE:

1) Red squirrels have to compete with each other (their own species) for food.

2) They also have to compete with grey squirrels (a different species).

4) Some species are better at competing than others.
5) Some organisms are also better at competing than others from their own species.
   This is because they show variation due to differences in their genes (see previous page).

Variation Leads to **Natural Selection**

1) Organisms with characteristics that make them better at competing
   are more likely to survive and reproduce.
2) This means they're more likely to pass on the genes for their
   useful characteristics to their offspring (children).
3) So, over time, lots of individuals end up with the useful characteristic.
4) When a useful characteristic gradually becomes more common like this, it's called natural selection.

EXAMPLE: Giraffes have long necks due to natural selection.

1) To start with there is variation — some giraffes have longer necks than others.

2) Giraffes with longer necks can reach leaves easily — so they're better at competing for food. They're more likely to survive and reproduce.

3) The gene for a longer neck gets passed on to the next generation. This process keeps happening until all giraffes have long necks.

Section Four — Inheritance, Variation and Survival

Extinction and Preserving Species

Organisms that can't compete <u>don't survive</u> for long. It's a <u>cruel world</u> out there.

Many Species Are at Risk of Becoming Extinct

1) If the environment <u>changes</u> in some way, some organisms will be badly affected. They may struggle to <u>compete successfully</u> for the things they need.

2) If this happens to a <u>whole species</u>, then that species may <u>die out</u>, so there are <u>none of them left at all</u>.

3) This means the species has become <u>extinct</u> (like the woolly mammoth). ➡️

4) Species <u>at risk</u> of becoming extinct are called <u>endangered species</u>.

Humans Can Suffer When Species Become Extinct

1) Humans <u>rely</u> on <u>plants</u> and <u>animals</u> for loads of things. For example:

2) We need to <u>protect</u> the organisms we already use.

3) We also need to make sure organisms we <u>haven't discovered yet</u> don't become extinct — they might end up being really important.

4) Organisms <u>rely</u> on other organisms to <u>survive</u> (see page 37). So if one species becomes extinct, this can have a <u>knock-on effect</u> for <u>other species</u> — including <u>humans</u>.

5) So it's important that we always have a <u>variety</u> of <u>species</u> on Earth — this is Earth's <u>BIODIVERSITY</u>.

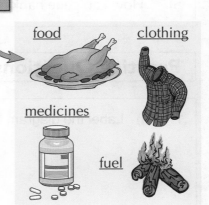

food   clothing

medicines

fuel

Gene Banks May Help to Prevent Extinction

1) A <u>gene bank</u> is a <u>store</u> of the <u>genes</u> of different species.

2) If a species becomes <u>endangered</u> or <u>extinct</u>, we could use stored genes to <u>create new members</u> of that species.

3) So gene banks could be a way of <u>maintaining biodiversity</u> in the future.

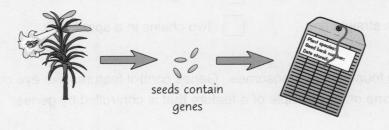

EXAMPLE: Plants

1) <u>Seeds</u> can be <u>collected</u> from plants and <u>stored</u> in <u>seed banks</u>.

seeds contain genes

2) If the plants become <u>extinct</u> in the wild, <u>new plants</u> can be <u>grown</u> from the seeds kept in storage.

EXAM TIP

It's not just animals that suffer when they go extinct

<u>Underline</u> key words in exam questions to make sure your answer covers exactly what the question <u>asks</u> — it's no good telling them all about gene banks if you won't get marks for it.

Warm-Up and Practice Questions

If you don't take the time to warm up you're risking some serious brain-strain. So take a look at these quick questions and get your mind in gear. Then launch yourself slowly into the practice questions.

Warm-Up Questions

1) True or false? Chromosomes are short lengths of DNA.

2) What did Watson and Crick build the first model of?

3) Characteristic features are caused by genes and what else?

4) Are different blood groups an example of continuous or discontinuous variation?

5) Name two resources that organisms compete for.

6) How can gene banks help to prevent species becoming lost from the Earth forever?

Practice Questions

1   (a)   Label the diagram below by drawing a line from each box to the correct letter.

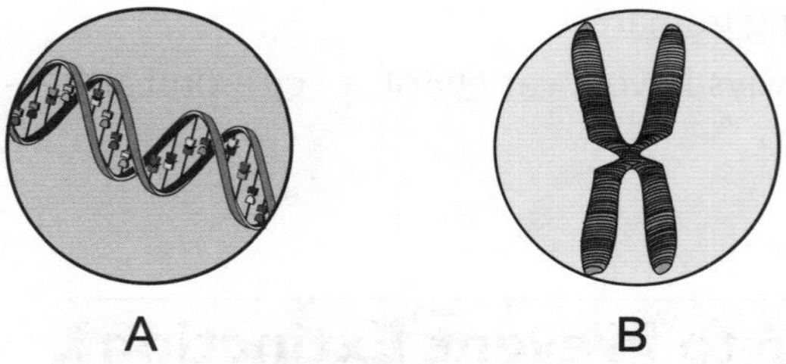

A   B

| Chromosome | DNA | Nucleus |

(2 marks)

(b)   (i)   What is the purpose of DNA?

(2 marks)

(ii)   Which is the best description of the structure of DNA? Tick **one** box.

☐ a circle   ☐ a single chain in a spiral

☐ a straight line   ☐ two chains in a spiral

(1 mark)

(c)   Genes are found on chromosomes. Genes control features like eye colour.
(i)   Give **one** other example of a feature that is controlled by genes.

(1 mark)

(ii)   Give **one** example of a feature that is **not** controlled by genes.

(1 mark)

(iii)   What is the name of the process that describes how genes are passed on from parents to their offspring? Tick one **box**.

☐ fertilisation   ☐ heredity   ☐ variation   ☐ selection

(1 mark)

Practice Questions

2   Kate wants to get a pet rabbit. She looks at several rabbits in the pet shop and notices that the rabbits have either long, straight ears or large, floppy ears.

(a) (i)   Kate says "the rabbits must be different species because there is variation in their ear type". Explain why Kate is wrong.

(1 mark)

(ii)   Is this variation in ear type continuous or discontinuous? Explain your answer.

(2 marks)

(b)   The picture below shows a typical rabbit.

Fill in the missing words to give a description of how rabbits may have evolved to have large ears. Use words from the box.

food	uncommon	predators
parents	common	offspring

Rabbits with larger ears were able to hear .... better and avoid being eaten. This meant rabbits with larger ears were more likely to survive and reproduce and pass on their big ear gene to their .... Over time, the gene for big ears (and so the characteristic) became more ....

(3 marks)

3   Some species are classified as 'endangered' by international conservation organisations.

(a)   What is the meaning of the term 'endangered species'? Tick **one** box.

☐   A species that has died out.

☐   A species that is at risk of extinction.

☐   A species that is dangerous to other species.

(1 mark)

(b)   Give **two** things that humans rely on other species for.

(2 marks)

(c)   It is thought that a particular endangered plant could one day be used to make a medicine to treat a disease. Explain how scientists might use a gene bank in this situation.

(2 marks)

Section Four — Inheritance, Variation and Survival

Revision Summary for Section Four

There are one or two fancy words in Section Four which might cause you trouble.
You should make the effort to learn exactly what they mean, before you start these questions.
These questions test exactly what you know and find out exactly what you don't.
They test all the basic facts, so you need to make sure you can answer them all.
Practise these questions over and over again until you can just sail through them.

1) Where do you find chromosomes? ☑

2) What are chromosomes made of? ☑

3) What is a gene? What does it do? ☑

4) True or false? A baby gets an equal mix of its parents' genes. ☑

5) What does heredity mean? ☑

6) Name the two scientists who first built a model of DNA.
Name the other two scientists whose data helped them. ☑

7) Describe the structure of a DNA molecule. ☑

8) What does variation mean? ☑

9) Why do different species look different? ☑

10) True or false? There is no variation within a species. ☑

11) What is a characteristic feature? ☑

12) Is height an example of continuous or discontinuous variation? Say why. ☑

13) Give one way in which a graph showing continuous variation would be different from a graph
showing discontinuous variation. ☑

14) Why is it important that organisms are good at competing for the things they need? ☑

15) Why are some organisms better at competing for resources than others of the same species? ☑

16) Why are genes for useful characteristics likely to become more common over time?
What is this process called? ☑

17) Why could it be bad news for an organism if its environment changes? ☑

18) What does extinct mean? ☑

19) What is biodiversity? Give one reason why it's important for us to maintain Earth's biodiversity. ☑

20) What is a gene bank? What are they used for? ☑

21) What part of a plant is usually stored in a gene bank? ☑

Section Four — Inheritance, Variation and Survival

Solids, Liquids and Gases

The first page in this section is all about states of matter and there are only three you need to know.

The **Three States of Matter** — Solid, Liquid and Gas

1) Materials come in three different forms...

SOLIDS — for example, gold.   LIQUIDS — for example, water.   GASES — for example, oxygen.

2) These forms are called the three states of matter.

Solids, Liquids and Gases Have **Different Properties**

A property of a substance is just how it behaves.

Property	Solids	Liquids	Gases
Volume This is how much space something takes up.	Solids have a definite volume	Liquids have a definite volume	Gases have no definite volume — they always fill the container they're in
Shape	Solids have a definite shape	Liquids match the shape of the container	Gases become the same shape as the container
Density This is how heavy something is for its size.	Solids usually have a high density (they're heavy for their size)	Liquids usually have medium density	Gases have a very low density (they're light for their size)
Compressibility This is how much you can squash something.	Solids are not easily squashed	Liquids are not easily squashed	Gases are easily squashed
Ease of Flow	Solids don't flow	Liquids flow easily	Gases flow easily

Particle Theory

Particle theory — <u>sounds</u> pretty <u>fancy</u>. But actually, it's pretty <u>straightforward</u>.

It's all about the **Arrangement** of **Particles**

1) All materials are made up of <u>tiny particles</u> — you can just think of them as tiny balls.

2) The way the particles are <u>arranged</u> is <u>different</u> in <u>solids</u>, <u>liquids</u> and <u>gases</u>. Look:

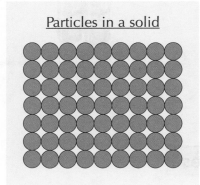

Particles in a solid

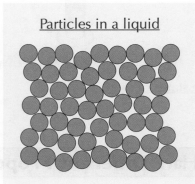

Particles in a liquid

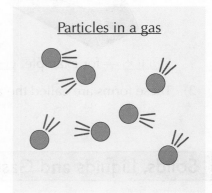

Particles in a gas

3) <u>Particle theory</u> explains how the arrangement of particles affects a material's <u>properties</u>.

Solids — Particles are Held **Very Tightly Together**

1) <u>Strong forces</u> hold the particles <u>very close together</u>.

2) This makes solids <u>dense</u> and <u>hard to squash</u>.

3) The particles <u>can't move</u> very much. They do <u>vibrate</u> (jiggle) a bit.

4) This means solids <u>keep</u> the <u>same shape</u> and <u>volume</u>.

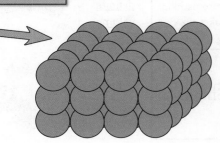

Liquids — Particles are **Close** but They Can **Move**

1) <u>Weak forces</u> hold the particles <u>quite close together</u>.

2) This makes liquids <u>quite dense</u> and <u>hard to squash</u>.

3) The particles are also free to <u>move</u> past each other.

4) This means liquids can <u>flow</u>.

5) It also means liquids <u>don't</u> always keep the <u>same shape</u>. They can form <u>puddles</u>.

6) Liquids <u>do</u> keep the <u>same volume</u>.

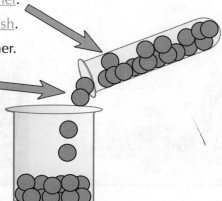

Particle Theory and Diffusion

So now you know what <u>solid</u> and <u>liquid particles</u> are up to. Time to complete the set and cover <u>gases</u>...

Gases — Particles are **Far Apart** and **Whizz About a Lot**

1) The particles in a gas are <u>far apart</u>.
   There are <u>very weak forces</u> between the particles.

2) There's <u>lots of space</u> between the particles, so gases are <u>easy to squash</u>.

3) Gases are <u>not dense</u>.

4) In gases, the particles <u>move quickly</u> in <u>all directions</u>.

5) This means gases <u>don't</u> keep the <u>same shape</u> or <u>volume</u>.
   They always <u>spread out</u> to <u>fill a container</u>.

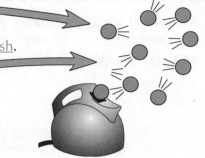

Diffusion is Just Particles **Spreading Out**

1) Particles "want" to <u>spread out</u> — this is called <u>diffusion</u>.
   An example is when a <u>smell</u> spreads slowly through a room.

2) The smell particles <u>move</u> from where there are <u>lots of them</u> to where there <u>aren't as many</u>.

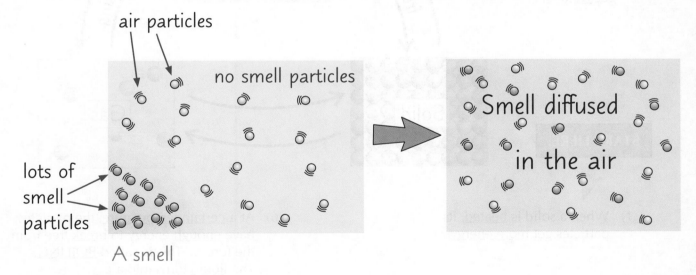

air particles

no smell particles

lots of smell particles

A smell

Smell diffused in the air

The particles in gases are far apart and have lots of energy

As the saying goes, a <u>picture is worth a thousand words</u>. Well it's the same here. The <u>diagrams</u> on these pages help explain why solids, liquids and gases have <u>different properties</u>. Without looking, have a go at <u>drawing</u> the <u>particle arrangements</u> for each one. Then jot down their <u>properties</u> next to each diagram. If you get stuck, have a <u>quick peek</u>. Then have another go.

Changes of State

Make sure you're happy with the three states of matter (p.49) and what they look like in particle theory (p.50-51). Now it's time to look at what happens as a material changes from one state to another.

Changes of State Involve a Change in Energy

1) Materials can change from one state of matter to another. For example, water changes from a LIQUID to a SOLID when it freezes.

2) Materials change state when the arrangement and energy of the particles changes.

> Changing state is an example of a physical change. There's loads more on physical changes on p.109-110.

3) At a certain temperature, the particles have enough energy to break free from their positions. This is called MELTING. The solid turns into a liquid.

4) When a liquid is heated, its particles get even more energy.

5) This energy makes the particles move faster. This weakens the forces holding the liquid together.

2) This makes the particles move more. The forces that hold the particles together get weaker.

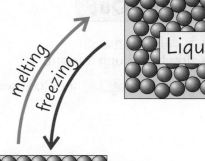

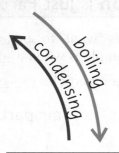

Liquid

Gas

Solid

START HERE:

1) When a solid is heated, its particles get more energy.

6) At a certain temperature, the particles have enough energy to break free from the forces. This is called BOILING. The liquid turns into a gas.

A red arrow means energy is supplied

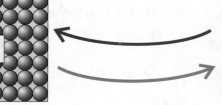

A blue arrow means energy is given out

Matter can move from solid to liquid to gas and back again

It can be tough to remember the difference between the changes of state, so try to think of some everyday examples for each. For example, solid ice cream melts to form a liquid when it's left out in the sun. Liquid water freezes to form solid ice cubes in the freezer. When you breathe on glass, it mists up as the water vapour in your breath condenses from a gas to a liquid.

Warm-Up and Practice Questions

There's a bit too much gas in this section in my opinion. Just tackle the Warm-Up Questions first, then move on to the trickier Practice Questions.

Warm-Up Questions

1) True or false? Liquids can be easily squashed.
2) What happens to the energy of particles as they are heated?
3) Which state of matter do you get when you freeze a liquid?
4) What change of state occurs if a gas gets turned into a liquid?

Practice Question

1   A student has a can of deodorant.

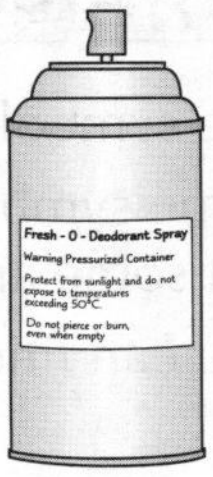

(a) The deodorant can is a solid. Which of the following are generally properties of a solid? Tick **two** boxes.

☐ Has a definite volume

☐ Has a high density

☐ Flows easily

☐ Matches the shape of the container

(2 marks)

(b) When the deodorant is sprayed, it changes from a liquid into a gas.
Complete the diagrams below to show the arrangement
of the particles in a liquid and in a gas.
Show each particle as a circle.

liquid

gas

(2 marks)

(c) The student uses the deodorant in the corner of a changing room.
After a while everyone in the room can smell the deodorant.

(i)   Explain, in terms of particles, why this is.

(1 mark)

(ii) Name this process.

(1 mark)

Atoms and Elements

If you've ever wondered what <u>everything</u> is <u>made of</u>, then the simple answer is <u>atoms</u>.

Everything on Earth is Made up of Atoms

1) <u>ATOMS</u> are pretty much the <u>smallest</u>, <u>simplest</u> type of <u>particle</u>.
2) An <u>ELEMENT</u> is a substance that contains only <u>one type of atom</u>.
3) These substances are all elements:

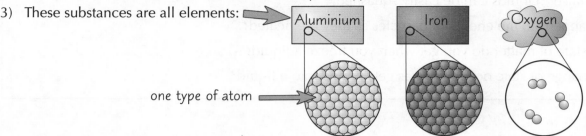

one type of atom

Every Element Has a Name and a Symbol

1) The symbol for an element can be <u>one or two letters</u>.
2) Some symbols <u>make sense</u> (like <u>O</u> for <u>o</u>xygen).
   But some are a bit <u>weird</u> — like <u>Fe</u>, the symbol for <u>iron</u>.
3) You can find the symbols for <u>all the elements</u> in the <u>periodic table</u>.

- The symbol for <u>oxygen</u> is <u>O</u>.
- The symbol for <u>aluminium</u> is <u>Al</u>.

The Periodic Table Lists All the Elements

1) Elements in the periodic table are arranged in <u>GROUPS</u> and <u>PERIODS</u>.

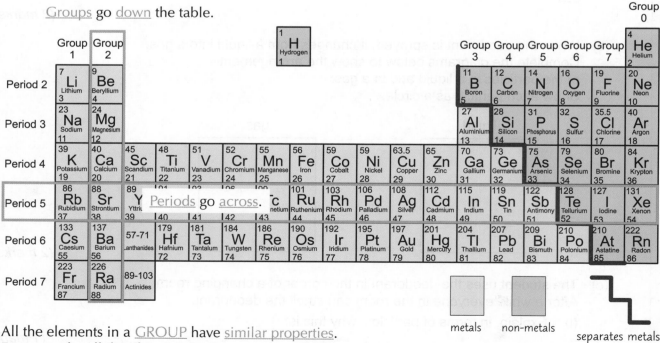

2) All the elements in a <u>GROUP</u> have <u>similar properties</u>.
   For example, all the elements in <u>Group 1</u> are <u>soft, shiny metals</u>.
3) But the <u>properties</u> of elements <u>change</u> slightly as you go <u>DOWN</u> a group.
   E.g. all the Group 1 metals <u>react</u> with <u>water</u>.
   But elements at the <u>bottom of the group</u> react <u>more violently</u> than elements at the <u>top</u>.

Section Five — Classifying Materials

Compounds

Compounds form when different atoms join together.

Compounds Contain **Two or More** Elements **Joined Up**

1) Molecules are formed when atoms join.

2) Compounds are formed when atoms from different elements join.

3) The "join" is known as a chemical bond.

4) You need to know the difference between elements and compounds:

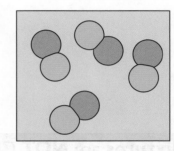

A CO₂ molecule

"join" or "bond" in molecule

An ELEMENT which is made up of atoms:

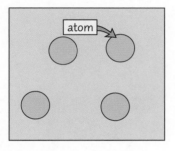

atom

The atoms are all the same.
It must be an element.

An ELEMENT which is made up of molecules:

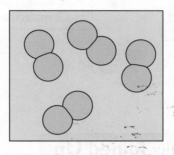

The atoms are joined, but they're all the same.
It must be an element.

Molecules in a COMPOUND:

The atoms are different and joined together.
It must be a compound.

Compounds are Formed from **Chemical Reactions**

1) In a chemical reaction chemicals combine together or split apart to form new substances.

2) When a new compound is made, elements combine.

3) New compounds produced by a chemical reaction are different from the original elements.

An example of this is iron reacting with sulfur:

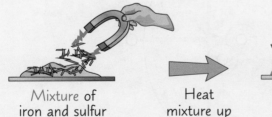

Mixture of iron and sulfur

Heat mixture up

nothing happens

Compound: iron sulfide

- Iron is magnetic.
- It reacts with sulfur to make iron sulfide.
- This is a totally new substance which is not magnetic.

All **Compounds** Have a **Chemical Formula**

1) The formula contains the symbols of the elements that make up the compound. For example:

The symbol for iron is Fe. The symbol for sulfur is S. The FORMULA for iron sulfide is FeS.

2) Numbers in the formula tell you if there's more than one atom of a particular element.

H_2O (water) has two H atoms and one O atom.

Mixtures

Mixtures in chemistry are like cake mix in the kitchen — all the components are mushed up together, but you can still pick out the raisins if you really want. Before you get to that though, there's a bit on pure substances.

Pure Substances Don't Contain Anything Else

1) A pure substance is made up of only one type of element OR only one type of compound.
2) It can't be separated into anything simpler without a chemical reaction.

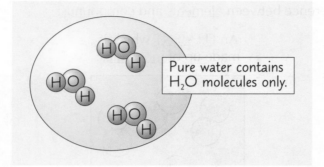

Pure water contains H_2O molecules only.

Mixtures are NOT Chemically Joined Up

1) A mixture contains two or more different substances.
2) These substances aren't chemically joined up. You can separate them fairly easily.
3) Air is a good example of a mixture. It contain several different gases.
   These gases aren't chemically combined together.
4) A mixture has the properties of the parts it's made from.

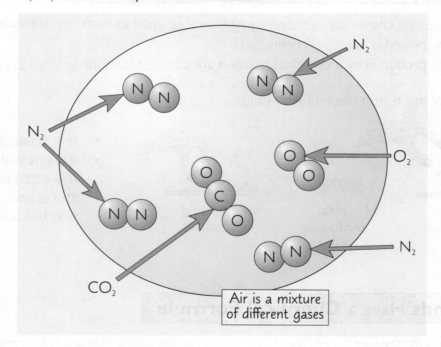

Air is a mixture of different gases

The components of a mixture are not chemically combined

I've said it already, but this is important — the parts of a mixture are not chemically-joined up at all. You can separate the substances fairly easily using physical methods (more on them in a couple of pages). A compound is different. You need a chemical reaction to separate one of these into something simpler.

Mixtures

If you've ever added some <u>sugar</u> to a cup of <u>tea</u>, you might have noticed that the sugar disappears from sight. It's <u>not magic</u> that causes this to happen — it's <u>dissolving</u>. Read on to find out more.

Dissolving isn't Disappearing

1) <u>Dissolving</u> is a common way mixtures are made. It involves adding a <u>solid</u> to a <u>liquid</u>.
2) This can <u>break</u> the <u>bonds</u> holding the solid particles together.
3) The solid particles then <u>mix</u> with the particles in the liquid. This makes a <u>solution</u>.

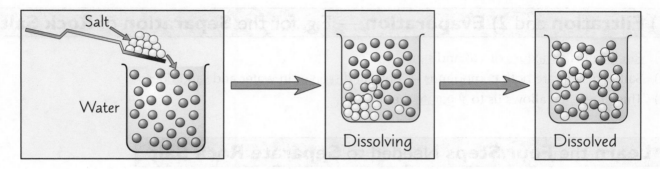

<u>Learn</u> these five words:

1) <u>Solute</u> – is the <u>solid</u> being dissolved.

2) <u>Solvent</u> – is the <u>liquid</u> it's dissolving into.

3) <u>Solution</u> – is a <u>mixture</u> of a solute and a solvent that does not separate out by itself.

4) <u>Soluble</u> – means a substance <u>WILL</u> dissolve.

5) <u>Insoluble</u> – means a substance will <u>NOT</u> dissolve.

4) When something <u>dissolves</u> it doesn't <u>vanish</u>. It's still <u>there</u> — <u>no mass</u> is lost.

20g salt   Added to 100g water =   120g solution

5) If you <u>evaporate</u> off the <u>solvent</u> (the liquid), you will see the <u>solute</u> (the solid) again (see next page).

There is no change in a solute's mass when it dissolves

It may <u>look</u> like salt disappears in water, but it's <u>still there</u> and it still has the same <u>mass</u>. Make sure you remember that, and learn the <u>five words</u> in the box. Right, now it's time to see how to <u>separate mixtures</u>.

Separating Mixtures

There are all sorts of ways you can separate mixtures. You've got to know <u>four</u> of them.

Mixtures Can be Separated Using Physical Methods

Here are the <u>four separation methods</u> you need to know:

1) <u>FILTRATION</u>   2) <u>EVAPORATION</u>

3) <u>CHROMATOGRAPHY</u>   4) <u>DISTILLATION</u>.

> Physical methods involve physical changes (see p.109).

1) Filtration and 2) Evaporation — E.g. for the Separation of Rock Salt

1) <u>Rock Salt</u> is a <u>mixture</u> of <u>salt</u> and <u>sand</u>.

2) Salt and sand are both <u>compounds</u> — but <u>salt dissolves</u> in water and <u>sand doesn't</u>.

3) This <u>difference</u> allows us to <u>separate</u> them.

Learn the Four Steps Needed to Separate Rock Salt

1) <u>Grinding</u>   2) <u>Dissolving</u>   3) <u>Filtering</u>   4) <u>Evaporating</u>

Grind up the rock salt with a <u>pestle and mortar</u>.

Dissolve in water and <u>stir</u>.

Filter through filter paper in a <u>funnel</u>.

Evaporate in an <u>evaporating dish</u>.

You can <u>evaporate off</u> the water by <u>boiling</u> the mixture. The liquid water will turn into a <u>gas</u> and <u>escape</u>. This leaves behind <u>salt crystals</u>.

- The sand <u>doesn't dissolve</u> in the water (it's <u>insoluble</u>). It stays as <u>big grains</u>.
- These big grains <u>won't fit</u> through the <u>tiny holes</u> in the filter paper. So the sand <u>collects on the filter paper</u>.
- The salt <u>does dissolve</u> in the water, so it goes <u>through</u> the filter paper. The salt forms <u>crystals</u> in the <u>evaporating dish</u> when the water is <u>evaporated</u>.

Grind, dissolve, filter, evaporate

It's pretty easy to separate <u>rock salt</u> into <u>rock</u> (sand) and <u>salt</u>. Salt <u>dissolves</u> in water, but sand <u>does not</u>. So all you need to do is <u>mash up</u> the rock salt, <u>dissolve</u> the salt, and fish out the sand with a <u>filter</u>. Then you can get rid of the water by <u>evaporating it off</u>. Easy when you know how — make sure you do.

Separating Mixtures

Two separation methods down, two more to go. Dive right in...

3) Chromatography is Ideal for Separating Dyes in Inks

Ink is a mixture of several different dyes (colourings).

You can use chromatography to separate the dyes in ink. Here's how:

1) Draw a pencil line near the bottom of some chromatography paper.

2) Put spots of inks along the line.

3) Roll the paper up and put it in a beaker of shallow solvent, for example water.

4) The solvent seeps up the paper. The ink dyes are carried with it.

5) The dyes travel up the paper at different speeds. So each dye will form a spot in a different place.

6) You end up with a pattern of spots like the one here. You can compare the pattern of spots in an unknown ink to the pattern of spots in some known inks to see which it is.

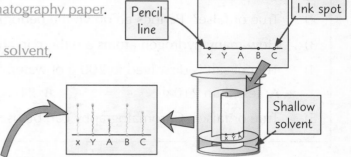

4) Distillation Separates Liquids from Solids

1) Simple distillation can be used for separating out a mixture of a liquid and a solid. For example, salt water.

2) The mixture is heated in a flask and the water boils off to form a gas.

3) The gas is cooled and turns back to a liquid in a condenser.

4) The liquid water is collected in a beaker.

5) The salt is left behind in the flask.

6) Simple distillation can also be used to get pure water from dirty water.

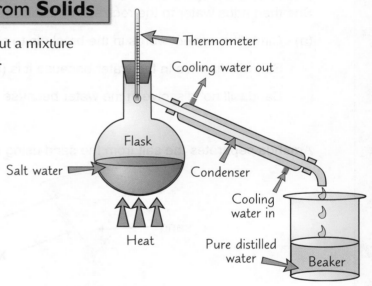

Check Purity with Melting and Boiling Points

1) A pure chemical substance has fixed melting and boiling points.

   For example, pure water boils at 100 °C and pure ice melts at 0 °C.

2) We know the melting and boiling points of a huge range of substances.

3) This helps us to identify substances if we're not sure what they are. For example, a liquid that boils at exactly 100 °C is likely to be pure water.

4) Impurities (other chemicals) change melting and boiling points. For example, impurities in water cause it to boil above 100 °C.

5) This means you can test the purity of a substance you've separated from a mixture. So if you want to test the purity of some water, boil it and check the temperature it boils at.

Section Five — Classifying Materials

Warm-Up and Practice Questions

Phew, that's enough stuff on mixtures to last a lifetime. Time to test whether it all went in though. Have a go at these Warm-Ups. Once you're happy with them, move on to the Practice Questions.

Warm-Up Questions

1) What is an element?

2) True or false? Periods go down the periodic table.

3) How many hydrogen atoms are there in a molecule of methane, CH_4?

4) 10 g of salt is dissolved in 200 g of water. What will the mass of the solution be?

   A: less than 210 g   **B:** 210 g   **C:** more than 210 g

5) True or false? Chromatography can be used to separate a mixture of dyes in an ink.

Practice Questions

1   Rock salt is a mixture of salt and sand. Amanda grinds up some rock salt.
    She then adds water to the rock salt and stirs.

   (a) Circle the correct words in the brackets to complete the following sentences.

        Salt will dissolve in the water because it is (**soluble / insoluble**).

        Sand will not dissolve in the water because it is (**soluble / insoluble**).

        (2 marks)

   Amanda separates the salt from the sand using the apparatus shown below:

   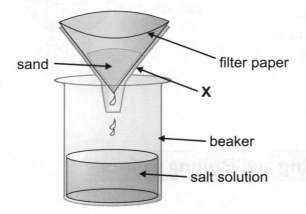

   (b) What is the piece of equipment labelled **X** on the diagram above? Tick **one** box.

   ☐ condenser   ☐ evaporating dish   ☐ funnel

        (1 mark)

   (c) What is this separation technique called?

        (1 mark)

   (d) Describe how Amanda could get salt crystals from the salt solution.

        (1 mark)

Section Five — Classifying Materials

Practice Questions

2   When Sally adds salt to water and stirs it, the salt dissolves in the water.

   (a)   Draw lines to match up the scientific words on the left
          to the substances on the right:

solvent		salt water
solution		water
solute		salt

(3 marks)

   (b)   Sally uses simple distillation to purify the salt water.

      (i)   The steps in the process of simple distillation are given below.
             Put the steps into the correct order.
             The first two statements have been done for you.

      A   The mixture is heated in a flask. — **Step 1**
      B   The water boils to form steam. — **Step 2**
      C   The water drips into a beaker.
      D   A condenser is used to cool the steam.
      E   The steam turns into water.

(2 marks)

      (ii)   How could Sally check that the distilled water is pure?

(1 mark)

3   The diagrams below represent the arrangement of atoms and
     molecules in four different substances, A, B, C and D.

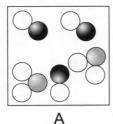 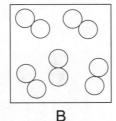 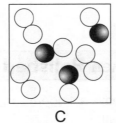 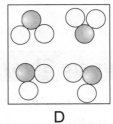

      A   B   C   D

   (a)   Which substance is a pure element?

(1 mark)

   (b)   Which substance is a mixture of two compounds?

(1 mark)

   (c)   Which substance would you expect to find in the periodic table?

(1 mark)

   (d)   Which substance is most likely to be pure Quater, H_2O?

(1 mark)

Properties of Metals

Metals are jolly <u>useful</u>. We use them all the time in <u>wires</u>, <u>bridges</u>, <u>musical instruments</u> and more. So it's only fair that you learn these two pages of fab <u>facts</u> about them in return...

1) Metals Can be Found in the Periodic Table

1) <u>Most</u> of the elements in the periodic table are metals.
2) Some are shown here in grey, to the <u>left</u> of the <u>zig zag</u>.

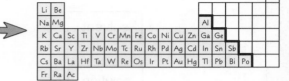

2) Metals Conduct Electricity

1) This means metals allow <u>electrical current</u> to pass through them <u>easily</u>.
2) So metals are used to make <u>wires</u> to allow <u>electricity</u> to move around a <u>circuit</u>.

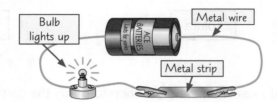

3) Metals Conduct Energy

1) Metals <u>transfer energy</u> from a <u>hot place</u> to a <u>cold place</u> quickly and easily.
2) That's why <u>saucepans</u> are usually made out of metal.

4) Metals are Strong and Tough

1) Metals have high <u>tensile strength</u>. This means they can be <u>pulled hard</u> without breaking.
2) So they make good <u>building materials</u>.

5) Metals are Shiny When Polished

1) <u>Polished</u> or <u>freshly cut</u> metals have a <u>smooth surface</u>.
2) This means they <u>reflect</u> light well.
3) So they look <u>shiny</u>.

6) Metals are Sonorous

1) This means they make a nice <u>"donnnnggg"</u> sound when they're hit.
2) If you think about it, it's <u>only metals</u> that do that.

Section Five — Classifying Materials

Properties of Metals

7) Metals are Malleable

1) Metals are easily shaped (malleable).
2) This means metals can be hammered into thin sheets or bent.
3) Shaped metal is used in cars and planes.

8) Metals are Ductile

1) This means they can be drawn into wires.
2) This means metals aren't brittle like non-metals are (see page 65).
3) Metals just bend and stretch.

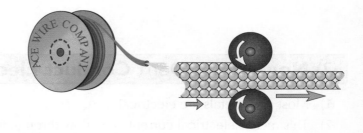

9) Metals have High Melting and Boiling Points

1) A lot of energy is needed to melt metals.
2) This is because their atoms are joined together with strong bonds.
3) Things that get really hot (like ovens) are usually made of metal, so they don't melt.

10) Metals have High Densities

1) Density is all to do with how much stuff there is squeezed into a certain space.
2) Metals feel heavy for their size — they're very dense. It's because they have a lot of atoms in a small space.

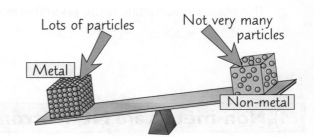

Lots of particles

Not very many particles

Metal

Non-metal

11) Some Metals are Magnetic

1) Magnetic means attracted to magnets.
2) Most metals aren't magnetic.
3) Iron, nickel and cobalt are magnetic.

Iron or nickel or cobalt

Most metals have similar properties to one another

Quite a few properties of metals to learn here. Make sure you understand each one before moving on.

Properties of Non-Metals

The properties of non-metal elements <u>vary</u> a lot. As you will slowly begin to realise...

1) **Non-metals** Can be Found in the **Periodic Table**

1) Non-metals are on the <u>right</u> of the <u>zigzag</u>.
2) There are <u>fewer</u> non-metals than metals.

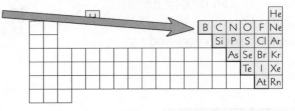

2) **Non-metals** Don't **Conduct Electricity**

1) Most non-metals are electrical <u>insulators</u>.
2) This means electrical current <u>can't</u> flow through them.
3) This is <u>useful</u> — non-metals are used to make things like <u>plugs</u> and electric cable <u>coverings</u>.

One exception to this rule is <u>graphite</u>. It's a <u>non-metal</u> made of <u>carbon</u>. But graphite <u>can conduct electricity</u>.

3) **Non-metals** Don't **Conduct Energy** by **Heating** Well

1) Non-metals <u>don't</u> transfer energy from a <u>hot place</u> to a <u>cold place</u> quickly or easily.
2) This makes non-metals really good thermal <u>insulators</u>.
3) <u>Oven gloves</u>, <u>saucepan handles</u> and <u>loft insulation</u> are normally made of <u>non-metals</u>.

4) **Non-metals** are **NOT Strong** or **Hard-Wearing**

1) The <u>forces</u> between the particles in non-metals are <u>weak</u>.
2) This means non-metals <u>break</u> easily.
3) It's also easy to <u>scrub</u> atoms or molecules off them — so they <u>wear away</u> quickly.

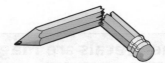

5) **Non-metals** are **Dull**

1) Most non-metals don't <u>reflect</u> light well.
2) Their surfaces are not usually as <u>smooth</u> as metals.
3) This makes them look <u>dull</u>.

Not much reflection

carbon

Properties of Non-Metals

6) Non-metals are Brittle

1) Non-metal <u>structures</u> are held together by <u>weak forces</u>.
2) This means they can <u>shatter</u> all too easily.

7) Non-metals Have Low Melting Points and Boiling Points

1) The <u>forces</u> which hold the particles in non-metals <u>together</u> are <u>very weak</u>.
This means they <u>melt</u> and <u>boil</u> very <u>easily</u>.
2) At <u>room temperature</u>, most non-metals are <u>gases</u> or <u>solids</u>. Only one is <u>liquid</u>.

8) Non-metals Have Low Densities

1) This means they <u>don't</u> have many <u>particles</u> packed into a certain <u>space</u>.
2) Non-metals which are <u>gases</u> have <u>very low densities</u>.
Some of these gases will even <u>float</u> in <u>air</u>.
These are ideal for <u>party balloons</u>.
3) Even the liquid and solid non-metals have <u>low densities</u>.

9) Non-metals are Not Magnetic

1) Only a few <u>metals</u> (iron, cobalt and nickel) are <u>magnetic</u>.
2) <u>All non-metals</u> are definitely <u>non-magnetic</u>.

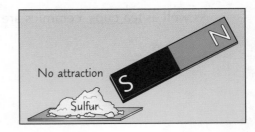

Non-metals — nine properties you need to know

Try making a <u>mind map</u>. Start with a <u>bubble</u> with the word "<u>non-metal</u>" in the middle.
Then have nine <u>little bubbles</u> coming off it showing the <u>nine properties</u>. And then around
each mini-bubble, you can write <u>everything you know</u> about the <u>property</u>. As a matter of
fact, it might be a good idea to make <u>two</u> mind maps — one for <u>metals</u> as well.

Properties of Other Materials

As well as metals and non-metals, you need to learn all about some compounds and mixtures of compounds. First up, it's polymers and ceramics.

Polymers Have Many Useful Properties

Another name for polymers is plastics. Nylon, polythene and PVC are all polymers.

1) Polymers are usually insulators. It's difficult for energy to be transferred through them electrically or by heating.

2) They're often flexible. They can be bent without breaking.

3) They can be very light for their size and strength. So they're ideal for making things that need to be strong but not heavy.

4) They're easily moulded. They can be used to manufacture equipment with almost any shape.

Polymers are used to make everything from kayaks to carrier bags.

Ceramics are Stiff but Brittle

Ceramics include glass, porcelain and bone china (for posh tea cups). They are:

1) Insulators of heat and electricity.

2) Brittle — they aren't very flexible and will break instead of bending.

3) Stiff — they can withstand strong forces before they break.

As well as tea cups, ceramics are used for brakes in cars.

Eat, sleep, learn some properties, repeat...

Remembering some examples of each type of material will help you to learn their properties. E.g. you can hold a tea cup without the tea burning you, so ceramics must be insulators of heat. They smash if you drop them, so they're brittle too. Have a go at making a list of some examples that'll help you remember the properties of the different types of material.

Properties of Other Materials

There's one more type of material that you need to know about — composites. Read on to find out more...

Composites are Made of Different Materials

1) Composite materials are made from two or more materials stuck together.

2) This can make a material with more useful properties than either material alone. For example:

Fibreglass

1) Fibreglass is made up of glass fibres fixed in plastic.

2) It has a low density (like plastic) but is very strong (like glass).

3) So fibreglass is used to make skis, boats and surfboards.

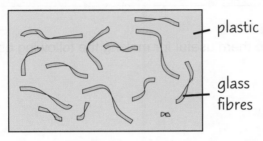

plastic

glass fibres

FIBREGLASS

Concrete

1) Concrete is made from a mixture of sand and gravel mixed in cement.

2) It can cope with being squashed without breaking.
So it's great at supporting heavy things.

3) This makes it ideal for use as a building material, for example in skate parks, shopping centres, and airport runways.

CONCRETE

Fibreglass and concrete are composite materials

Two or more materials are COMbined to make a COMposite. See — not so difficult when you know how. Now just remember a couple of examples and you're flying...

Warm-Up and Practice Questions

Take a look at these Warm-Up Questions and test yourself. If you get any wrong,
go back and have a look at the parts you didn't know, then test yourself again.   Simple.

Warm-Up Questions

1) Name a metal that is magnetic.

2) Out of metals and non-metals, which are the:
a) densest,   b) most brittle,   c) shiniest,   d) best electrical insulators?

3) Name two useful properties of polymers.

4) True or false? Concrete is made from glass fibres mixed in cement.

Practice Questions

1   Metals and non-metals have different properties.

(a)   Which property of metals would make them useful for making the following objects?
Tick **one** box for each object.

(i)   a bridge

☐   good conductor of electricity

☐   strong

☐   dense

(1 mark)

(ii)   a trophy

☐   shiny when polished

☐   magnetic

☐   high melting point

(1 mark)

(iii)   a frying pan

☐   sonorous

☐   ductile

☐   good conductor of heat

(1 mark)

(b)   Sulfur is found on the right-hand side of the periodic table.

(i)   Would you expect sulfur to be a good conductor of energy by heating?
Give a reason for your answer.

(1 mark)

(ii)   Complete the sentences below by selecting
the correct option in each of the brackets.

Sulfur is (**magnetic** / **non-magnetic**). Its surface has a (**shiny** / **dull**)
yellow colour. Sulfur is also (**brittle** / **flexible**).

(3 marks)

Practice Questions

2   Elements can be metals or non-metals.
     The diagram below shows some elements in the periodic table.

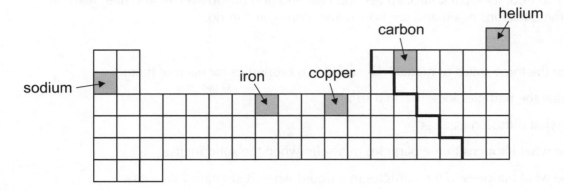

(a)   From the elements shown above, give the name of one element which
      (i)   is a metal.
      (ii)   is a non-metal.
      (iii) will be attracted by a magnet.

                                                                          (3 marks)

(b)   Does the periodic table contain more metals or non-metals?

                                                                          (1 mark)

3   Sophie is designing a bottle for a drinks company.
(a)   The bottle needs to be light, flexible and have an interesting shape.
      (i)   Suggest a material that the bottle could be made from.

                                                                          (1 mark)

      (ii)   Give **one** reason why a metal might **not** be a good material to use for the bottle.

                                                                          (1 mark)

(b)   Sophie is also designing a set of ceramic cups for the company.
      The cups need to be designed for hot drinks. Give **one** property of ceramics
      that allows someone to hold a hot drink without being burned.

                                                                          (1 mark)

(c)   Sophie is given a surfboard made of fibreglass as a present from the company.
      (i)   Fibreglass is a composite material.
             Explain what is meant by a composite material.

                                                                          (1 mark)

      (ii)   Circle the **two** properties of fibreglass that make it
             a good choice of material for a surfboard.

             good insulator of heat   **strong**   **non-magnetic**

                     high melting point   **low density**

                                                                          (2 marks)

Section Five — Classifying Materials

Revision Summary for Section Five

You may have noticed that we've moved on to Chemistry now.
Makes a refreshing change from all that slimy Biology anyway.
You know the drill: work through these questions and try to answer them.
For any you can't do, look back through Section Five and find the answer — and then learn it.
Then try all the questions again and see how many more you can do.

1) What are the three states of matter? Describe two properties for each of them. ☑

2) Draw what the particles look like in a solid. ☑

3) Explain what diffusion is. ☑

4) Describe what happens to the particles in a solid when the solid melts. ☑

5) Describe what happens to the particles in a liquid when it changes into a gas. ☑

6) What is an atom? ☑

7) Do groups go down the periodic table or across? ☑

8)* Using the periodic table on page 54, give the chemical symbol for each of these:
    a) sodium   b) magnesium   c) oxygen   d) iron   e) sulfur
    f) aluminium   g) carbon   h) chlorine   i) calcium   j) zinc. ☑

9) True or false? All elements in a group have similar properties. ☑

10) What is a compound? ☑

11) Give one way that iron sulfide is different to a mixture of iron and sulfur. ☑

12)* Which two elements are in the compound H_2O? (Use the periodic table on page 54 to help you.) ☑

13)* Which two elements are in the compound $CaCl_2$? (Use the periodic table on page 54 to help you.) ☑

14) What is a pure substance? ☑

15) What is a mixture? ☑

16) Describe what happens when a substance dissolves. ☑

17) List four techniques for separating a mixture.
    Give an example of a mixture that you could separate with each one. ☑

18) List the 11 properties of metals that you need to know. ☑

19) List the 9 properties of non-metals that you need to know. ☑

20) Out of metals and non-metals, which are the:
    a) best conductors   b) strongest? ☑

21) What are ceramics useful for? ☑

22) Name a composite and describe what it's made of. ☑

*Answer on page 192

Equations

Chemistry is full of equations. Luckily, you'll find all you need to know about them here.

Chemicals are **Formed** in **Chemical Reactions**

1) In a chemical reaction, chemicals combine together or split apart to form new substances.
2) The chemicals you start with are called the REACTANTS.
3) The chemicals you end up with are called the PRODUCTS.

Word Equations Show **What's Happening** in a Reaction

1) You can show what's happening in a chemical reaction by writing an equation.
2) A word equation has the names of all the chemicals written out in full.

EXAMPLE:

This equation means that sodium and water join together...   ...to make sodium hydroxide and hydrogen.

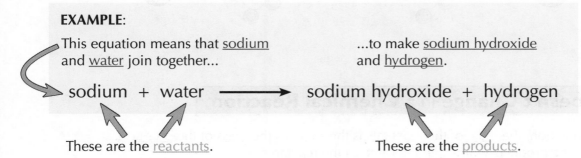

sodium + water ⟶ sodium hydroxide + hydrogen

These are the reactants.   These are the products.

Scientists Usually Use **Symbol Equations**

1) Remember, all elements have a symbol in the periodic table (see page 54).
2) The formula for a compound (see page 55) is made up of the symbols of the elements inside it.
3) A symbol equation uses symbols and formulas to show what's happening in a chemical reaction.
4) The big numbers show you the amounts of reactants and products in the reaction.

EXAMPLE:

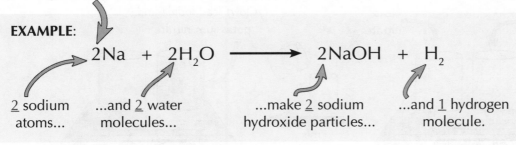

$$2Na + 2H_2O \longrightarrow 2NaOH + H_2$$

2 sodium atoms...   ...and 2 water molecules...   ...make 2 sodium hydroxide particles...   ...and 1 hydrogen molecule.

'H_2' means the same as '$1H_2$'. You don't need to write a big '1' each time there's only one of something in a symbol equation.

5) Here are some examples of formulas you'll see a lot in symbol equations:

H_2O
(water)

NaCl
(table salt)

CO_2
(carbon dioxide)

Chemical Reactions

In a chemical reaction, all that's really happening is the <u>atoms are moving around</u> into new positions. The reactants might give out energy or make a loud bang, but the <u>mass won't change</u>.

Atoms Move About During Chemical Reactions

1) In a <u>chemical reaction</u> atoms are <u>not</u> made or destroyed.

2) The atoms <u>move around</u> during a chemical reaction, but they're <u>not changed</u>.

3) The atoms at the <u>start</u> of a reaction are <u>still there</u> at the <u>end</u>.

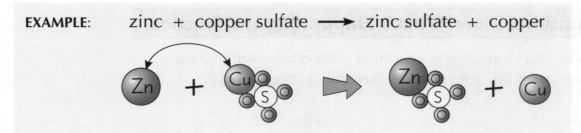

EXAMPLE: zinc + copper sulfate ⟶ zinc sulfate + copper

The Mass Doesn't Change in a Chemical Reaction

1) In a chemical reaction, the <u>mass</u> of the <u>reactants</u> is the <u>same</u> as the <u>mass</u> of the <u>products</u>. In other words, the products will <u>weigh the same</u> as the reactants.

2) You might be able to <u>see</u> changes in the reaction mixture — these show that a reaction has taken place. For example — a <u>gas</u> comes off, a <u>solid</u> is made, or the <u>colour</u> changes.

EXAMPLE:

1) When colourless <u>potassium iodide</u> solution reacts with colourless <u>lead nitrate</u> solution, you get <u>potassium nitrate</u> and <u>lead iodide</u>.

2) The mixture goes <u>bright yellow</u> and <u>heats up</u>.

3) But the <u>mass stays the same</u>.

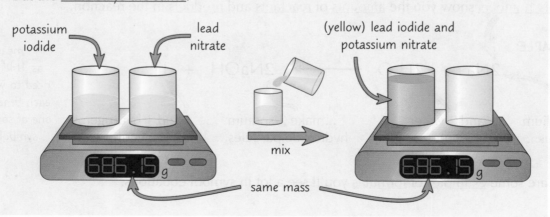

potassium iodide   lead nitrate   (yellow) lead iodide and potassium nitrate

mix

686.15 g   same mass   686.15 g

Chemical reactions — just a case of atoms moving around

Some <u>chemical reactions</u> involve colour changes, heating up, stinky gases and even explosions, but there's one thing that always stays the <u>same</u> — the total <u>mass</u>, before and after the reaction.

Examples of Chemical Reactions

This page contains three common examples of chemical reactions.

Combustion is Burning in Oxygen

1) Combustion is burning — a fuel reacts with oxygen to release energy.
2) Three things are needed for combustion:

   1) Fuel
   2) Heating
   3) Oxygen

3) Hydrocarbons are fuels containing only hydrogen and carbon.
4) When it's hot enough and there's enough oxygen, hydrocarbons combust (burn) to give water and carbon dioxide:

> **hydrocarbon + oxygen ⟶ carbon dioxide + water (+ energy)**

5) Combustion is useful because energy is transferred away by light and by heating.

Oxidation is the Gain of Oxygen

1) When a substance reacts with oxygen, it's called an oxidation reaction.
2) Combustion is an oxidation reaction.
3) Rusting is also an oxidation reaction.
4) Rusting is when iron reacts with oxygen in the air to form iron oxide (rust).

> **iron + oxygen ⟶ iron oxide (rust)**

Thermal Decomposition is Breaking Down by Heating

1) Thermal decomposition is when you heat a substance and it breaks down.
2) For example, if you heat copper carbonate it breaks down into copper oxide and carbon dioxide.

EXAMPLE:

$$\text{copper carbonate} \longrightarrow \text{copper oxide} + \text{carbon dioxide}$$
$$CuCO_3 \qquad\qquad CuO \quad + \quad CO_2$$

This is green...  ...and this is black.

3) Only certain substances break down when they're heated — usually things just melt.

Thermal decomposition only needs one reactant

Here are three common types of chemical reaction to read about and learn. A good way to learn key phrases and equations is to use flash cards — create some for this topic.

More on Chemical Reactions

Chemical reactions always involve a transfer of energy to or from the surroundings.

In an Exothermic Reaction, Energy is Given Out

An EXOTHERMIC REACTION is one which TRANSFERS ENERGY TO the surroundings

1) Energy is usually given out by heating.
2) So exothermic reactions involve an INCREASE in temperature.
3) The best example of an exothermic reaction is combustion (see page 73).
   This gives out a lot of energy — it's very exothermic.
4) Many neutralisation reactions (page 76) and oxidation reactions (page 73) are exothermic.
5) Everyday uses of exothermic reactions include hand warmers and self-heating cans of coffee.

In an Endothermic Reaction, Energy is Taken in

An ENDOTHERMIC REACTION is one which TAKES IN ENERGY from the surroundings

1) Energy is usually taken in by heating.
2) So endothermic reactions involve a DECREASE in temperature.
3) Thermal decompositions (page 73) are endothermic reactions.
   They involve a substance taking in energy, then breaking down.
4) Everyday uses of endothermic reactions include sports injury packs.
   They take in energy and get very cold.

Catalysts Make Reactions Faster

A CATALYST is a substance which SPEEDS UP a chemical reaction. It is not CHANGED or USED UP in the reaction itself.

1) Catalysts speed up reactions — so more product can be made in the same amount of time.
2) Catalysts allow reactions to happen at lower temperatures.
3) In industry, high temperatures make reactions expensive to run.
   So catalysts make reactions cheaper.
4) Catalysts come out of a reaction the same as when they went in.
   This means catalysts can be reused.

"exo-" means out and "endo-" means in

"Exothermic" and "endothermic" sound pretty similar, but don't get them confused — they have very different meanings. Most reactions you'll see in the chemistry lab are exothermic. Exothermic reactions are usually the ones that are easier to spot — a flame is a good clue.

Acids and Alkalis

The pH scale is what scientists use to describe how acidic or alkaline a substance is.

The pH Scale Shows the Strength of Acids and Alkalis

1) The pH scale goes from 0 to 14.
2) Anything with a pH below 7 is an acid. The strongest acid has pH 0.
3) Anything with a pH above 7 is an alkali. The strongest alkali has pH 14.
4) A neutral substance has pH 7 (like water).

Indicators Are Dyes Which Change Colour

An indicator is something that changes colour depending on whether it's in an acid or in an alkali.

1) Litmus paper is an indicator. Acids turn litmus paper red. Alkalis turn it blue.
2) Universal indicator solution is a liquid indicator.
3) It gives the colours shown in a pH chart.

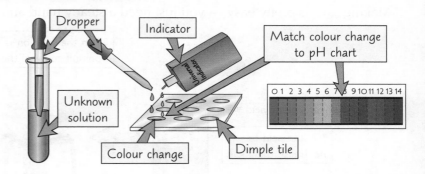

A pH Chart Shows How Strong an Acid or Alkali is

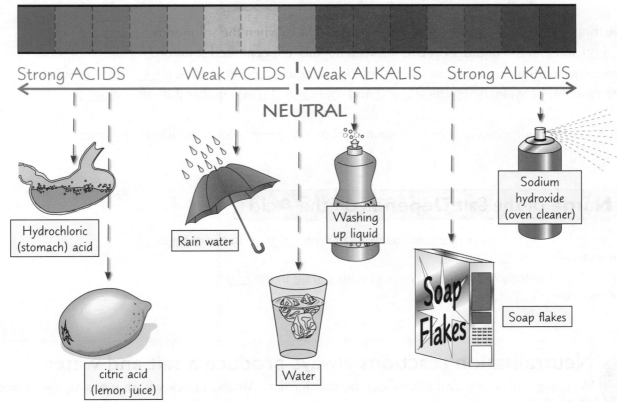

Section Six — Chemical Changes

Neutralisation Reactions

You might have done something like this in the lab. If not, I bet you will pretty soon.

Acids and Alkalis Neutralise Each Other

1) Acids react with alkalis to form a salt and water:

> You can get different kinds of salt — not just table salt.

$$\text{acid + alkali} \longrightarrow \text{salt + water}$$

2) This is a neutralisation reaction. The products have a neutral pH (a pH of 7).

Making Salts by Neutralisation

Making salts is pretty easy — you just need a steady hand and a lot of time.

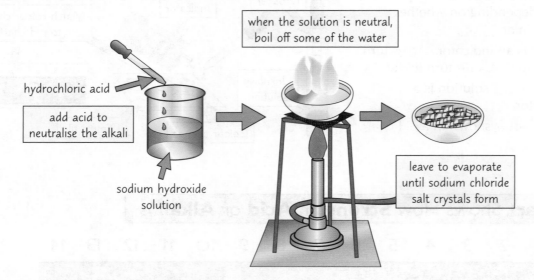

when the solution is neutral, boil off some of the water

hydrochloric acid

add acid to neutralise the alkali

sodium hydroxide solution

leave to evaporate until sodium chloride salt crystals form

1) Wearing eye protection, add an acid to an alkali. Stop when the solution is neutral.
2) Boil off some of the liquid so you're left with a really concentrated solution.
3) Leave the solution overnight for the rest of the water to evaporate. Nice big salt crystals will form.
4) The reaction between hydrochloric acid and sodium hydroxide makes the salt sodium chloride:

$$\text{hydrochloric acid + sodium hydroxide} \longrightarrow \text{sodium chloride + water}$$

The Name of the Salt Depends on the Acid

1) Hydrochloric acid always reacts to make a salt with chloride in the name.
   For example, sodium chloride.
2) Sulfuric acid always reacts to make a salt with sulfate in the name.
   For example, copper sulfate.

Neutralisation reactions always produce a salt and water

Working with acids and alkalis can be dangerous. Always check you're wearing the correct protective clothing when you're using them, e.g. safety goggles, gloves and a lab coat.

Section Six — Chemical Changes

Warm-Up and Practice Questions

You need to learn all the stuff in this section. Might as well make a start on it now.
It's not a lot of fun, but it's the only way to get good marks.

Warm-Up Questions

1) 92 g of sodium reacts with 142 g of chlorine to make sodium chloride.
   Work out the total mass of the sodium chloride produced from this reaction.

2) True or false? A catalyst can be used more than once.

3) What is the highest number on the pH scale?

4) True or false? Acids have a pH below 7.

5) What would you see if an indicator was added to an acid or an alkali?

6) What kind of acid would you use to make zinc sulfate?

Practice Questions

1 Chemical reactions can be endothermic or exothermic.
   (a) Complete the sentences below. Use words from the box.

surroundings	**decreasing**	**products**
reactants		**increasing**

   In an endothermic reaction, energy is taken in from the _____.
   This is often shown by the temperature _____.

   (2 marks)

   (b) Combustion and oxidation are both types of **exothermic** reaction.
      (i) Circle the **three** things needed for **combustion** to take place.

      | light | | a salt | | heat | | fuel |

      | water | | oxygen | | acid |

      (3 marks)

      (ii) Complete the word equation for the following **oxidation** reaction.

      iron + oxygen $\longrightarrow$ _____

      (1 mark)

2 Channing heats some copper carbonate ($CuCO_3$).
   Copper oxide (CuO) and carbon dioxide are produced.
   (a) What type of reaction is this? Tick **one** box.

   ☐ combustion   ☐ thermal decomposition   ☐ neutralisation

   (1 mark)

   (b) Suggest **one** way in which Channing could tell that a reaction has taken place.

   (1 mark)

Section Six — Chemical Changes

Practice Questions

3   Use the pH chart below to answer this question.

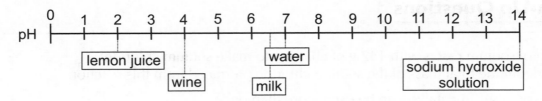

(a)   Give **one** substance on the chart that is:
    (i)   acidic

(1 mark)

    (ii)   alkaline

(1 mark)

    (iii)   neutral

(1 mark)

(b)   Suggest **one** substance on the chart that could neutralise
    sodium hydroxide solution. Explain your answer.

(2 marks)

4   Nish is making sodium chloride. He slowly adds hydrochloric acid to a
sodium hydroxide solution until the sodium hydroxide had all reacted.

(a)   Complete the general word equation for this kind of reaction:

$$\text{acid} + \text{alkali} \longrightarrow \text{.............................} + \text{.............................}$$

(1 mark)

(b)   Describe how Nish could use universal indicator solution
    to find out when all of the sodium hydroxide had reacted.

(2 marks)

5   Nitrogen gas reacts with hydrogen gas to form ammonia.

(a) NH_3 is the chemical formula for ammonia.
    How many nitrogen atoms and hydrogen atoms are there in a molecule of ammonia?

(1 mark)

(b)   One molecule of nitrogen gas (N_2) reacts with three molecules of hydrogen gas (H_2).
    Two molecules of ammonia are formed.
    Use this information to write a symbol equation for this reaction.

(2 marks)

(c)   When this reaction is carried out in industry, an iron catalyst is used.
    Which of the following statements about catalysts is **not** true? Tick **one** box.

    ☐   Catalysts speed up reactions.

    ☐   Catalysts are not used up in reactions.

    ☐   Catalysts increase the temperature of reactions.

    ☐   Catalysts make industrial processes cheaper.

(1 mark)

Reactivity Series and Metal Extraction

You need to know which metals are most reactive — and which are least reactive.

The **Reactivity Series** — How **Well** a Metal **Reacts**

The Reactivity Series lists metals in order of how reactive they are.

The Reactivity Series

Make sure you learn this list:

Potassium	K	} Very reactive
Sodium	Na	
Calcium	Ca	
Magnesium	Mg	} Fairly reactive
Aluminium	Al	
(Carbon)	non-metal	
Zinc	Zn	}
Iron	Fe	
Lead	Pb	} Not very reactive
(Hydrogen)	non-metal	
Copper	Cu	
Silver	Ag	} Not at all reactive
Gold	Au	

Carbon and hydrogen are non-metals, but it's useful to know where they are in the reactivity series.

Some **Metals** Can Be **Extracted** With **Carbon**

1) Metals are usually mined as ores — rocks containing metal compounds. These compounds are usually metal oxides — see page 81.

2) A metal can be extracted (removed) from its ore using REDUCTION.

3) Reduction means removing oxygen from the ore to leave behind the metal. Reduction of a metal ore can be done using carbon.

   For example, carbon is used to remove oxygen from iron oxide:

   iron oxide + carbon ⟶ iron + carbon dioxide

4) Only metals below carbon in the reactivity series can be extracted from their ore using carbon.

5) Metals above carbon (like aluminium and magnesium) can't be extracted from their ores like this. You need electricity to get those out.

Potassium
Sodium
Calcium
Magnesium
Aluminium

—CARBON—

Zinc
Iron
Lead
Copper

A metal's reactivity shows how it will behave in reactions

It's a good idea to learn a phrase that helps you remember the order of the elements in the reactivity series. For example, Peter Stopped Calling Me After Certain Zebra Infants Lost His Cool Safety Goggles. The 'P' in 'Peter' is for Potassium, the 'S' in 'Stopped' is for Sodium etc.

Reactions of Metals with Acids

One more page on metals to learn. You don't need to know about each individual reaction, just how the reactivity of each metal affects it.

Reacting Metals with **Dilute Acid**

$$\text{metal} + \text{acid} \longrightarrow \text{salt} + \text{hydrogen}$$

1) Metals above hydrogen in the reactivity series (see previous page) will react with acids to make a salt and hydrogen.
2) The metals below hydrogen in the reactivity series don't react with acids.
3) The reaction becomes less and less exciting as you go down the series.

More Reactive Metals React More **Violently**

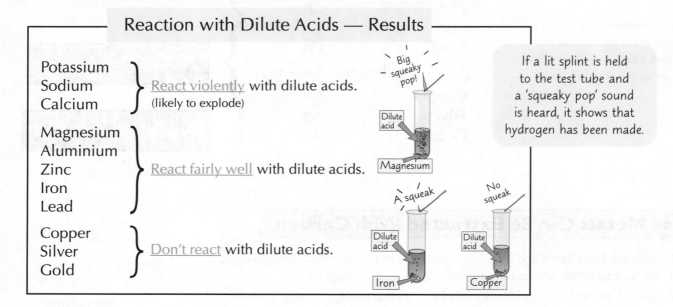

Reaction with Dilute Acids — Results

Potassium
Sodium
Calcium
} React violently with dilute acids.
(likely to explode)

Magnesium
Aluminium
Zinc
Iron
Lead
} React fairly well with dilute acids.

Copper
Silver
Gold
} Don't react with dilute acids.

If a lit splint is held to the test tube and a 'squeaky pop' sound is heard, it shows that hydrogen has been made.

Big squeaky pop!
Dilute acid
Magnesium

A squeak
Dilute acid
Iron

No squeak
Dilute acid
Copper

EXAMPLES:

1) zinc + sulfuric acid $\longrightarrow$ zinc sulfate + hydrogen
$$Zn + H_2SO_4 \longrightarrow ZnSO_4 + H_2$$

Zinc takes the place of hydrogen in the acid because zinc is more reactive than hydrogen.

2) sodium + hydrochloric acid $\longrightarrow$ sodium chloride + hydrogen
$$2Na + 2HCl \longrightarrow 2NaCl + H_2$$

Sodium takes the place of hydrogen in the acid because sodium is more reactive than hydrogen.

The more reactive the metal, the more violent the reaction

It might seem like there's loads going on here, but it's just the same principle repeated over and over. All the metals that react have roughly the same reaction — some are just more violent than others.

Reactions of Oxides with Acids

Oxides are exactly what they sound like — they're chemicals with oxygen in them somewhere...

Metals React With Oxygen to Make Oxides

Metals react with oxygen to make metal oxides.

> **EXAMPLE**: magnesium + oxygen ⟶ magnesium oxide

Metal Oxides are Alkaline

1) Metal oxides in solution have a pH which is higher than 7. They're alkaline.
2) So metal oxides react with acids to make a salt and water.

pH more than 7

> **acid + metal oxide ⟶ salt + water**

> **EXAMPLES**:
> • hydrochloric acid + copper oxide ⟶ copper chloride + water
> • sulfuric acid + zinc oxide ⟶ zinc sulfate + water

Non-metals React With Oxygen to Make Oxides

Non-metals also react with oxygen to make oxides.

> **EXAMPLE**: sulfur + oxygen ⟶ sulfur dioxide

Non-metal Oxides are Acidic

1) The oxides of non-metals have a pH below 7. This means they're acidic.
2) So non-metal oxides will react with alkalis to make a salt and water.

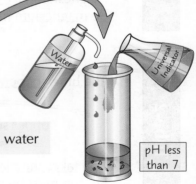

pH less than 7

> **alkali + non-metal oxide ⟶ salt + water**

> **EXAMPLE**: sodium hydroxide + silicon dioxide ⟶ sodium silicate + water
>
> ↑ an alkali   ↑ a non-metal oxide

REVISION TIP

Metal oxides are alkaline, non-metal oxides are acidic

You can put either of these facts into "acid + alkali → salt + water" (see p.76) to get the two word equations on this page. That way, you only have to learn one equation instead of three.

Displacement Reactions

This page will make more sense if you can remember the reactivity series (page 79).

'Displacement' Means 'Taking the Place of'

Learn this rule:

A MORE REACTIVE metal will displace a LESS REACTIVE metal from its compound.

1) In other words, a more reactive metal will take the place of a less reactive metal in a compound.
2) The less reactive metal gets "kicked out" of its compound.
   It then coats itself on the reactive metal.

A **Reactivity Series** Investigation

You can use displacement reactions to investigate the reactivity of metals.

Method: 1) Put a bit of metal into some salt solutions.   2) See what happens.

Tube 1   **Tube 2**   **Tube 3**

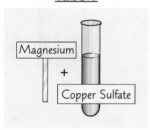   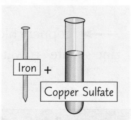   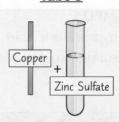

Tube 1

- The blue copper sulfate solution goes colourless.
- The copper coats the magnesium strip.

magnesium + copper sulfate $\longrightarrow$ magnesium sulfate + copper

- Magnesium takes the place of copper in the sulfate compound.
  So magnesium must be more reactive than copper.

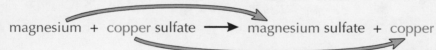

Result: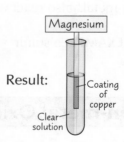

Tube 2

- The blue copper sulfate solution goes green. The copper coats the nail.

iron + copper sulfate $\longrightarrow$ iron sulfate + copper

- Iron takes the place of copper in the sulfate compound.
  So iron must be more reactive than copper.

Result: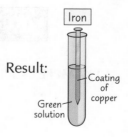

Tube 3

- There's no reaction.
- Copper can't displace zinc — it's not reactive enough.

copper + zinc sulfate $\longrightarrow$ no change

Result: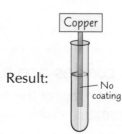

Warm-Up and Practice Questions

The good thing about the last few pages is that they all involve the same thing — the reactivity series. You need to get your head round that if you want to stand a good chance in any tests you might take.

Warm-Up Questions

1) Is potassium above or below gold in the reactivity series?

2) Name one non-metal in the reactivity series.

3) Why can't carbon be used to extract magnesium from its ore?

4) True or false? Iron will react with sulfuric acid (H_2SO_4).

5) Why does no reaction occur when zinc is added to magnesium sulfate solution?

Practice Questions

1   Some metals can be extracted from their ores using carbon reduction.

(a)   Complete the sentences below. Use words from the box.

less	more	react
displace		dissolve

Aluminium cannot be extracted from its ores using carbon reduction

because carbon is .... reactive than aluminium.

This means carbon cannot .... aluminium from aluminium ores.

(2 marks)

(b)   What does reduction mean in the extraction of metals? Tick **one** box.

☐ The removal of hydrogen.

☐ The addition of oxygen.

☐ Breaking the metal up into small pieces.

☐ The removal of oxygen.

(1 mark)

(c)   Part of the reactivity series is shown on the right.
Using this reactivity series, name **two** metals that
cannot be extracted by carbon reduction methods.

potassium
sodium
carbon
iron
lead
hydrogen
copper
gold

(2 marks)

Practice Questions

2   The table below shows some reactions of different metals.

metal	reaction with dilute acids
mercury	no reaction
lithium	reacts quickly, releasing hydrogen gas
magnesium	reacts slowly, releasing hydrogen gas

(a) Put these three metals in the order of their reactivity,
      beginning with the most reactive.

(2 marks)

(b) Complete the word equation for the reaction of magnesium with hydrochloric acid.

magnesium + hydrochloric acid ⟶ .... + hydrogen

(1 mark)

3   Stephen poured copper oxide and zinc powders onto an upturned dish.
      He used a Bunsen burner to heat the powders. A reaction occurred.

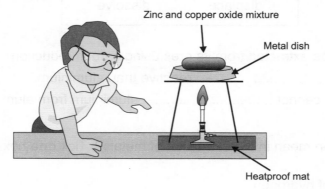

Zinc and copper oxide mixture

Metal dish

Heatproof mat

(a) Look at the diagram above.
      Give **one** safety precaution which Stephen took in this experiment.

(1 mark)

(b) In this reaction, copper and zinc oxide were produced.
      (i)   Write a word equation to show this reaction.

(1 mark)

      (ii) What kind of reaction is this?

(1 mark)

(c) Why wouldn't there have been a reaction if Stephen had used aluminium oxide
      instead of copper oxide?

(1 mark)

(d) Stephen separates the zinc oxide produced in the reaction from the copper.
      He adds some acid to the zinc oxide.
      Would you expect a reaction to occur? Explain your answer.

(2 marks)

Section Six — Chemical Changes

Revision Summary for Section Six

Good work, you've made it through another section of Chemistry. Now it's time to sum it all up with a handy set of questions that test everything you need to know. Luckily for you, that's exactly what this page is for. You must have heard it all before by now — work through the questions one by one, make sure you know everything, then maybe treat yourself to something sweet.

1) In a chemical reaction, what are the chemicals you start with called? What are the chemicals you end up with called? ☑

2) Name the two types of equation you can use to show what happens in a chemical reaction. ☑

3) Which of the equations you named in question 2) shows how many atoms are on each side? ☑

4) What's the chemical formula for a) water, b) table salt, c) carbon dioxide? ☑

5) What happens to the atoms in a chemical reaction? ☑

6) Does the mass change during a chemical reaction? Why or why not? ☑

7) What's combustion? ☑

8) A substance reacts with oxygen. What type of reaction is this? ☑

9) What's thermal decomposition? ☑

10) What's formed when copper carbonate breaks down by thermal decomposition? ☑

11) What's the main difference between exothermic and endothermic reactions? ☑

12)*If you put sodium in water, it catches fire and burns up.
Is this reaction exothermic or endothermic? ☑

13)*When ammonia breaks down to nitrogen and hydrogen, the temperature drops.
Is this reaction exothermic or endothermic? ☑

14) How does a catalyst affect the speed of a reaction? ☑

15) How do catalysts make a reaction cheaper to run? ☑

16) What pH does the strongest acid on a pH chart have? And the strongest alkali? ☑

17) What pH does a neutral solution have? ☑

18) What colour would universal indicator go if it was mixed with:
a) a strong acid,   b) a neutral solution,   c) a strong alkali? ☑

19) Hydrochloric acid makes chloride salts — what salts does sulfuric acid make? ☑

20) List the reactivity series in the correct order. Include carbon and hydrogen. ☑

21) Which metals in the reactivity series can be extracted from their ores using carbon? ☑

22) What do metals produce when they react with an acid? ☑

23) Which metal will react the most violently with acid? ☑

24) Are metal oxides in solution acidic, neutral or alkaline? ☑

25) Are non-metal oxides in solution acidic, neutral or alkaline? ☑

26) What does displacement mean? ☑

27) What is the rule for displacement reactions? ☑

28) Can magnesium displace copper from copper sulfate? ☑

*Answers on page 193.

Section Six — Chemical Changes

The Earth's Structure

Ever wondered what the planet's like on the inside? Well you're in for a treat with this page then.

The Earth Has a **Crust**, a **Mantle** and a **Core**

The Earth is almost a sphere and it has a layered structure. A bit like a scotch egg. Or a peach.

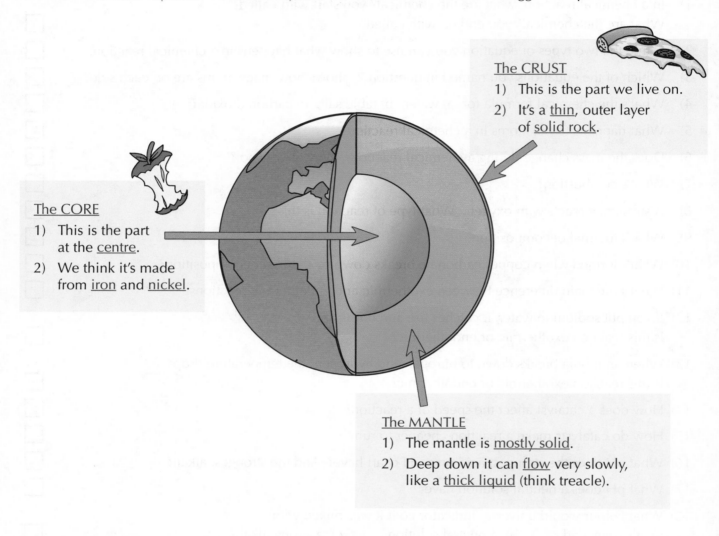

The CRUST
1) This is the part we live on.
2) It's a thin, outer layer of solid rock.

The CORE
1) This is the part at the centre.
2) We think it's made from iron and nickel.

The MANTLE
1) The mantle is mostly solid.
2) Deep down it can flow very slowly, like a thick liquid (think treacle).

The **Earth's Surface** is Broken Into **Plates**

1) The crust and the upper part of the mantle are cracked into a number of large plates.
2) These plates are a bit like big rafts that 'float' on the mantle. They're able to move around slowly.
3) Sometimes, the plates move very suddenly, causing an earthquake.

The part of Earth we live on is called the crust

You need to know the structure of Earth, i.e. what it would look like if you cut it open (which I wouldn't recommend) and what it's made of. That diagram above is your friend — learn it and learn it well. And, while we're on the subject, you'll need to learn all the words too. On the whole page.

Minerals and Rock Types

There's <u>more than one</u> sort of rock you know — they're all covered on these two pages.

The Crust Contains **Minerals**

1) The Earth's <u>crust</u> is made up of <u>rocks</u>. These are made from different types of <u>mineral</u>.
2) Minerals are made of <u>elements</u> and <u>compounds</u>.

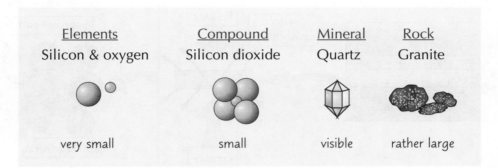

<u>Elements</u>	<u>Compound</u>	<u>Mineral</u>	<u>Rock</u>
Silicon & oxygen	Silicon dioxide	Quartz	Granite
very small	small	visible	rather large

There are **Three Different** Types of **Rock**

1) **Igneous** Rocks

1) These are formed from <u>magma</u> (melted underground rock).
2) Some magma gets <u>pushed up</u> to the <u>surface</u> of the crust — and often out through <u>volcanoes</u>.
3) It then <u>cools</u> and forms rocks <u>above</u> ground.
4) Sometimes it cools <u>below</u> ground.

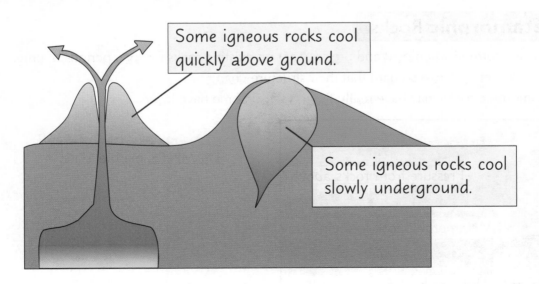

Some igneous rocks cool quickly above ground.

Some igneous rocks cool slowly underground.

<u>EXAMPLES</u>: basalt (cooled above ground),
granite (cooled below ground)

More on Rock Types

2) **Sedimentary** Rocks

1) These are formed from <u>layers</u> of sediment (tiny bits of rock).
2) The layers get <u>laid down</u> in lakes or seas over <u>millions</u> of years.
3) The layers are <u>stuck</u> together by <u>other minerals</u>.

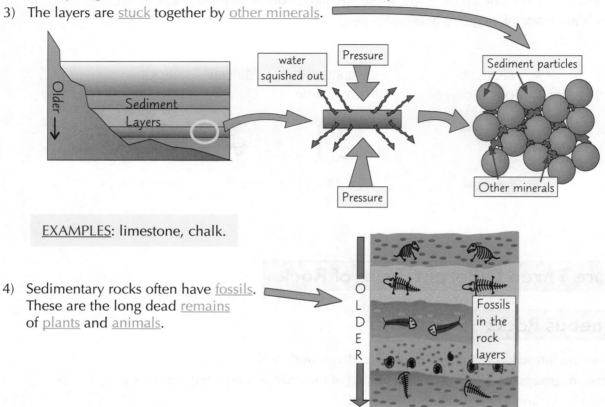

<u>EXAMPLES</u>: limestone, chalk.

4) Sedimentary rocks often have <u>fossils</u>. These are the long dead <u>remains</u> of <u>plants</u> and <u>animals</u>.

3) **Metamorphic** Rocks

1) These are formed when <u>heat</u> and <u>pressure</u> act on existing rocks for <u>long</u> periods of time.
2) The rocks get <u>squished</u> so hard that their structure <u>changes</u>.
3) Metamorphic rocks may have really <u>tiny crystals</u>. Some have layers.

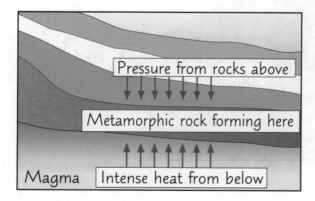

<u>EXAMPLES</u>: marble, slate.

The Rock Cycle

The rock cycle involves changes to rocks both <u>inside</u> and <u>outside</u> the Earth.

The **Rock Cycle** Takes **Millions** of **Years** to **Complete**

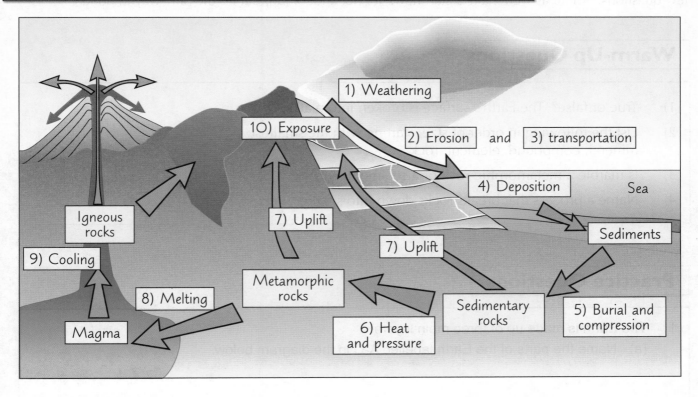

The three types of rock are <u>igneous</u>, <u>sedimentary</u> and <u>metamorphic</u> (see page 87-88).
The rock cycle involves <u>changing</u> the three types of rock from one to another. This happens by:

1) <u>WEATHERING</u>: <u>breaking down</u> rocks into <u>smaller bits</u>.

2) <u>EROSION</u>: <u>wearing down</u> rocks, for example, by rain.

3) <u>TRANSPORTATION</u>: <u>moving</u> the eroded bits of rock round the world by <u>wind</u> and <u>water</u> (mostly).

4) <u>DEPOSITION</u>: laying down of <u>sediment</u>.

5) <u>BURIAL and COMPRESSION</u>: <u>squeezing</u> and <u>compressing</u> the layers —
                              eventually they form <u>SEDIMENTARY ROCKS</u>.

6) <u>HEAT and PRESSURE</u>: further <u>squashing</u> and <u>heating</u> turns the rocks into <u>METAMORPHIC ROCKS</u>.

7) <u>UPLIFT</u>: rocks are <u>pushed up</u> to the surface.

8) <u>MELTING</u>: lots of <u>heat</u> makes the rocks <u>melt</u> a little — that changes them to magma.

9) <u>COOLING</u>: The molten (melted) rock turns to <u>solid IGNEOUS ROCK</u>.

10) <u>EXPOSURE</u>: <u>back</u> to weathering and erosion again.

Rocks can change between different forms over time

<u>Ten stages</u> of the rock cycle to learn there — make sure you know <u>what happens</u> at each stage,
and how each of the stages are <u>linked</u>. Why not try writing a <u>summary</u> in your own words?

Warm-Up and Practice Questions

You'll need to learn all the stuff in this section if you want to make it through Key Stage 3 Science. There were loads of difficult words over the previous few pages, so you might need to put in that extra bit of time to get them in your head. The best way to check you've learnt them all is to try answering a few questions. Might as well make a start now. It's not a lot of fun, but it's the only way to do it.

Warm-Up Questions

1) True or false? The Earth's surface is broken into plates.

2) List the following in order of size, starting with the smallest: mineral, compound, element, rock.

3) Is marble a metamorphic rock or a sedimentary rock?

4) Name a process that breaks rocks down into smaller pieces.

Practice Questions

1 The Earth is made up of three main layers.

(a) Name the parts of the Earth labelled A-C in the diagram below.

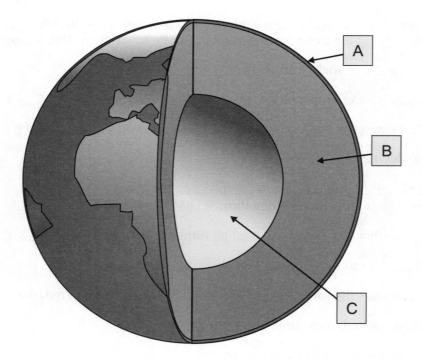

(3 marks)

(b) Which layer is thought to be made of iron and nickel?

(1 mark)

Section Seven — The Earth and The Atmosphere

Practice Questions

2   The diagram below shows part of a small volcanic island.

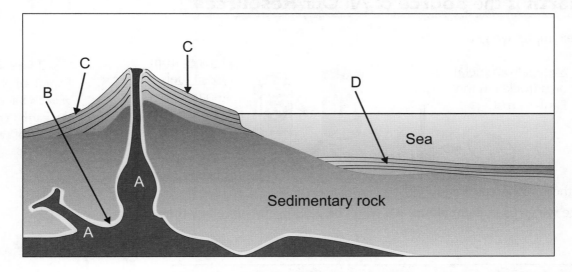

(a)   Magma has cooled and formed rocks A and C.

(i)   What type of rock are A and C?

(1 mark)

(ii)   Over time, rock B can be turned into rock A.
Which of the following processes is involved in turning rock B into rock A?

☐   Deposition

☐   Melting

☐   Erosion

(1 mark)

(iii)   Rock C can be changed by weathering. What is weathering?

(1 mark)

(b)   D will eventually become a sedimentary rock.

(i)   What is D?

(1 mark)

(ii)   In order for D to become a sedimentary rock, the water must be removed.
Explain how this happens.

(2 marks)

(iii)   There are often fossils in sedimentary rock.
What are fossils formed from?

(1 mark)

(c)   Rock B is metamorphic. It was formed from a sedimentary rock.
Describe how a sedimentary rock can be turned into a metamorphic rock.

(1 mark)

Section Seven — The Earth and The Atmosphere

Recycling

Every time you recycle something you're doing your bit to <u>save limited resources</u>.

The **Earth** is the **Source** of All Our **Resources**

1) For example, we get:

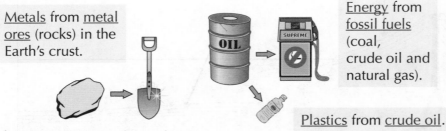

<u>Metals</u> from <u>metal ores</u> (rocks) in the Earth's crust.

<u>Energy</u> from <u>fossil fuels</u> (coal, crude oil and natural gas).

Fossil fuels are made from dead plants and animals buried in the Earth's crust for millions of years.

<u>Plastics</u> from <u>crude oil</u>.

2) But these resources are <u>limited</u>.
3) Once we've <u>used</u> them all up, we <u>won't</u> be <u>getting any more</u> any time soon.

There are **Lots** of **Good Reasons** for **Recycling**

Recycling means taking <u>old</u>, <u>unwanted products</u> and using the <u>materials</u> to make <u>new stuff</u>. <u>Recycling</u> is usually <u>better</u> than <u>making things from scratch</u> because:

1) It uses <u>fewer limited resources</u>.

2) It uses <u>less energy</u> — so fewer <u>fossil fuels</u> are <u>burnt</u>.

3) It <u>saves money</u>.

4) It makes <u>less rubbish</u>.

<u>Example — recycling aluminium cans saves energy and money:</u>

1) If aluminium <u>wasn't recycled</u>, more aluminium would have to be <u>mined</u> (dug up).
2) Mining costs <u>money</u> and uses loads of <u>energy</u>.
3) The aluminium then needs to be <u>transported</u> and <u>extracted</u> (page 79). This uses <u>more energy</u> and costs <u>more money</u>.
4) It also <u>costs money</u> to send the <u>used aluminium</u> to <u>landfill</u> (big rubbish dumps).

For every <u>1 kg</u> of aluminium cans that are recycled, you <u>save</u> about:
- <u>95%</u> of the <u>energy</u> needed to mine and extract 'fresh' aluminium,
- <u>4 kg</u> of aluminium ore,
- a <u>lot</u> of waste.

This means it's really <u>efficient</u> to recycle aluminium.

Recycle this book — but wait till you've finished KS3 science

Not all materials are as efficient to recycle as aluminium. But even if the <u>energy</u> and <u>money</u> saved is relatively small, you could still be <u>saving limited resources</u> and <u>creating less waste</u>.

The Carbon Cycle

Carbon is a very important element because it's part of all living things.
It's never completely used up — it just gets recycled through the environment.
It's constantly passed between living things until it's returned to the environment, and the cycle starts again.

The **Carbon Cycle** Shows How **Carbon** is **Recycled**

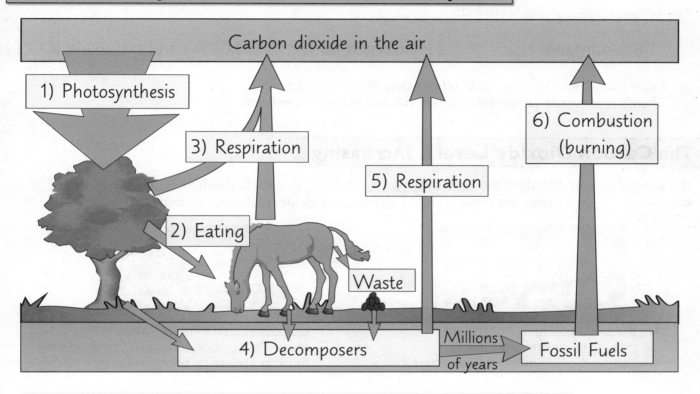

1) PLANTS take carbon dioxide out of the air by PHOTOSYNTHESIS (see page 31).

2) When plants are EATEN by ANIMALS the carbon in the plants goes into the animals.

3) When plants and animals RESPIRE (see page 4) carbon dioxide goes back into the air.

4) Dead organisms and waste are BROKEN DOWN by decomposers.

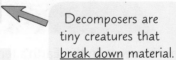

Decomposers are tiny creatures that break down material.

5) Decomposers RESPIRE and release carbon dioxide back into the air.

6) The COMBUSTION (burning) of fossil fuels also releases carbon dioxide into the air.

REVISION TASK

Carbon is recycled through the environment

Another cycle to learn here I'm afraid. Try covering up the diagram at the top of the page and sketching it out on a piece of paper. If you don't remember all the labels, take a good look at the diagram, then try again. Then see if you can remember what each of the labels means.

The Atmosphere and Climate

It's important to know exactly what you're breathing in and out. So read this page and find out.

The **Earth's Atmosphere** is Made Up of **Different Gases**

1) The gases that surround a planet make up that planet's atmosphere.
2) The Earth's atmosphere is around:

| 78% nitrogen (N$_2$) | 21% oxygen (O$_2$) | 0.04% carbon dioxide (CO$_2$) |

3) It also contains small amounts of other gases, like water vapour.
(There's more water vapour than carbon dioxide in the atmosphere.)

The **Carbon Dioxide Level** is **Increasing**

The level of carbon dioxide in the Earth's atmosphere is rising — and it's down to human activities and some natural causes. Here are some examples of human activities that affect carbon dioxide levels:

1) Burning fossil fuels in cars and power stations releases lots of carbon dioxide into the atmosphere.

2) Deforestation (chopping down trees) means less carbon dioxide is removed from the atmosphere by photosynthesis.

Carbon Dioxide **Affects** the **Earth's Climate**

1) Carbon dioxide traps energy from the Sun in the Earth's atmosphere.
2) This stops some energy from being lost into space and helps to keep the Earth warm.
3) But the level of carbon dioxide is increasing.
4) And the Earth has been getting hotter. Most scientists think this is because of the rise in carbon dioxide levels.

5) This increase in the Earth's temperature is called global warming.
6) Global warming seems to be having some serious effects. For example:

- Rainfall patterns are changing, which might make it harder for some farmers to grow crops.
- Ice on land (like the large sheets of ice covering Greenland) might melt faster. This could cause sea levels to rise, leading to floods.

The atmosphere and the climate are dead important
The link between carbon dioxide levels in the atmosphere and climate change is a great example of scientists basing theories on what they see in the real world.

Warm-Up and Practice Questions

There's only been a few pages of stuff to learn since the last set of questions, so hopefully you'll still remember most of it by this point. The best way to make sure you know all the important stuff covered is to try out some questions and see if you get them right. Well, what are you waiting for?

Warm-Up Questions

1) Give a material that can be made from crude oil.

2) True or false? Photosynthesis releases carbon dioxide into the air.

3) What gas is most of the Earth's atmosphere made up of?

4) True or false? Changing the amount of carbon dioxide in the atmosphere can affect the Earth's climate.

Practice Questions

1   Mushrooms and earthworms are both types of decomposer.
Decomposers help to break things down. They are part of the carbon cycle.

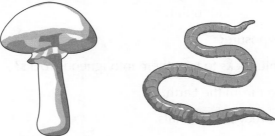

(a) Name **one** thing that decomposers help to break down.

(1 mark)

(b) (i) Through what process do decomposers release carbon into the atmosphere?

(1 mark)

     (ii) Name the gas that decomposers release into the atmosphere during this process.

(1 mark)

2   In the UK, local councils collect materials so that they can be recycled.

(a) A council is making a leaflet to encourage the locals to recycle more.
The leaflet includes these three points:

> 1. Recycling releases less carbon dioxide into the atmosphere than making new materials from scratch.
> 2. Recycling aluminium uses less energy than mining and extracting more aluminium from the Earth.
> 3. Recycling saves money because it is completely free.

Say whether each statement is **true** or **false**.

(3 marks)

(b) Many of Earth's resources are limited.
Explain why it is important to recycle limited resources.

(1 mark)

Section Seven — The Earth and The Atmosphere

Revision Summary for Section Seven

Well there we are. The end of Section Seven. All you have to do now is learn it all. And yes you've guessed it, here are some lovely questions I prepared earlier. It's no good going through them and only answering the one or two that take your fancy. Make sure you can answer all of them.

1) The Earth is covered with a thin outer layer of rock. What is this layer called?

2) What is the name of the structure between the outer layer of rock and the Earth's core?

3) Which two metals do we think the Earth's core is made of?

4) What's the Earth's crust broken into?

5) How are igneous rocks formed?

6) How do sedimentary rocks form?

7) The dead remains of plants and animals can become trapped in sedimentary rocks. What are these remains called?

8) How do metamorphic rocks form?

9) Give one example of: a) an igneous rock, b) a sedimentary rock, c) a metamorphic rock.

10) In the rock cycle, describe what happens during:
   a) erosion   b) deposition   c) uplift.

11) Which rock cycle stages follow exposure?

12) What must happen to metamorphic rocks to turn them into igneous rocks?

13) Name two limited resources we get from the Earth.

14) Give four reasons why it's good to recycle materials.

15) Which living things remove carbon dioxide from the air?

16) How does carbon get passed from plants to animals?

17) What percentage of the Earth's atmosphere is: a) nitrogen, b) oxygen, c) carbon dioxide?

18) Name one other gas present in the Earth's atmosphere.

19) Give two human activities that are affecting the level of carbon dioxide in the atmosphere. Say why each one affects the level of carbon dioxide.

20) How does carbon dioxide help to keep the Earth warm?

21) What is global warming? What's causing it?

22) Describe two possible effects of global warming.

Energy Stores

Energy is everywhere, so this is a pretty important page.

Learn These Seven **Energy Stores**...

1. **Kinetic** (Movement) Energy Store

Anything that moves has energy
in its kinetic energy store.

2. **Thermal** Energy Store

1) Everything has some energy in
   its thermal energy store.

2) The hotter something is,
   the higher its temperature.

3) The hotter something is, the more
   energy in its thermal energy store.

3. **Elastic Potential** Energy Store

1) Anything stretched has energy
   in its elastic energy store.

2) For example, rubber bands
   and springs.

4. **Magnetic** Energy Store

Two magnets that attract or repel each other
have energy in their magnetic energy stores.

There's more on
magnets on page 154.

5. **Electrostatic** Energy Store

Two electric charges that attract or
repel each other have energy in their
electrostatic energy stores.

positive   negative
charge   charge

See page 153
for more.

6. **Chemical** Energy Store

1) Anything with energy
   which can be released by
   a chemical reaction.

2) Things like food, fuels and
   batteries have lots of energy
   in their chemical energy stores.

7. **Gravitational Potential** Energy Store

1) Anything in a gravitational field has energy
   in its gravitational potential energy store.

2) The higher the object is,
   the more energy is in this store.

3) For example, a ski jumper in the air.

In physics, a field is a region in which a
particular force can act on objects.
So if something's in a gravitational field, it means
it's in a region where gravity can act on it.

Energy Transfer

And now it's time to see how <u>energy</u> can be <u>moved between stores</u>...

There are **Four Ways** of **Transferring** Energy

The four main ways you can transfer energy between stores are:

Mechanically

When a <u>force</u> makes something <u>move</u> (see page 99). E.g. if an object is <u>pushed</u>, <u>pulled</u>, <u>stretched</u> or <u>squashed</u>.

Electrically

When <u>electric charges</u> move around an electric <u>circuit</u> due to a potential difference (see page 148).

By **Light** and **Sound**

When <u>light</u> or <u>sound</u> waves (see Section 10) carry energy from <u>one place</u> to <u>another</u>.

By **Heating**

When energy is transferred from <u>hotter</u> objects to <u>colder</u> objects (see page 100).

Examples of Energy Transfer

Here are some <u>real-life examples</u> to help you understand how energy is transferred.

EXAMPLE 1: Dropping an object

1) When you <u>drop</u> an object, it <u>moves</u> through a <u>gravitational field</u>.

2) This causes energy to transfer <u>from</u> its <u>gravitational potential energy</u> store to its <u>kinetic energy</u> store.

3) The force of <u>gravity</u> makes the object <u>move</u>, so energy is transferred <u>mechanically</u>.

EXAMPLE 2: Electric circuits

1) When you turn on a <u>battery-powered fan</u>, you <u>complete</u> an <u>electric circuit</u>.

2) Energy is transferred <u>electrically</u> from the <u>chemical energy</u> store of the battery to the <u>kinetic energy</u> store of the fan.

EXAMPLE 3: Food

1) <u>Food</u> has energy stored in <u>chemical energy</u> stores.

2) When you eat food, it is <u>metabolised</u> (changed by chemical processes in your body), which <u>transfers</u> the energy in the food to <u>different stores</u> in your body.

EXAMPLE 4: Burning fuel

1) When you <u>burn</u> fuel, energy is transferred from the fuel's <u>chemical energy store</u>.

2) Energy is transferred to the <u>thermal energy</u> store of the surroundings <u>by heating</u>.

EXAMPLE 5: A stretched spring

1) A <u>stretched spring</u>, has energy in its <u>elastic potential energy</u> store.

2) When it's released, energy is <u>transferred</u> from the spring's <u>elastic potential energy store</u> to its <u>kinetic energy</u> store as it moves back to its original shape.

3) A <u>force</u> is making the spring <u>move</u>, so the energy is transferred <u>mechanically</u>.

Energy Transfer and Force

Now it's time for more on <u>mechanical energy transfers</u> — when a <u>force</u> makes an object <u>move</u>...

Energy is Transferred When a Force Moves an Object

> **When a <u>force moves</u> an object through a <u>distance</u>, <u>energy is transferred</u>.**

Energy transferred is the same as work done — see page 124.

1) Objects need a <u>force</u> (some sort of '<u>effort</u>') to make them <u>move</u>.

2) <u>Energy</u> is needed to <u>supply</u> this force. This energy can come from <u>food</u>, <u>fuel</u> etc.

3) The energy supplied is <u>transferred</u> to the object's <u>kinetic energy store</u>, so the object moves.

EXAMPLE: Pushing a broom

1) In order to <u>move</u> a broom, the person has to supply a <u>force</u> to the broom.

2) The <u>energy</u> the person uses to do this comes from the <u>food</u> they have eaten.

3) This energy is <u>transferred</u> to the <u>kinetic energy store</u> of the broom. So the broom moves.

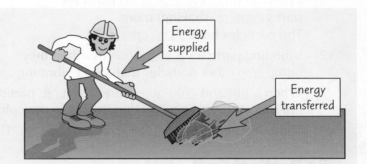

One More Thing About Energy Transfer and Forces...

If you give a machine a <u>set amount</u> of energy to transfer, it can either:

1) apply a <u>large force</u> over a <u>small distance</u>,

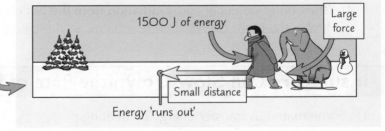

OR

2) apply a <u>small force</u> over a <u>large distance</u>.

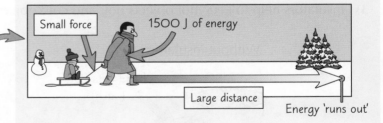

In these examples the 'machine' is a man. But the same rule applies for other machines such as cars and cranes.

Objects need a force to make them move

If you want to understand how <u>forces</u> cause <u>energy transfers</u>, it'd help to be clued-up about the previous three pages. If it's not making sense, go back to the beginning of the section and have another go.

Energy Transfer by Heating

Energy can be <u>transferred</u> between <u>objects</u> by heating.

Energy is Transferred From Hotter to Cooler Objects

1) When two objects are at <u>different temperatures</u>, the <u>hotter</u> object transfers <u>energy</u> to the <u>cooler</u> object.
2) This carries on until both objects reach the <u>same temperature</u>.
   At this point we say they've reached <u>THERMAL EQUILIBRIUM</u>.

   You need to know about <u>two ways</u> in which energy can be transferred between objects by <u>heating</u>:

1) Conduction

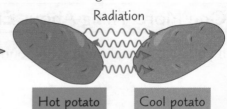

a particle   Energy transfer

Hot object   Cold object

1) When an object is <u>heated</u>, its particles
   start <u>vibrating</u> (shaking) more.
   The particles have <u>more energy</u>.
2) Vibrating particles <u>transfer</u> energy when they
   <u>bump into</u> other particles that aren't vibrating as much.
3) When a <u>hot</u> and <u>cold</u> object are <u>touching</u>, particles in the
   hot object <u>transfer energy</u> to particles in the cold object.
4) The hot object <u>loses energy</u> so it <u>cools down</u>. The cold object <u>gains energy</u> so it <u>heats up</u>.

2) Radiation

1) <u>All objects</u> radiate (send out) invisible <u>waves</u> (called <u>radiation</u>) to the surroundings.
   These waves can <u>transfer energy</u> from one place to another.
2) Objects can also <u>absorb</u> (take in) radiation.
3) The hotter object (like this hot potato)
   <u>radiates more energy than it absorbs</u>, so it <u>cools down</u>.
4) The cooler object <u>absorbs</u> radiation from the hot object.
   It <u>absorbs more energy</u> than it radiates, so it <u>heats up</u>.

Radiation

Hot potato   Cool potato

Insulators Can Slow Down the Rate of Energy Transfer

1) Some materials transfer energy by heating <u>more quickly</u> than others.
2) Materials like <u>plastic</u> and <u>cardboard</u> transfer energy <u>slowly</u>. These materials are called <u>INSULATORS</u>.
3) Insulators help to <u>keep</u> hot objects hot, and cold objects cold.

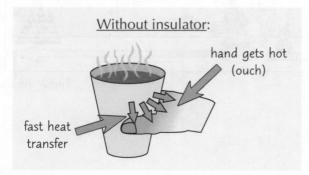

Without insulator:

hand gets hot
(ouch)

fast heat
transfer

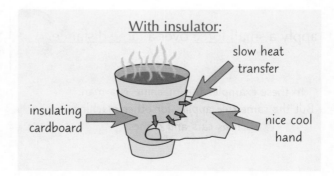

With insulator:

slow heat
transfer

insulating
cardboard

nice cool
hand

REVISION
TIP

Make sure you can describe both methods of energy transfer

The big difference is that <u>conduction</u> needs two objects to be <u>touching</u>, but <u>radiation doesn't</u>.

Conservation of Energy

Energy has to be transferred. Not always in a useful way though.

Some **Laws** About **Energy**

You need to know two important laws relating to energy:

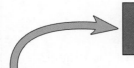

> **Energy can never be <u>CREATED</u> nor <u>DESTROYED</u>
> — it's only ever <u>TRANSFERRED</u> from one store to another.**

This means energy is conserved (it never disappears).

> **Energy is <u>ONLY USEFUL</u> when it's <u>TRANSFERRED</u> from one store to another.**

Most **Energy Transfers** are Not Perfect

1) Useful devices transfer energy from one store to another.

2) Some of the energy put into the device will be transferred usefully. Some will be wasted — usually by heating.

3) BUT no energy is destroyed:

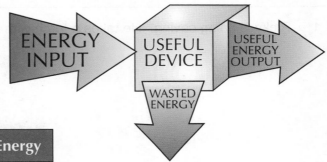

> **Energy INPUT = USEFUL Energy + WASTED Energy**

You Can Also Draw **Energy Transfer Diagrams**

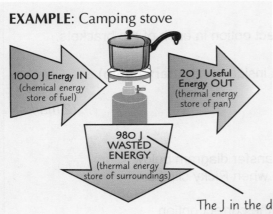

EXAMPLE: Camping stove

1000 J Energy IN (chemical energy store of fuel)

20 J Useful Energy OUT (thermal energy store of pan)

980 J WASTED ENERGY (thermal energy store of surroundings)

The J in the diagram stands for 'joules'. A joule is a unit of energy.

1) You can show how energy moves between stores by drawing an energy transfer diagram.

2) Rectangles are used to represent the different stores.

3) Draw an arrow to show energy being transferred and label it with the method of transfer.

4) If there's more than one transfer, draw an arrow for each one, each going to a different store.

CHEMICAL ENERGY STORE OF FUEL	by heating →	THERMAL ENERGY STORE OF PAN
	by heating →	THERMAL ENERGY STORE OF SURROUNDINGS

Warm-Up and Practice Questions

Feeling energised? I hope so, because it's time to see how much of all that energy transfer stuff you've taken in over the previous few pages. You know what to do...

Warm-Up Questions

1) Name three types of energy stores.

2) Give one way in which energy is transferred from a lightbulb.

3) When a force moves an object, energy is transferred to which energy store of the object?

4) What happens to the temperature of an object if the object gains energy during conduction?

5) True or false? Energy can never be created.

Practice Questions

1 Ricky is going caving. He takes a torch with him to help him see inside the cave.

(a) Complete the sentence below by selecting the correct option in each of the brackets.

When the torch is switched off, the energy is stored inside the (**battery** / **bulb**)
in its (**kinetic** / **chemical**) energy store.

(2 marks)

(b) Ricky climbs up the wall of the cave. The energy transfer diagram below
shows some of the energy transfers that take place when Ricky climbs.

Complete the energy transfer diagram by selecting the correct option
in each of the brackets.

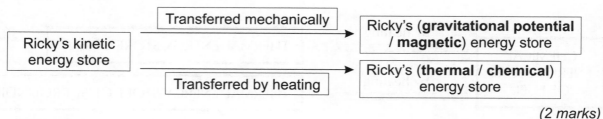

(2 marks)

Practice Questions

2 (a) Complete the sentence below by selecting the correct option in each of the brackets.

Coal is burnt in a fireplace to warm a room.
Energy in the (**chemical** / **kinetic**) energy store of the
coal is transferred (**by heating** / **electrically**) to the
(**chemical** / **thermal**) energy stores of the room.

(3 marks)

(b) A skydiver jumps out of a plane.
Which of the following statements is **true**? Tick **one** box.

☐ Energy in the skydiver's gravitational potential energy store is transferred away mechanically.

☐ Energy in the skydiver's elastic potential energy store is transferred away by heating.

☐ Energy in the skydiver's magnetic energy store is transferred to the skydiver's kinetic energy store.

(1 mark)

3 Simon uses an electric blender to mix some ingredients.
Simon plugs the blender into a power supply and switches it on. 3000 J of energy is transferred to the blender. 450 J of this energy is wasted heating up the blender.

3000 J Energy IN

450 J Heat Energy OUT

2550 J Rest Of Energy OUT

(a) How was the energy from the power supply transferred to the blender?

(1 mark)

(b) Suggest **one** thing that might have happened to the rest of the energy that was transferred to the blender.

(1 mark)

4 Amy is investigating energy transfer by heating using a cup of hot water.
(a) Amy places her hand near the cup of hot water. She notices that her hand feels warmer. Briefly explain what causes Amy's hand to feel warmer.

(1 mark)

(b) Amy notices that the table around the hot cup feels warm.
She decides that energy must have been transferred from the cup by conduction.
(i) Explain what conduction is. Write about the particles involved in your answer.

(1 mark)

(ii) Amy places a plastic coaster under the cup.
Explain how the coaster stops the table from heating up.

(2 marks)

Energy Resources

The <u>Sun</u>'s a useful old thing. It provides us with loads of <u>energy</u>.

The **Sun** is the **Source** of Our **Energy Resources**

1) Most of the <u>energy</u> around us originally <u>came from</u> the <u>Sun</u>.
2) The Sun is really useful for supplying us with the energy we need.
3) Often the Sun's energy is <u>transferred</u> into <u>different stores</u> before we use it as an <u>energy resource</u>.

Five **Examples** of Our **Energy Resources**

1. Sun's Energy ⟶ Coal, Oil, and Gas (Fossil Fuels)

Sun ⟹ light ⟹ photosynthesis ⟹ dead plants/animals ⟹ FOSSIL FUELS

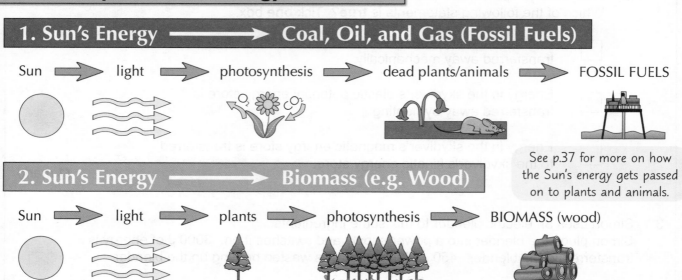

See p.37 for more on how the Sun's energy gets passed on to plants and animals.

2. Sun's Energy ⟶ Biomass (e.g. Wood)

Sun ⟹ light ⟹ plants ⟹ photosynthesis ⟹ BIOMASS (wood)

3. Sun's Energy ⟶ Wind Power

Sun ⟹ heats atmosphere ⟹ air moves ⟹ causes WINDS

We can use all of these energy resources to produce electricity — see the next page.

Land warm   Sea cool

4. Sun's Energy ⟶ Wave Power

Sun ⟹ heats atmosphere ⟹ causes WINDS ⟹ causes WAVES

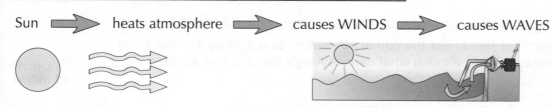

5. Sun's Energy ⟶ Solar Cells

Sun ⟹ light hits solar cells ⟹ generates ELECTRICITY

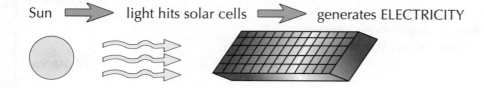

Section Eight — Energy and Matter

Generating Electricity

We can use the <u>energy</u> we get from the Sun to <u>generate electricity</u>, in lots of different ways...

There Are **Different Ways** of **Generating Electricity**

1) We can use <u>energy resources</u> to <u>generate</u> (make) <u>electricity</u>.

2) At the moment we generate most of our electricity by burning <u>fossil fuels</u>.

3) Most ways of <u>generating electricity</u> turn a <u>turbine</u> and a <u>generator</u>. The generator transfers energy from <u>kinetic energy stores</u> away <u>electrically</u>.

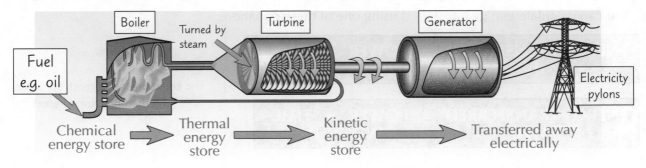

See previous page for more on energy resources.

4) Energy resources that we use to generate electricity can be split into two groups — <u>non-renewable</u> and <u>renewable</u>.

Non-renewable Energy Resources **Will Run Out**

1) <u>Fossil fuels</u> are a non-renewable energy resource.

2) <u>Fossil fuels</u> take <u>millions</u> of years to form. They only take <u>minutes</u> to burn.

3) Eventually, we'll <u>run out</u> of fossil fuels — this could have a <u>very big impact</u> on our lives. We need to <u>reduce</u> the amount of fossil fuels we use, so they won't run out <u>as quickly</u>.

Renewable Energy Resources **Won't Run Out**

As long as the Sun still shines...

1) The <u>WIND</u> will always <u>blow</u> — and turn <u>turbines</u> to generate electricity.

2) <u>PLANTS</u> will always <u>grow</u> — which can be <u>burnt</u> to generate electricity.

3) <u>WAVES</u> will always be <u>made</u> — and <u>drive generators</u> to make electricity.

4) <u>SOLAR</u> cells will always <u>work</u> — and use light to make electricity.

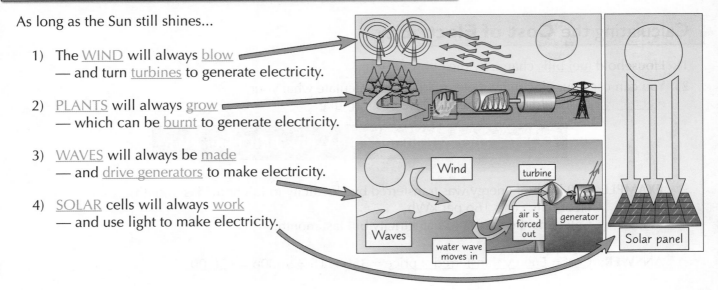

REVISION TIP

Think over this page — it affects all of us

A common mistake is to call renewable energy resources "<u>re-usable</u>". They can be <u>renewed</u> — e.g. trees will grow again if replanted. But once a tree is burnt you can't <u>re-use</u> it.

The Cost of Electricity

Electricity <u>isn't free</u> you know — ask your mum and dad. At least the <u>cost</u> is pretty easy to <u>calculate</u>.

You Can **Calculate** the **Energy** That an **Appliance Transfers**

1) Anything that needs <u>electricity to work</u> is an <u>electrical appliance</u>.
2) Electrical appliances <u>transfer</u> energy between stores (see page 98).
3) Energy transferred can be measured in <u>joules</u> (J), <u>kilojoules</u> (kJ) or <u>kilowatt-hours</u> (kWh).
4) <u>Power</u> is usually measured in <u>watts</u> (W) or <u>kilowatts</u> (kW).
5) You can calculate <u>energy transferred</u> using one of these equations:

$$\text{ENERGY TRANSFERRED (J)} = \text{POWER (W)} \times \text{TIME (seconds)}$$

$$\text{ENERGY TRANSFERRED (kWH)} = \text{POWER (kW)} \times \text{TIME (hours)}$$

The equations are <u>almost</u> the same — just the <u>units</u> are different.

Electricity Meters Record Electricity Usage

1) <u>Electricity meters</u> record the amount of <u>energy</u> transferred in <u>kWh</u>.
2) You can use them to work out the <u>energy transferred</u> over a <u>given time</u>.

EXAMPLE: Here are two meter readings. How much energy has been transferred between 6 pm and 6 am?

4 4 3 8 0 kWh	→	4 4 3 8 5 kWh
6 pm		6 am

ANSWER: Energy transferred from 6 pm to 6 am = <u>44385 − 44380</u>
= <u>5 kWh</u>

You need to work out the difference between the two meter readings.

Calculating the Cost of Electricity

1) Household <u>fuel bills</u> charge by the <u>kilowatt-hour</u>.
2) You can use your electricity meter readings to calculate what your <u>electricity bill</u> should be. You need to use this <u>formula</u>:

$$\underline{\text{COST}} = \text{Energy transferred (kWh)} \times \underline{\text{PRICE}} \text{ per kWh}$$

EXAMPLE: 350 kWh of energy was transferred by electricity to Jo's home last month. Electricity costs 16p per kWh. Calculate the cost of Jo's electricity bill last month.

ANSWER: <u>Cost = Energy transferred × price</u> = 350 × 16 = 5600p = <u>£56.00</u>

Calculate energy transferred using power and time
Energy transferred can be given in either <u>joules</u> (J) or <u>kilowatt-hours</u> (kWH). Make sure you check the <u>units</u> of any data you have and use the right equation.

Comparing Power Ratings and Energy Values

You can work out how much energy an appliance transfers if you know its power rating. And to find out how much energy is in your food, just check the label. This energy stuff's everywhere.

Power Ratings of Appliances

1) The power rating of an appliance tells you how fast it transfers energy.
2) You can use an appliance's power rating to work out the energy it transfers in a certain time.
3) To do this you need to use the equations on the previous page.

The **Energy Transferred** Depends on the **Power Rating**

1) The higher the power rating of an appliance, the more energy it transfers in a given time.
2) You can compare how much energy is transferred by appliances with different power ratings.

> **EXAMPLE:** A 1.5 kW heater is left on for 1.5 hours.
> A 4 kW heater is also left on for 1.5 hours.
> Compare the energy transferred by both heaters.
>
> **ANSWER:** Energy transferred (kWh) = power rating (kW) × time (h).
> Energy transferred by the 1.5 kW heater = 1.5 × 1.5 = 2.25 kWh.
> Energy transferred by the 4 kW heater = 4 × 1.5 = 6 kWh.
>
> Difference in the energy transferred by the two heaters = 6 − 2.25 = 3.75 kWh.
>
> So the 4 kW heater transfers 3.75 kWh more energy than the 1.5 kW heater in 1.5 hours.

Food Labels Tell You **How Much Energy** is in Food

1) All the food we eat contains energy.
2) The energy in food is measured in kilojoules (kJ).
3) You can compare the amount of energy in different foods by looking at their labels.

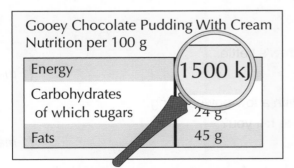

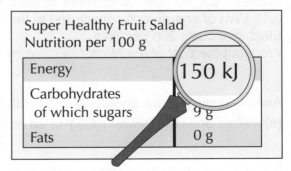

And that's why you should always read the label

To work out the energy transferred by an appliance you just need its power rating and the length of time it was used for. Again, be careful with units — the power rating can be given in W or kW.

Warm-Up and Practice Questions

It's time for another set of questions. Energy can be a bit of a tricky topic to understand, so take your time to work through these questions until you're sure you get it.

Warm-Up Questions

1) Where did most of our energy originally come from?

2) True or false? Plants are a renewable energy resource.

3) What does an electricity meter in your home measure?

4) What is the equation you would use to calculate the cost of electricity?

Practice Questions

1 Energy resources can be renewable or non-renewable.

(a) Explain what is meant by a 'non-renewable energy resource'.

(1 mark)

(b) Circle **two** examples of **renewable** energy resources.

　　　Coal　　　　　　　　**Solar power**　　　　　　　　**Crude oil**
　　　　　Natural gas　　　　　　　**Wave power**

(2 marks)

(c) Why it is important to use more renewable energy resources? Tick **one** box.

☐ Renewable resources are more powerful than non-renewable resources.

☐ Renewable resources won't run out but non-renewable resources will run out.

☐ Renewable resources generate electricity faster than non-renewable resources.

(1 mark)

2 Andrew uses his new kettle to boil some water.
0.15 kWh of energy was transferred to the kettle.
Electricity costs 20p per kWh.
Work out the cost of the electricity used by Andrew's kettle.

(1 mark)

3 Anne is testing a new energy-saving lightbulb with a low power rating.

(a) What does the 'power rating' of an appliance tell you?

(1 mark)

(b) The new energy-saving lightbulb is a 10 W bulb. Anne usually uses a 60 W bulb.
Anne turns both bulbs on for 60 seconds. How much more energy will be
transferred by the 60 W bulb compared to the 10 W bulb in 60 seconds?
Use the formula: energy transferred = power × time.

☐ 50 J　　　☐ 600 J　　　☐ 3000 J　　　☐ 3600 J

(1 mark)

Physical Changes

A change in the conditions (e.g. temperature) can cause a substance to change physically.

Physical Changes Can Lead to a Change in State

1) A substance can either be a solid, a liquid or a gas.
   These are called states of matter.

2) A substance can change from one state of matter to another (see page 52).
   For example, water can change from a liquid to a solid.
   This is called a physical change.

3) A physical change is different to a chemical change.
   In a physical change there is no chemical reaction and no new substances are made.
   For example, ice is still water — just in a different (physical) state.

4) You need to learn these six different processes that can bring about a physical change:

1. Melting

A solid changes into a liquid.

2. Evaporating

A liquid changes into a gas.

3. Condensing

A gas changes into a liquid.

4. Freezing

A liquid changes into a solid.

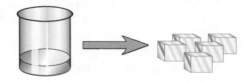

5. Dissolving

A solid mixes with a liquid to form a solution.

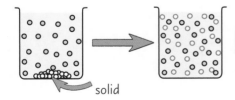

solid

See p.57 for more on dissolving.

6. Sublimation

A solid changes into a gas.

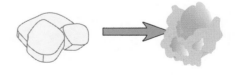

5) All of these processes are reversible — this means they can be 'undone' by another process.
   For example, if you melt some ice you get liquid water.
   If you want to reverse this process you can freeze the liquid water to get ice again.

Physical Changes

Changing from one state to another is an physical change, so it makes sense that the physical properties of the substance will change as well. Nothing is lost, however, so the mass will always stay the same.

Physical Changes Don't Involve a Change in Mass

When a substance changes from one state of matter to another, its mass doesn't change.

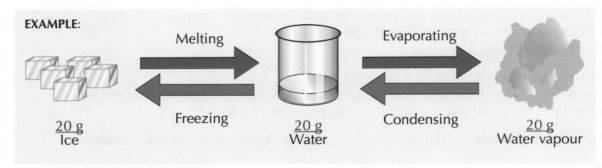

EXAMPLE:

Melting → Freezing

20 g
Ice

Evaporating → Condensing

20 g
Water

20 g
Water vapour

Changes of State Affect Physical Properties

1) The particles in solids are packed together tightly compared to gases and liquids. This means solids have a higher density than gases and liquids.

2) When you heat a substance, it changes from a solid, to a liquid, to a gas. The particles move further apart and the substance becomes less dense.

> There's more about particles on p.50.

3) Ice is different though.
When you heat ice (so that it melts) the particles actually come closer together. So liquid water has a higher density than solid ice. That's why icebergs float on water.

Changes of state change a substance's physical properties

Remember, physical changes aren't the same as chemical reactions (pages 71-74). Physical changes just cause a substance to change state. Ice is really just water, but with the particles in a more structured formation. If ice melts, it goes back to being water without losing any mass at all.

Movement of Particles

Particles can move around by bashing into each other and bouncing off in a new direction.

Brownian Motion is the Random Movement of Particles

1) Brownian motion is the random movement of any particle suspended (floating) within a liquid or gas.

2) It's a result of collisions between particles:

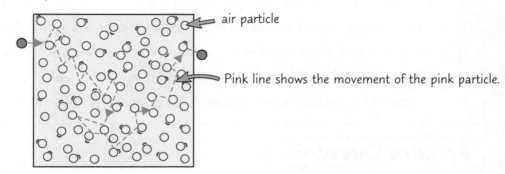

air particle

Pink line shows the movement of the pink particle.

3) Remember — atoms and molecules are both types of particle. (See pages 54 and 55).

Diffusion is Caused by the Random Motion of Particles

1) The particles in a liquid or gas move around at random.

2) Particles eventually bump their way from an area of high concentration (a place where there are lots of them) to an area of low concentration (a place where there aren't as many of them).

3) They constantly bump into each other, until they're evenly spread out across the substance.

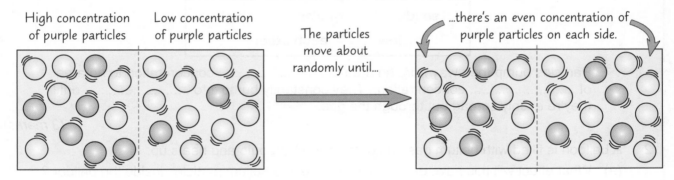

High concentration of purple particles

Low concentration of purple particles

The particles move about randomly until...

...there's an even concentration of purple particles on each side.

Movement of Particles Increases With Temperature

1) An increase in temperature causes particles to move around more.

2) So the spaces between the particles get bigger. This causes the substance to expand.

3) This explains how a thermometer works.

EXAMPLE:

When a thermometer is heated the volume of liquid in the bulb expands. The particles move apart with their extra energy.

So the liquid moves up the thin tube of the thermometer.

Section Eight — Energy and Matter

Warm-Up and Practice Questions

You're nearly done with this section now. Take time to make sure you've really understood everything so far — these questions will help you discover any gaps in your knowledge.

Warm-Up Questions

1) Describe what is meant by a physical change.

2) True or false? When a substance condenses it changes from solid to a gas.

3) What happens to the mass of a substance when it changes from a liquid to a gas?

4) True or false? Liquid water has a higher density than solid ice.

5) Explain why particles move randomly when they are suspended in a liquid or gas.

Practice Questions

1   Particles in a gas will become evenly spread out over time.

   (a) What name is given to this process?

    ☐ Dissolving   ☐ Diffusion   ☐ Evaporation

(1 mark)

   (b) Complete the sentences below about the movement of particles in a gas.
Use options from the box.

solids	**similar**	**high**
low	**each other**	

     Particles bump their way from an area of .... concentration to an area of .... concentration. They constantly bump into .... until they're evenly spread out through the gas.

(3 marks)

2   A balloon is filled with helium gas. It floats near a light bulb and heats up.

   (a) What effect will this have on the movement of the helium particles inside the balloon?

(1 mark)

   (b) Why does the balloon increase in size when this happens? Tick **one** box.

     ☐ The particles of gas have increased in size.

     ☐ There is more space between the particles of gas.

(1 mark)

3   Solids and liquids have different physical properties.

   (a) Describe the difference in density between ice and liquid water.

(1 mark)

   (b) 40 g of ice melts.
What mass of liquid water is produced in this process?

(1 mark)

Revision Summary for Section Eight

Ah, the section summary — on the home stretch at last. In this section you've looked at the wonderful world of energy and matter. Take the time to work through these questions below — they'll help you make sure you're up to scratch with everything you've seen in Section Eight. You can have the odd peek back at the right page if you're stuck, but keep trying until you can do them all without looking.

1) Give four ways of transferring energy.

2) Give one example of energy being transferred to a kinetic energy store.

3) What store of energy does a stretched slingshot transfer energy from when it's released?

4)* Two identical cranes each transfer 20 kJ of energy to move a weight. One crane applies a big force, the other applies a small force. Which crane can lift the weight the furthest?

5) What does thermal equilibrium mean?

6) Name two ways in which energy can be transferred by heating between two objects. Briefly describe how energy is transferred in each of these ways.

7) How does adding an insulator to an object affect the rate of energy transfer?

8) True or false? Energy is sometimes destroyed.

9) Why are most energy transfers NOT perfect?

10) Give two energy resources created using the Sun's energy.

11) Give an example of a non-renewable energy resource.

12)*Calculate the energy transferred by a 1.5 kW remote-control helicopter used for one hour.

13) What unit is household electricity measured in?

14)*Electricity costs 15p per kWh. Calculate the cost of an electricity bill for 298.2 kWh.

15)*Which will transfer more energy — a 200 W device left on for 1 hour, or a 300 W device left on for 1 hour?

16) What unit is the energy in food usually measured in?

17) Where could you find out the energy contained in a packet of chocolate-covered sugar cubes?

18) Why is a physical change different to a chemical change?

19) Melting is a process that brings about a physical change. Name five other processes that bring about a change of state.

20) True or false? Melting is not a reversible process.

21) Give one difference between the physical properties of a gas and a solid of the same substance.

22) What's meant by Brownian motion?

23) What is diffusion?

24) Explain why gases expand when they're heated.

*Answers on page 195.

Section Eight — Energy and Matter

Speed

Yes, it's a page on speed. Make sure you can do these calculations — don't zoom through.

Speed is **How Fast** You're **Going**

1) Speed is a measure of how far you travel in a set amount of time.
2) You can use this formula to do speed calculations:

$$\text{Speed} = \frac{\text{Distance}}{\text{Time}}$$

 This line means divided by.

3) Use the word SIDOT to help you remember the formula: SIDOT — Speed Is Distance Over Time.

Units are Really **Important**

There are three common units for speed.

metres per second — m/s
miles per hour — mph or miles/h
kilometres per hour — km/h

Always use UNITS.

Work Out **Speed** Using **Distance** and **Time**

To work out speed you need to know the distance travelled and the time taken.

Example: A sheep moves down a farmer's track.
It takes the sheep exactly 5 seconds to move between two fence posts.
The posts are 10 metres apart.
What is the sheep's speed?

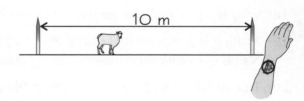
10 m

Answer:
Step 1) Write down what you know:
  distance = 10 m   time = 5 s
Step 2) Use the formula:
  Speed = Distance ÷ Time = 10 ÷ 5 = 2 m/s

The answer is in metres per second (m/s) because the distance was given in metres and the time in seconds.

 MATHS TIP

Speed units are always a distance unit per a time unit

The unit for speed depends on the units of the distance and time you put into the formula.
So if the distance was in km and the time was in hours, the speed will be in km per hour or km/h.

Distance-Time Graphs

Distance-time graphs can seem confusing — read this page extra-carefully.

Distance-Time Graphs Tell You About an Object's **Motion**

A distance-time graph shows the distance travelled by an object over time.

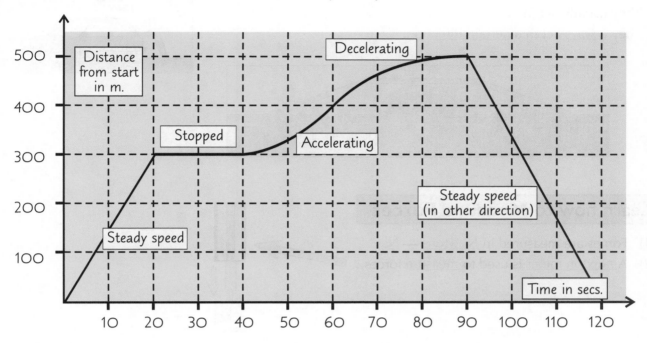

1) The slope of the line (gradient) shows the speed at which the object is moving.

2) A steeper line means the object is moving faster.

3) Flat sections are where it's stopped.

4) Downhill sections mean it's moving back toward its starting point.

5) Curves mean the speed is changing.

6) A curve that gets steeper means the object is speeding up (accelerating).

7) A curve levelling off means the object is slowing down (decelerating).

The slope of the line is really important

If the line on a distance-time graph is flat, the object's not moving. If it's straight but not flat, the object's moving at a steady speed. If the line is curved, the object is speeding up (accelerating) or slowing down (decelerating). Get that learnt and these graphs will make all sorts of sense.

Forces

Well, I can't <u>force</u> you to read this page — but if I were you, I'd <u>push</u> on with it...

Forces are Usually **Pushes** and **Pulls**

1) Forces <u>can't</u> be seen — but the <u>effects</u> of a force <u>can</u> be seen.
2) They usually act in <u>pairs</u>.
3) They <u>always</u> act in a <u>certain direction</u>.

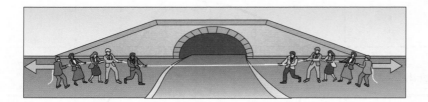

Learn how to **Measure Forces**

1) Forces are measured in <u>Newtons</u> — <u>N</u>.
2) A <u>newton meter</u> is used to <u>measure</u> forces.

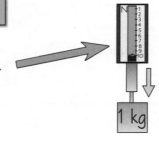

Forces Can Occur Between Objects That **Aren't Touching**

1) Forces usually occur between two objects that are <u>touching each other</u>. But this <u>isn't always the case</u>.
2) Forces due to <u>gravity</u> (p.158), <u>magnetism</u> (p.154) and <u>static electricity</u> (p.153) are all <u>NON-CONTACT FORCES</u>.
3) This means they can happen between two objects that <u>AREN'T touching</u> each other. For example:

<u>Gravity</u> makes the skydiver fall without touching him.

The <u>magnet</u> attracts the paperclips without touching them.

The strands of the girl's hair are not touching but are pushing each other away. This is because of <u>static charge</u>.

REVISION TASK

Forces mean lots of arrows to draw

Forces are a <u>simple enough</u> idea, but you still need to know <u>all of the details</u> on this page. Jot down each of the three <u>headings</u>, then <u>cover</u> the page and see which points you can remember for each of them. The final step is to <u>re-read</u> the page and see what you missed.

Force, Movement and Friction

Friction is a force that stops you falling over, but slows you down when you try to move. It's a mixed bag.

Forces Can Make Objects do Five Things

1) Speed Up or Start Moving

Like kicking a football.

2) Slow Down or Stop Moving

Like air resistance (see next page).

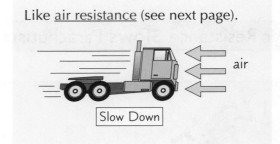

3) Change Direction

Like hitting a ball with a bat.

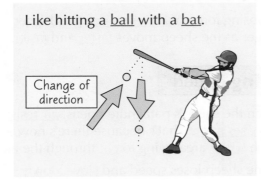

4) Change Shape

Like stretching and compressing (see p.124), bending and twisting.

5) Turn

Like turning a spanner.

If the forces acting on an object are balanced, the object will be moving at a steady speed or be stationary — see pages 121-122.

Friction Tries to Stop Objects Sliding Past Each Other

1) Friction is a force that always acts in the opposite direction to movement.
2) To start something moving, a push or pull force must be bigger than resisting forces like friction.
3) So to push an object out of the way, you need to overcome friction.
4) You get friction when:

- two surfaces rub together.
- an object passes through air or water.

Air and Water Resistance

Like friction, air resistance is good at <u>slowing things down</u>. Don't let it turn studying into a drag.

Air and Water Resistance Slow Down Moving Objects

1) Air and water resistance are <u>frictional forces</u>.
2) They <u>push against</u> objects which are moving through air or water and <u>slow</u> them down.

Air Resistance Slows Parachutists Down

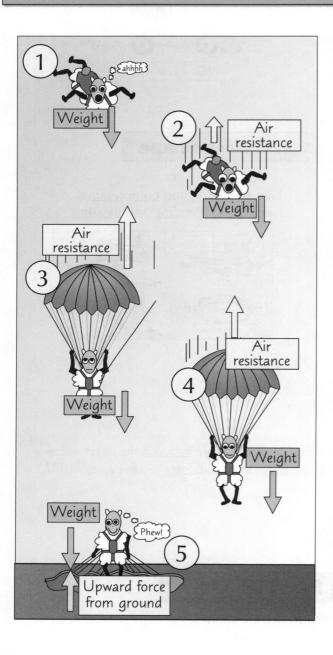

1) Gains Speed

1) At the start, the sheep only has the <u>force</u> of its <u>weight</u> pulling it down.
2) So the sheep starts to <u>move faster</u>.

2) Still Gaining Speed

The opposing force of <u>air resistance</u> gets bigger and bigger as the sheep moves <u>faster</u> and <u>faster</u>.

3) Losing Speed

1) When the sheep's parachute opens, <u>air resistance increases a lot</u>. That's because there's now a much <u>larger</u> area trying to <u>cut</u> through the air.
2) So the sheep loses speed and <u>slows down</u> gracefully.

4) Steady Speed

1) The <u>air resistance</u> very quickly becomes <u>equal</u> to the <u>weight</u>.
2) This means the two forces are <u>balanced</u>. The sheep now moves at a <u>steady speed</u>.

5) No Speed

1) Back on the <u>ground</u>, the sheep <u>doesn't move</u> at all.
2) The <u>weight</u> acting downwards is balanced by an equal <u>upward force</u> from the ground.

Parachuting sheep — don't try this at home

Anything moving through air or water feels a <u>resistance</u> trying to slow it down. Some objects like boats and cars are <u>streamlined</u> to reduce resistance. You'll also need to understand that resistance eventually makes objects fall at a <u>steady speed</u> by pushing in the <u>opposite direction</u> to gravity.

Warm-Up and Practice Questions

Here's another set of Warm-Up and Practice Questions. Take time to give these questions a good go — they'll help you to find out which pages you've understood really well, and which pages could do with a bit more attention. Go on, you know you want to...

Warm-Up Questions

1) Give the equation that is used to calculate speed.

2) Give three common units for speed.

3) A girl cycles 180 metres in 30 seconds. What is her speed? (Speed = distance ÷ time)

4) How would you show acceleration on a distance-time graph?

5) Give one example of a force which occurs between two objects that aren't touching.

6) True or false? A parachutist keeps on accelerating until he reaches the ground.

Practice Questions

1 A tennis player tosses her ball in the air before serving.

(a) What force causes the ball to begin falling back
down towards Earth?

(1 mark)

(b) The girl hits the ball with her racket.

(i) Which of the following statements are most likely to be true?
Tick **two** boxes.

☐ There is a non-contact force between the racket and ball.

☐ The force causes the ball to change direction.

☐ The force makes the ball speed up.

☐ The racket does not change the ball's direction or speed.

(2 marks)

(ii) Suggest **one** way in which the force of the
racket changes the shape of the ball.

(1 mark)

(c) The ball leaves the tennis player's racket and travels a distance of 20 m in 0.4 seconds.

(i) Calculate the speed of the ball. Use the formula: speed = $\frac{distance}{time}$.
Give your answer in m/s.

(2 marks)

(ii) The diagram shows the ball moving
horizontally through the air.
Force **X** is slowing down the ball.
What is force **X**?

direction of motion

force **X**

(1 mark)

Practice Questions

2   Trevor is playing with his model train set.

(a) Trevor places a model carriage on a horizontal track a short distance behind the engine. A magnet is attached to the front of the carriage and the back of the engine, as shown below. The magnets attract, so that the carriage moves towards the engine.

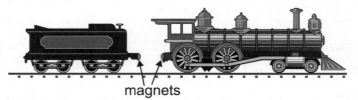

magnets

Circle the correct word to complete the following sentence.

The force between the engine and carriage was a **(contact / non-contact)** force.

(1 mark)

(b) Trevor's model train travels along a metal track. One part of the track is rusty.

Suggest how the model train's motion may change as it travels over the rusty part of the track. Explain your answer.

(2 marks)

Trevor plays with his model train for 80 seconds. The graph below shows how the train's distance from its start point changed over this time period.

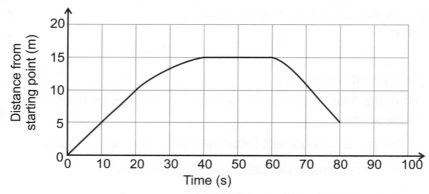

Use the graph to answer the following questions:

(c) Between 10 and 20 seconds:
   (i)   how far does the model train travel?

(1 mark)

   (ii) how fast is the model train going?

(2 marks)

(d) After 40 seconds, the model train stops at a station.
   (i)   How far is the station from the starting point?

(1 mark)

   (ii) How many seconds does the model train stop at the station for?

(1 mark)

(e) In what direction is the train travelling between 60 and 70 seconds?

(1 mark)

Section Nine — Forces and Motion

Force Diagrams

Force diagrams. They're <u>diagrams</u> that show <u>forces</u>. Bet you weren't expecting that...

Use **Force Diagrams** to **Show** the **Forces Acting** on Objects

1) Force diagrams use <u>arrows</u> to show the <u>forces</u> acting on an object.
2) The <u>direction</u> of an arrow shows the <u>direction</u> that the force is acting in.
3) The <u>size</u> of an arrow shows the <u>size</u> of the force.

EXAMPLE:

1) The car in the diagram has <u>three horizontal forces</u> acting on it.
2) The <u>red arrows</u> represent forces acting to the <u>left</u>.
3) The <u>blue arrow</u> represents the <u>friction force</u> acting to the <u>right</u>.
4) The force of the rocket is the <u>biggest</u> — it's shown by the <u>biggest arrow</u>.
5) There are <u>vertical forces</u> acting on the car too (e.g. weight). These <u>aren't shown</u>.

Stationary Objects have **Balanced Forces**

A <u>stationary</u> object <u>doesn't move</u>.

EXAMPLE: Stationary mug force diagram

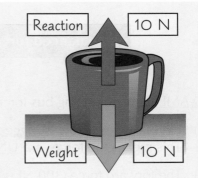

1) This mug on the right is <u>stationary</u>.
2) The mug's <u>weight</u> is a <u>force</u> acting <u>downwards</u> on the table. It's the <u>red</u> arrow.
3) A <u>reaction force</u> from the table's surface <u>pushes up</u> on the mug. This is the <u>blue</u> arrow.
4) The <u>reaction force</u> and <u>weight</u> are <u>EQUAL</u> and <u>OPPOSITE</u>. The <u>arrows</u> are the <u>same size</u> and point in <u>opposite directions</u>.
5) This means the <u>forces</u> on the mug of coffee are <u>BALANCED</u>. So it stays <u>stationary</u> (not moving).

Learn this <u>important rule</u>:

> **Balanced forces produce no change in movement.**

Weight = Reaction Force for an object sitting on a surface

The car in the diagram at the top of this page also has <u>weight acting downwards</u> on it and a <u>reaction force</u> from the road pushing <u>up</u> on it. Unless an object is in Space, it'll always have weight. And, there'll usually be some force acting upwards on it too (e.g. a reaction force or air resistance).

Force Diagrams

This is where it gets tricky. <u>Balanced forces</u> don't always mean an object is <u>stationary</u>...

Movement at a **Steady Speed** Needs **Balanced Forces**

Just like stationary objects, moving objects can also have <u>balanced forces</u> acting on them...

<u>EXAMPLE</u>: Steady bus force diagram

1) The <u>red</u> arrow shows the bus has a <u>forward force</u> of <u>100 N</u>.

2) The <u>blue</u> arrow shows a <u>frictional force</u> of <u>100 N</u> acting in the <u>opposite direction</u>.

3) The arrows are <u>the same size</u> — so the <u>forces</u> are <u>balanced</u>.

4) If the forces acting on a <u>moving object</u> are <u>balanced</u>, it <u>keeps moving</u> at a <u>steady speed</u> in the <u>same direction</u>.

Overall force = 100 − 100 = 0 N
Forces are balanced.
Bus continues at same speed.

Unbalanced Forces mean Acceleration

If the forces acting on an object are <u>not balanced</u>, the object <u>won't</u> stay still or continue at a steady speed.

> Unbalanced forces change the speed or direction of moving objects.

<u>EXAMPLE</u>: Accelerating bus force diagram

1) Here, the <u>red</u> arrow is <u>bigger</u> than the <u>blue</u> arrow. This means the forces are <u>UNBALANCED</u>.

2) The <u>forward</u> force (300 N) is <u>bigger</u> than the force acting in the <u>opposite</u> direction (100 N).

3) So there's an <u>overall force</u> (of 200 N) in the <u>forward</u> direction.

4) This means the bus is <u>speeding up</u> (<u>accelerating</u>).

5) If the <u>opposing</u> force was <u>bigger</u> than the <u>forward</u> force, the bus would slow down (<u>decelerate</u>).

Overall force = 300 − 100 = 200 N
Forces are NOT balanced.
Bus accelerates.

Use the force — look at a diagram, find out if it's accelerating

Remember: if the arrows on a force diagram are <u>equal</u> and <u>opposite</u>, the object <u>isn't moving</u> or is moving at a <u>steady speed</u>. If they're <u>different sizes</u>, the <u>object</u> will <u>accelerate</u> or <u>decelerate</u>.

Moments

Don't wait a lifetime to learn moments like this — memorise what's on this page now.

Forces Cause Objects to Turn Around Pivots

A pivot is the point around which rotation happens — like the middle of a seesaw.

A Moment is the Turning Effect of a Force

1) When a force acts on something which has a pivot, it creates a moment (turning effect).

2) Learn this important equation:

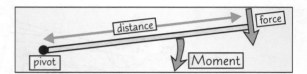

$$\text{Moment} = \text{force} \times \text{distance}$$

in newton metres, Nm   in newtons, N   in metres, m

Balancing Moments

Balanced moments mean that...

anticlockwise moments = clockwise moments

If the moments are not balanced, the ruler will turn in the direction of the bigger moment.

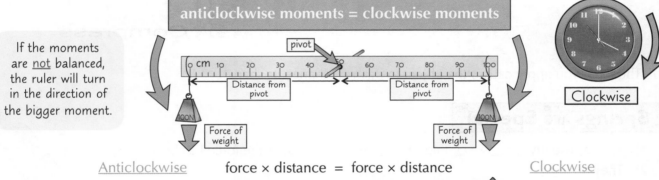

Clockwise

Anticlockwise   force × distance = force × distance   Clockwise
                        100 N × 0.5 m = 100 N × 0.5 m
                              50 Nm = 50 Nm   ✓ – BALANCED

50 cm = 0.5 m

Is it Balanced?

You can calculate moments to work out what will happen to these beams...

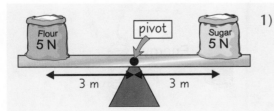

1) Anticlockwise   Clockwise
    5 × 3 = 15 Nm   5 × 3 = 15 Nm

The anticlockwise moment equals the clockwise moment. So the beam is BALANCED.

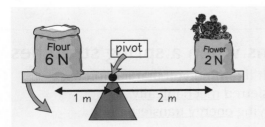

2) Anticlockwise   Clockwise
    6 × 1 = 6 Nm   2 × 2 = 4 Nm

The anticlockwise moment is bigger than the clockwise moment. The beam is NOT BALANCED.
It will turn in the anticlockwise direction.

Forces and Elasticity

It's not just about turning, pushing and pulling. Forces are also able to stretch or squash things.

You Can **Deform** Objects by **Stretching** or **Squashing**

1) You can use forces to:

Stretch...

...or Compress Objects

2) The force you apply causes the object to deform (change its shape).

Springs are Special

1) Springs usually spring back into their original shape after the force has been removed.
2) They are elastic.

Work is Done When a Force Deforms an Object

1) You might remember energy transfer from page 99 (if not, take a look).
2) Work done is the same thing.
3) Energy is transferred and work is done when an object is deformed.

EXAMPLE:
- When you stretch a spring, you're doing work.
- Energy is transferred from your kinetic energy store to the elastic potential energy store of the spring.

Energy

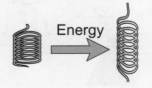

REVISION TIP

Learn the energy transfer that happens when a spring stretches

Do look back to the stuff on energy transfers on p.99. It'll remind you that if a force is making something move, then the energy is being transferred mechanically. And remember, work done is just a Physics-y way of saying energy transferred.

Forces and Elasticity

The more force you use to pull on a spring, the more it stretches. It makes sense really.

Hooke's Law Says Extension Depends on the Force

1) If a spring is supported at the top and then a weight is attached to the bottom, it stretches.

2) Hooke's Law says:

> **The amount a spring stretches (the extension), is directly proportional to the force applied (the weight).**

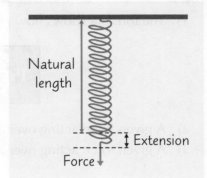

3) This just means that a graph of force against extension looks like this:

4) Hooke's Law only applies up to a certain force.

5) For springs, the force at which Hooke's Law stops working is much higher than for most materials. Springs are unusual.

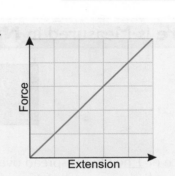

A Spring Holding a Weight Still is in Equilibrium

1) Equilibrium means all the forces are balanced.
2) When a stretched or compressed spring holds a weight still, the force of the weight is the same as the force of the spring.
3) So the forces are balanced and in equilibrium.

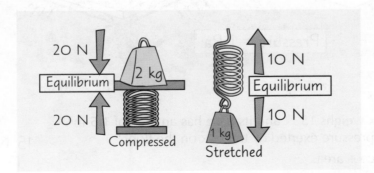

This page will stretch you — better do some work on it

It's true — there's a lot of stuff to learn here — including an important graph. So read through the page again, then cover it up and see if you can remember the two headings. Then draw the diagrams. Then learn the rest. You know what to do. It's the only way.

Pressure

Don't let pressure <u>get you down</u> — here's a lovely couple of pages that explain it all. Enjoy.

Pressure is How Much **Force** is Put on a Certain **Area**

1) The formula shows how <u>pressure</u>, <u>force</u> and <u>area</u> are linked:

$$\text{Pressure} = \frac{\text{Force}}{\text{Area}}$$

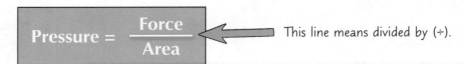 This line means divided by (÷).

2) A given force acting over a <u>BIG area</u> means a <u>SMALL pressure</u>.
3) A given force acting over a <u>SMALL area</u> means a <u>BIG pressure</u>.

Pressure is Measured in **N/m²** or **Pascals** (Pa)

$$1 \text{ newton/metre}^2 = 1 \text{ pascal}$$
$$1 \text{ N/m}^2 = 1 \text{ Pa}$$

If a force of <u>1 newton</u> is spread over an area of <u>1 m²</u> (like this) then it applies a pressure of <u>1 pascal</u>. Simple as that.

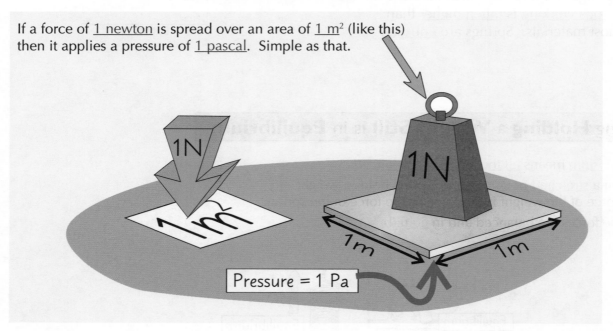

1N

1N

1m²

1m   1m

Pressure = 1 Pa

Example: A wooden box weighs 15 N and its base has an area of 1.5 m².
Calculate the pressure exerted by the box on the floor.

Answer: Pressure = force ÷ area.
15 ÷ 1.5 = <u>10 N/m²</u> or <u>10 Pa</u>.

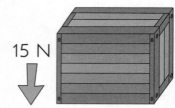

15 N

MATHS TIP

Don't feel too pressured about this stuff

Using <u>equations</u> can be tricky — double check you've put the numbers in the right way around. Remember, pressure is in N/m², so the force in <u>newtons</u> (N) goes on the top.

Pressure

You can't see air — but it's applying pressure to you all the time (unless you are reading this in Space).

Atmospheric Pressure is **All Around Us** All the Time

1) At sea level, there's a lot of atmosphere (air) above you.
   The atmosphere weighs quite a bit, so it applies a high pressure.

> Weight is a force.
> So atmospheric pressure =
> weight of the atmosphere ÷ area.

2) At the top of a mountain, there's less atmosphere above you. The atmosphere weighs less, so the pressure it applies is lower.

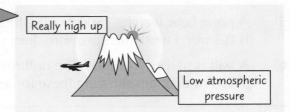

3) The higher you go, the lower the pressure.

The Pressure in **Liquids Increases** with **Depth**

For liquids like water, the pressure increases with depth.
So the pressure at the bottom of an ocean is higher than at the top.

Water Pressure Causes **Upthrust** and Makes Things **Float**

1) If you place an object in water, it experiences water pressure from all directions.

2) Water pressure increases with depth.
   So the force pushing upwards at the bottom of the object is bigger than the force pushing down at the top of the object.

3) This causes an overall upwards force, called upthrust.

4) If the upthrust is the same as the object's weight, the object will float.

5) If the upthrust is less than the object's weight, it will sink.

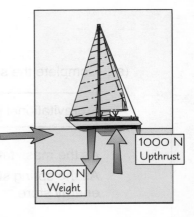

1000 N Upthrust

1000 N Weight

Pressure — it pushes down on you all the time

Remember: if you increase the amount of air (or water) above your head, you're increasing the force acting on your head and you'll get an increase in pressure on it. That's why pressure in liquids increases with depth and why air pressure decreases with height. Re-read this page to make sure you really understand it before moving on.

Warm-Up and Practice Questions

There are quite a lot of calculations to get to grips with here.
Go back over any ones you get wrong until you're confident about how to do them.

Warm-Up Questions

1) Draw a force diagram for a car moving at a steady speed with a driving force of 2000 N. Ignore the vertical forces on the car.

2) The engine of a motorbike is providing a forward force of 1000 N. The frictional force is 400 N. Explain whether the motorbike is moving with a steady speed or is accelerating.

3) Fill in the missing words in the following sentence. If the moments on an object are balanced, you know that: _____ moments = _____ moments.

4) True or false? If a stretched spring is still, the forces on it are balanced.

5) A polar bear weighs 1500 N. The total area of her paws that is in contact with the ground is 0.3 m². How much pressure does she exert on the ground? Give the units.

6) A ball is placed in water. The upthrust on the ball is less than the ball's weight. Sketch a diagram showing these forces. Will the ball sink or float?

Practice Questions

1 Arnold attaches a mass to a fixed spring. He then allows it to fall.

(a) Complete the sentences below. Use words from the box.

| gravitational potential | elastic potential | chemical | kinetic |

As the mass falls, energy is transferred to its .... energy store.
As the spring stretches, this energy is transferred to its ....
energy store.

(2 marks)

(b) Eventually the mass comes to rest and is held in equilibrium by the spring.
The weight of the mass is 5 N.
What is the size of the force being exerted on the mass by the spring?

(1 mark)

Practice Questions

2   A dolphin takes in air. The dolphin then swims downwards towards the seabed.

(a)   How does the water pressure felt by the dolphin change as it swims downwards?

(1 mark)

(b)   The dolphin releases a bubble of air, which rises to the surface.
What force causes the bubble to rise? Tick **one** box.

☐ weight   ☐ upthrust   ☐ friction

(1 mark)

3   Stuart wants to make a mobile to hang above a baby's cot.
He has a teddy and a toy horse to hang from the mobile.
He hangs them from the rod shown below.

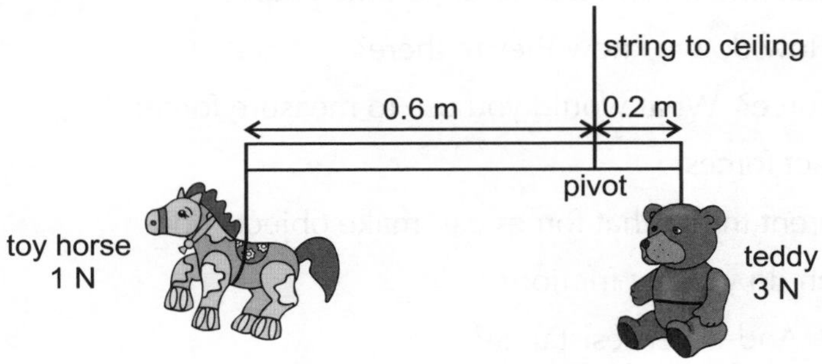

(a)   Calculate the clockwise moment (turning effect) of the weight of the teddy.
Give the units. Use the formula: moment = force × distance.

(3 marks)

(b)   Calculate the anticlockwise moment (turning effect) of the weight of the toy horse.
Give the units.

(3 marks)

(c)   Is the mobile balanced? Explain your answer.

(2 marks)

4   Maz and Pam both weigh exactly 700 N. Maz wears shoes with pointed heels.
Pam wears trainers. They both lean back so they are standing only on their heels.

(a)   Explain why Maz makes dents on the floor but Pam doesn't.
Use these words in your answer:

force   area   pressure

(2 marks)

(b)   Maz's heels each have an area of 0.0001 m². She balances on
one heel so that all of her weight acts through it onto the floor.
Calculate the total pressure that Maz is putting on the floor.
Use the formula: pressure = $\frac{force}{area}$

(3 marks)

Revision Summary for Section Nine

Section Nine is all about forces and motion. It's all pretty straightforward stuff really and the questions below will test whether you've learnt the basic facts.

If you're having trouble learning the stuff, try taking just one page on its own.
Start by learning part of it, then covering it up and scribbling it down again.
Then learn a bit more and scribble that down.
Soon you'll have learnt the whole section and be ready to face any question your teachers throw at you.

1)   What exactly is speed?

2)   How does SIDOT help you remember what speed is?

3)* A pea is flicked across a room. It travels 5 m in 2 seconds.
     Calculate the speed of the pea.

4)   When you are using the speed formula, you put in a distance in km
     and a time in hours. What units will the speed have?

5)   What does the gradient show on a distance-time graph?

6)   What does a straight, flat line mean on a distance-time graph?

7)   Can forces be seen? How do we know they're there?

8)   What are the units of force? What would you use to measure force?

9)   Name three non-contact forces.

10) What are the five different things that forces can make objects do?

11) What is friction? When do you get friction?

12) What is air resistance? And water resistance?

13) When a sheep first jumps out of a plane what happens to its speed?

14) As the sheep moves faster, what happens to the air resistance?

15) What happens to air resistance when the sheep's parachute opens?

16) Does the speed then change? When does the sheep's speed become steady?

17) Look at the force diagram of a book resting on a table.
     Why does the book remain stationary?

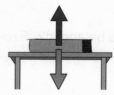

18) If the forces acting on a moving bus are balanced, what will happen to its speed?

19) What is a pivot?

20) What is a moment? Give the formula for a moment.

21) What does "balanced moments" mean?

22) Give two ways you can deform (change the shape of) objects.

23) What does Hooke's Law say?

24) What is pressure? Give the formula for calculating pressure.

25)* A force of 200 N acts on an area of 2 m². Calculate the pressure.

26) Is atmospheric pressure higher at the seaside or up a mountain? Why?

27)* A boat is put into the sea. The weight of the boat is 1000 N.
     The upthrust from the water is 1000 N. Will the boat sink or float?

*Answers on page 196

Section Nine — Forces and Motion

Water Waves

If you've ever gone swimming in the sea, you will have noticed that you bob up and down. This is because of water waves. Read on to find out more...

Water Waves are Transverse

1) Waves travelling across the ocean are transverse waves.
2) A transverse wave has undulations (up and down movements).
   These movements are at right angles to the direction the wave is travelling in.

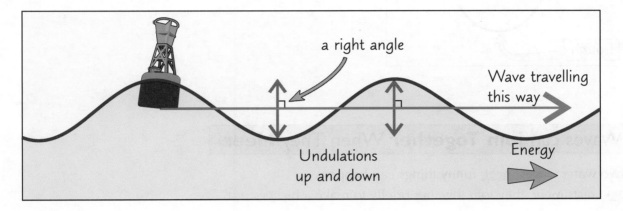

a right angle

Wave travelling this way

Undulations up and down

Energy

3) Waves transfer energy from one place to another.
   Energy is transferred in the direction the wave is travelling in.

Waves Can be Reflected

1) If a water wave hits a surface, it will be reflected.
2) This causes the direction of the wave to change.
3) All waves can be reflected. There's more on reflection on pages 134 and 143.

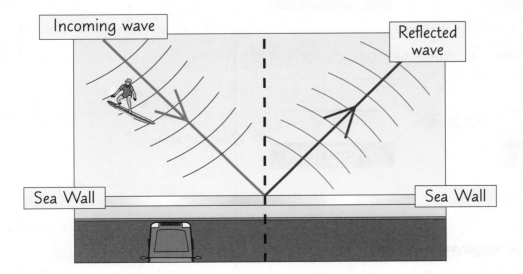

Incoming wave

Reflected wave

Sea Wall

Sea Wall

Water Waves

Transverse Waves Have Crests and Troughs

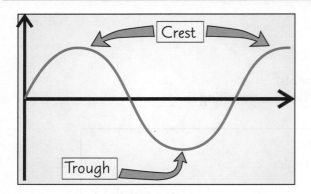

1) The <u>crest</u> is the <u>highest</u> part of the wave.
2) The <u>trough</u> is the <u>lowest</u> part of the wave.

You met <u>transverse waves</u> on the previous page.

Two Waves can Join Together When They Meet

When two water waves <u>meet</u>, funny things can happen:

1) If <u>two crests</u> meet, they <u>join together</u> briefly to make a <u>bigger crest</u>.

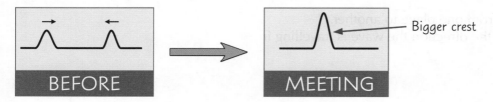

Bigger crest

2) If <u>two troughs</u> meet, they <u>join together</u> briefly to make a <u>bigger trough</u>.

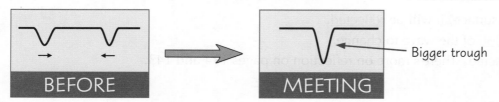

Bigger trough

3) If an identical <u>crest</u> and <u>trough</u> meet, they <u>cancel each other out</u> briefly.

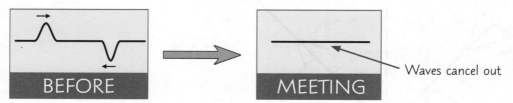

Waves cancel out

REVISION TASK

Transverse waves, crests, troughs — learn the labels

Waves are a bit tricky. So grab a piece of paper and <u>write</u> down all the <u>technical words</u> on these pages and what they <u>mean</u>. Then draw and explain the <u>diagrams</u>. Finally, do all that again with the book closed until you've memorised both pages — even the difficult bits...

Light Waves

You wouldn't know from looking, but light is actually a wave. Here's a page all about it...

Light is a **Wave** of **Energy**

1) Light is produced by luminous objects.
These include the Sun, light bulbs and flames.

2) Light is a wave. It always travels in a straight line.

Light Waves are Similar to Water Waves

	Water Wave	Light Wave
Is a transverse wave	✓	✓
Transfers energy	✓	✓
Can be reflected	✓	✓
Needs particles to travel	✓	✗

1) Water waves and light waves have lots of things in common.
These are shown by the ticks (✓) in the table above.

2) One big difference between them is that water waves
need particles to travel. Light waves DON'T.

3) Light waves are slowed down by particles.

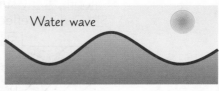

Water wave

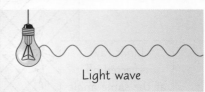

Light wave

Water waves and light waves
have the same shape —
they're both transverse waves.

Light Waves **Travel Fastest** in a **Vacuum**

1) Light travels faster when there are fewer particles to get in the way.

2) Light always travels fastest in a VACUUM.
A vacuum is where there is nothing at all — no air, no particles, nothing.

3) Space is mostly a vacuum. So light travels very fast in space.

4) The speed of light in a vacuum is ALWAYS 300 000 000 m/s
— that's three hundred million metres per second.

> **Speed of light in a vacuum: 300 000 000 m/s**

Light waves are similar to water waves — but not the same

Light is just like all those waves you see at the beach. Except that it doesn't need a load of water to get from A to B. Anything like water puts a load of particles in the way and slows the light waves down. Nope, light only hits top speed when it's in a vacuum with absolutely nothing in the way at all.

Reflection

Reflection is all about what happens to light rays when they hit something.

Mirrors Have Shiny Surfaces Which Reflect Light

1) A light wave is also known as a light ray.
2) Light rays reflect off mirrors and most other things.
3) Mirrors have a very smooth shiny surface.
4) The shiny surface allows each light ray to reflect off it at the same angle, giving a clear reflection. This is called SPECULAR REFLECTION.
5) Rough surfaces look dull because the light is reflected back in lots of different directions (scattered). This is called DIFFUSE SCATTERING.

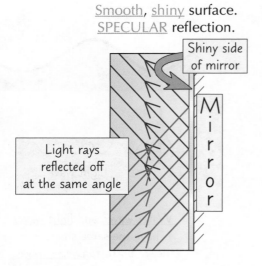

Smooth, shiny surface.
SPECULAR reflection.

Shiny side of mirror

Light rays reflected off at the same angle

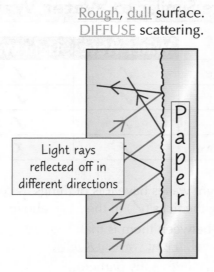

Rough, dull surface.
DIFFUSE scattering.

Light rays reflected off in different directions

Learn the Law of Reflection:

ANGLE OF INCIDENCE = ANGLE OF REFLECTION

1) The angle of incidence is the angle at which a light ray hits a surface.
2) The angle of reflection is the angle at which a light ray leaves a surface.
3) The normal is a line at a right angle (90°) to the surface.
4) The angle of incidence and the angle of reflection are always measured between the light ray and the normal.
5) You can draw all this in a ray diagram.

Make sure you draw straight lines and get the angles the same when drawing ray diagrams. Use a ruler and a protractor.

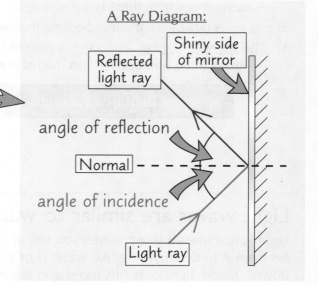

A Ray Diagram:

Shiny side of mirror

Reflected light ray

angle of reflection

Normal

angle of incidence

Light ray

Refraction

Refraction happens when light rays move to a <u>more</u> or <u>less</u> dense substance.

Refraction is When Light Bends

1) Light will travel through <u>transparent</u> (see-through) material.
   It <u>won't</u> go through anything <u>opaque</u> (not see-through).

2) Any <u>substance</u> that <u>light</u> or sound <u>travels through</u> is called a <u>MEDIUM</u>.

3) When light travels <u>from one</u> transparent medium <u>to another</u>, it <u>bends</u>.
   This is called <u>REFRACTION</u>.

<u>LEARN THESE:</u>

> When light goes from a <u>LESS dense</u> medium to a <u>MORE dense</u> medium:
> light bends <u>TOWARDS THE NORMAL</u>.

Example: <u>air</u> to <u>glass</u>.

> When light goes from a <u>MORE dense</u> medium to a <u>LESS dense</u> medium:
> light bends <u>AWAY FROM THE NORMAL</u>.

Example: <u>glass</u> to <u>air</u>.

Here's What Happens When Light Hits a Glass Block

1) <u>Light</u> hits the <u>glass</u> and <u>slows down</u>.

2) If the light ray hits the glass at an <u>angle</u>,
   it will <u>bend towards</u> the <u>normal</u>.

3) When the light ray <u>leaves</u> the glass block it
   <u>speeds up</u> — and bends <u>away</u> from the <u>normal</u>.

> Glass is much more dense than air.

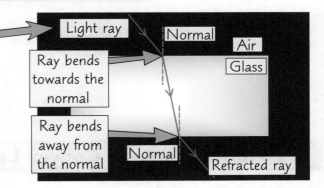

4) If a light ray hits the glass block
   <u>straight</u> on, it <u>doesn't bend</u>.
   There's <u>no refraction</u>.

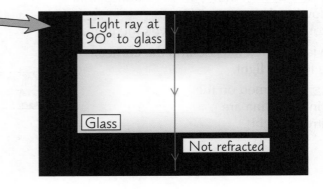

Don't get reflection and refraction mixed up

<u>Reflection</u> and <u>refraction</u> sound similar, but they are really <u>very different</u>. Make sure you <u>learn</u> what they are, and all the details about how they work. It really helps to learn the paths of the light rays. Reflected rays form a <u>V-shape</u>, and refracted rays form a <u>badly drawn Z-shape</u>.

Sight

Have you ever wondered <u>how we see</u>? Well it's time to stop wondering — you're about to find out...

We **See** Things Because **Light Reflects** into our **Eyes**

1) When an object produces light, the light <u>reflects</u> off <u>other objects</u>.

2) Some of the reflected light then goes <u>into our eyes</u>. This is how we <u>see</u>.

Lenses Can be Used to **Focus Light**

1) A lens <u>refracts</u> (bends) light.

2) A <u>convex</u> lens <u>bulges outwards</u>. It causes rays of <u>light</u> to move <u>together</u> to a <u>focus</u>.

> Take a look back at the previous page for a reminder of what refraction is.

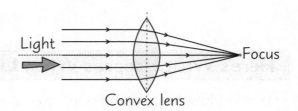

The **Human Eye** uses **Convex Lenses** to **Focus**

1) In the <u>human eye</u>, the <u>cornea</u> is a transparent 'window' with a <u>convex shape</u>. The cornea does most of the eye's <u>focusing</u>.

2) There is a convex <u>lens</u> behind the cornea. It also focuses light.

3) <u>Images</u> are formed on the <u>retina</u>. Cells in the retina are <u>photo-sensitive</u> (sensitive to <u>light</u>).

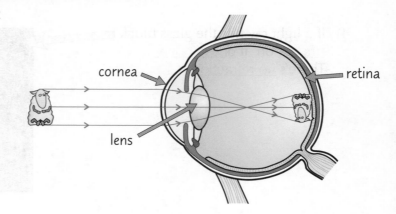

Our eyes focus light by refracting it

<u>Reflection</u> and <u>refraction</u> play a big part in you being able to <u>see things</u>. If you're struggling to understand the stuff on this page, take a look back at <u>pages 134-135</u>. It may just <u>do the trick</u>.

Cameras and Sight

An <u>important</u> page this one — it's all about how cameras produce <u>images</u>.

The **Pinhole Camera** is a **Simple Camera**

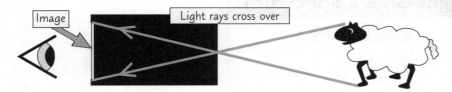

1) The light travels in a <u>straight line</u> from the sheep to the <u>photographic film</u> through the <u>pinhole</u>.

2) The hole is small, so <u>only one ray</u> gets in from <u>each point</u> on the sheep.

3) The <u>image</u> of the sheep seen by the farmer is <u>upside down</u> and <u>crossed over</u>.

4) This is because the rays of light <u>cross over</u> inside the camera:

Energy is **Transferred** From a Light **Source** to an **Absorber**

1) <u>Energy</u> is <u>transferred</u> by light waves (page 133).

2) Anything that <u>absorbs</u> this energy is called an <u>absorber</u>. For example a <u>retina cell</u> in the <u>eye</u>, or the <u>digital image sensor</u> in a <u>digital camera</u>.

3) Energy is <u>transferred</u> to the <u>absorber</u> when light waves hit it.

4) When light waves hit a <u>cell</u> in the <u>retina</u> it causes <u>chemical</u> and <u>electrical changes</u> that send signals to the <u>brain</u>.

5) In a <u>digital camera</u>, light causes the sensor to produce an <u>electrical charge</u>. The changes in charge are read by a <u>computer</u> and turned into an <u>image</u>.

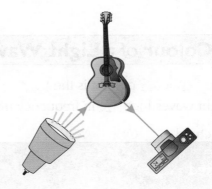

An image sensor in a digital camera absorbs light and makes an image

<u>Retina cells</u> in the eye do the <u>same thing</u>. Better <u>learn</u> all this stuff then — cast your gaze back to the top of the page and read it over <u>again</u>. Then <u>cover up</u> the book and see if you can remember everything.

Light and Colour

Ok, prepare yourself — there's a big plot twist coming up on this page. Wait for it... here we go:

White Light is Not Just a Single Colour

1) White light is actually a mixture of colours.
2) This shows up when white light hits a prism or a rain drop. It gets split up into a full rainbow of colours.
3) The splitting up of light is called dispersal.
4) The proper name for this rainbow effect is a spectrum.

Dispersal of White Light Gives a Spectrum

1) Learn the order that the colours come out in:

Red Orange Yellow Green Blue Indigo Violet

2) Remember it with this rhyme:

Richard Of York Gave Battle In Velvet

A prism

A spectrum

White light

red
orange
yellow
green
blue
indigo
violet

Violet light is bent the most

The Colour of a Light Wave is Related to Its Frequency

1) The frequency of light is the number of waves that pass a point per second.
2) Light waves increase in frequency from red (low frequency) to violet (high frequency).

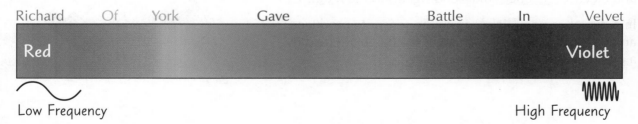

Richard	Of	York	Gave	Battle	In	Velvet

Red ... Violet

Low Frequency ... High Frequency

REVISION TIP

Red and yellow and pink and gr... hang on, that's not right

If you can learn the rhyme about dear old Richard, you're doing well. Even better if you can learn the colours that go with it. But remembering that red light has a lower frequency than violet light can be tricky. It might help to look at the number of letters in "red" and "violet". "Red" has a LOWER number of letters. This might remind you that it has a LOWER frequency.

Absorption and Reflection of Colour

The different colours that make up white light can be <u>reflected</u> and <u>absorbed</u>. Read on...

Coloured Filters Only let Their Colour Through

1) A <u>filter</u> only allows one <u>particular colour</u> of light to <u>go through it</u>.
2) <u>All other colours</u> are <u>ABSORBED</u> by the filter — so they <u>don't get through</u>.

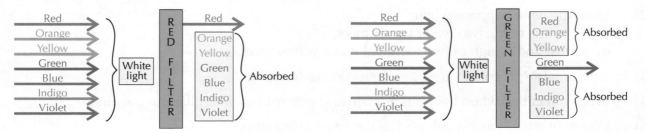

Coloured Objects Reflect Only That Colour

1) <u>Blue</u> jeans are <u>blue</u> because they <u>reflect</u> blue light and <u>absorb</u> all the other colours.
2) <u>White</u> objects <u>REFLECT all</u> colours.
3) <u>Black</u> objects <u>ABSORB all</u> colours.

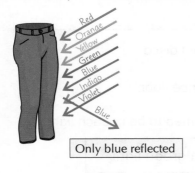

Only blue reflected

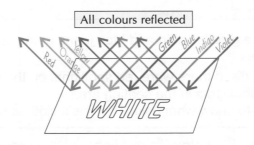

All colours reflected

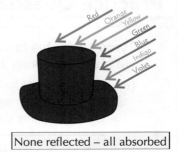

None reflected – all absorbed

Objects Seem to Have Different Colours in Different Coloured Light

IN WHITE LIGHT

1) The boot looks <u>red</u>. It reflects <u>red</u> light and <u>absorbs</u> all other colours.
2) The lace looks <u>green</u>. It reflects <u>green</u> light and absorbs all other colours.

IN RED LIGHT

1) The boot looks <u>red</u>. It reflects the <u>red</u> light.
2) The lace looks <u>black</u>. It has <u>no green light</u> to reflect. It absorbs all the <u>red</u> light.

IN GREEN LIGHT

1) The boot looks black. It has <u>no red light</u> to reflect. It absorbs the <u>green</u> light.
2) The lace looks <u>green</u>. It <u>reflects</u> the <u>green</u> light.

Red objects only reflect red light, blue objects only reflect blue light...

This stuff isn't too bad once you get your head around it. Make sure you <u>know it all</u> before moving on.

Warm-Up and Practice Questions

You're now over halfway through Section Ten. Time for a quick breather and a chance to check your understanding of the pages so far. Give these questions a go and make sure you haven't missed anything.

Warm-Up Questions

1) True or false? Transverse waves have crests and troughs.

2) Describe what happens when:
   a) the crests of the two water waves meet,
   b) a crest and trough of two identical water waves meet.

3) True or false? A convex lens uses reflection to focus light.

4) What is it called when light hits a prism and gets split up into different colours?

5) Which of the following colours has the lowest frequency?
   A: violet   **B**: yellow   **C**: green   **D**: red

6) Does a blue filter absorb blue light or let blue light pass through it?

Practice Questions

1   Tyrone wore his favourite green T-shirt and blue jeans at the school disco.
    He also wore white shoes.

   (a) When he got to the disco there were red spotlights on the dance floor.
        There were green spotlights in the seating area.
        Complete the table to show what colour Tyrone's clothes seemed to be in each light:

Tyrone's clothes	colour in red light	colour in green light
green T-shirt		
blue jeans	black	
white shoes		green

   (4 marks)

   (b) At the end of the disco the DJ put the main white lights on.
        Complete the sentences below. Use words from the box.
        You may use the words more than once.

blue	reflected	white
absorbed		green

   In the white light, Tyrone's jeans appear to be ....

   This is because the .... light is .... by the jeans

   and all the other colours are .... by the jeans.

   (4 marks)

Practice Questions

2 (a) The cells in the retina of the eye are photo-sensitive.
        What is meant by the word "photo-sensitive"? Tick **one** box.

   ☐ sensitive to light   ☐ sensitive to colour   ☐ sensitive to cameras
   (1 mark)

   (b) What is the role of the cornea in helping us to see.

   (1 mark)

3 Bruno is investigating the properties of light in the lab.
   He shines light rays at a piece of paper.
   The light is reflected back as shown in the diagram on the right.

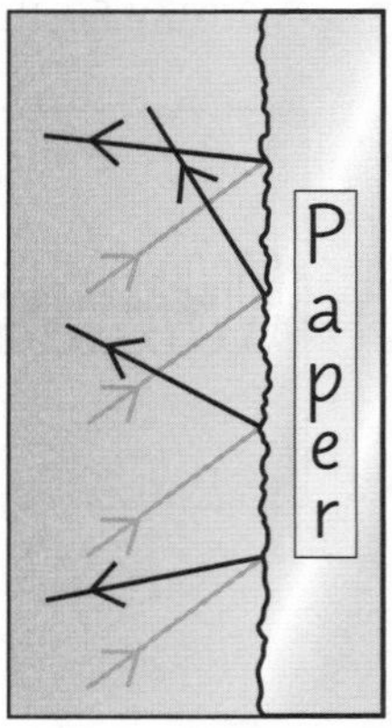

   (a) Explain why the paper looks dull.   *(2 marks)*

   (b) Bruno replaces the paper with a mirror.
        It gives a clear reflection.
        (i) What name is given to this kind of reflection?   *(1 mark)*

        (ii) The angle of incidence of the ray of light on the mirror is 39°.
              What is the angle of reflection?

   (1 mark)

4 (a) A student places a block of glass in the path of a light ray, as shown in
        the ray diagram below. The light bends when it enters the glass block.
        The light bends again when it leaves the far side of the glass block.

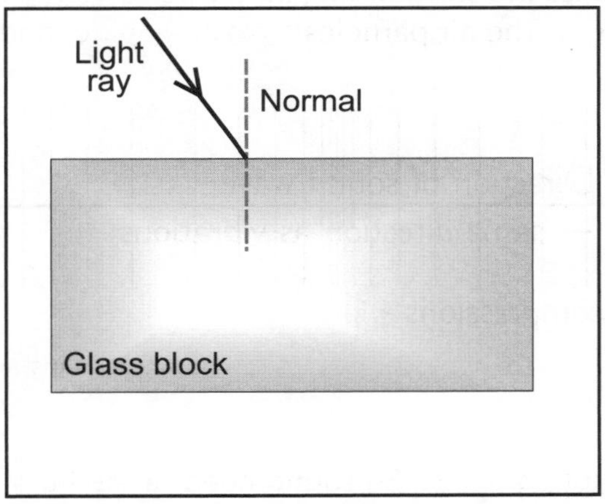

        (i) The glass block is much more dense than air. In which direction
             does the light bend when it enters the glass block? Tick **one** box.

        ☐ towards the normal   ☐ away from the normal

        ☐ towards the light source
        (1 mark)

        (ii) Complete the ray diagram to show the ray moving through and leaving the block.
        (1 mark)

   (b) How fast does light travel in a vacuum?

   (1 mark)

Sound

Like light, sound is a wave. It's a different type of wave to light though.

Longitudinal Waves Vibrate in the Same Direction as the Wave is Going

1) Longitudinal waves have vibrations in the same direction as the wave.
2) This means the vibrations are also in the direction of energy transfer.
3) Examples of longitudinal waves include:
   - Sound waves.
   - A slinky spring when you push the end.

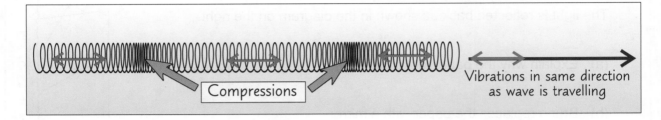

Compressions

Vibrations in same direction as wave is travelling

Sound Travels as a Longitudinal Wave

1) Sound waves are caused by vibrating objects.
2) When an object vibrates, it makes the surrounding air particles vibrate.
   This is how a sound wave travels. The air particles squash together and spread out.

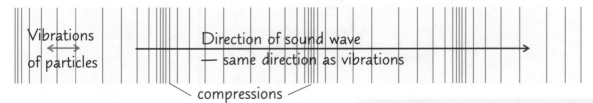

Vibrations of particles

Direction of sound wave — same direction as vibrations

compressions

Compressions are areas of squashed up particles.

3) Sound waves can't travel without particles. So sound needs a medium, like air, to travel.
4) Sound can't travel in space, because it's mostly a vacuum (there are no particles).

Learn the headings and you're halfway there...

REVISION TASK

... make sure you do that first. Then learn the diagrams and scribble them down from memory. Then do the same with the details. If you do that for five minutes, it might just help.

Sound

Sound Can be Reflected and Absorbed

1) Sound can be <u>reflected</u> and <u>refracted</u> — just like light (see pages 134-135).
2) An <u>ECHO</u> is sound that has been <u>reflected</u> from a surface.
3) Sound can also be <u>absorbed</u>.
4) <u>Soft</u> things like carpets and curtains <u>absorb</u> sound easily.

Sound's Speed Depends on What it's Passing Through

1) Sound usually travels <u>faster in SOLIDS</u> than in <u>LIQUIDS</u>.
2) It travels <u>faster in LIQUIDS</u> than in <u>GASES</u>.
3) Sound always travels <u>much slower</u> than light.

Frequency is the Pitch of Sound

1) The frequency of sound is the <u>number of waves</u> per second.
2) Frequency is a measure of how <u>high-pitched</u> (squeaky) the sound is.
   A <u>high frequency</u> means a <u>high-pitched</u> sound.
3) Frequency is measured in <u>hertz (Hz)</u>.

The speed of sound depends on what it's travelling through

<u>Sound</u> waves are caused by <u>vibrations</u>. If you've ever put a hand on a <u>bass speaker</u> (or turned <u>up</u> the volume and felt the <u>floor vibrate</u>) you'll have 'felt' a sound wave being made. <u>Higher-pitched</u> sounds work in the same way, but the vibrations are <u>more frequent</u>.

Hearing

You might be wondering how you can <u>hear</u> the <u>vibrations</u> in a <u>sound wave</u>. Well it's time to find out...

Sound Waves Make Your Ear Drum Vibrate

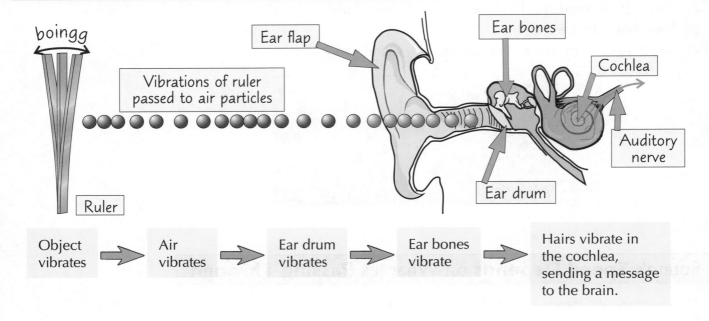

boingg

Vibrations of ruler passed to air particles

Ear flap

Ear bones

Cochlea

Auditory nerve

Ear drum

Ruler

| Object vibrates | → | Air vibrates | → | Ear drum vibrates | → | Ear bones vibrate | → | Hairs vibrate in the cochlea, sending a message to the brain. |

People and Animals Have Different Auditory Ranges

> Your <u>AUDITORY RANGE</u> is the range of <u>frequencies</u> that you can <u>hear</u>.

1) The auditory range of humans <u>varies</u>. But it's usually <u>20-20 000 Hz</u>.

2) This means we <u>can't hear</u> sounds with frequencies of <u>less</u> than 20 Hz or sounds with frequencies <u>above</u> 20 000 Hz.

3) <u>Dogs</u>, <u>bats</u> and <u>dolphins</u> can hear much <u>higher frequencies</u> than humans.

Take a look back at the previous page for more on frequency.

Frequency of sound in hertz

There's a fair bit of Biology on this page

The thing is, you still have to learn it. Remember, we <u>hear things</u> because the <u>air carries</u> the <u>vibrations</u> right into our <u>ear</u>. Learn the stuff about <u>auditory ranges</u> too — it's pretty important.

Energy and Waves

You might remember how waves <u>transfer energy</u> (page 131). Here's a whole page on how <u>useful</u> that is.

Information Can be Transferred by Waves

1) <u>All</u> waves <u>transfer energy</u> from one place to another.
   In doing so, they can also transfer <u>information</u>.
2) <u>Sound</u> waves do this through <u>vibrations</u> between <u>particles</u>.
3) This is very useful for <u>recording</u> and <u>replaying</u> sounds.

Sound Wave Energy is Detected by Diaphragms in Microphones

1) A diaphragm is a <u>thin paper</u> or <u>plastic</u> sheet.
2) The vibrations in a <u>sound wave</u> make the <u>diaphragm</u> inside a microphone <u>vibrate</u>.
3) The microphone converts the vibrations to <u>electric signals</u>.
4) Another device <u>records</u> the signals.

Loudspeakers Recreate Sound Waves

1) An <u>electrical signal</u> is fed into a loudspeaker.
2) This signal causes the <u>diaphragm</u> to <u>vibrate</u>.
3) This makes the air vibrate, producing <u>sound waves</u>.
4) It's a bit like a microphone <u>in reverse</u>.

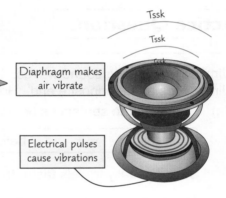

Diaphragm makes air vibrate

Electrical pulses cause vibrations

Tssk
Tssk

Ultrasound is High Frequency Sound That We Can't Hear

Ultrasonic Cleaning Uses Ultrasound

1) <u>High-frequency</u> sound waves can be used to <u>clean</u> things.
2) <u>Vibrations</u> from the sound waves remove the <u>dirt</u>.
3) You can use ultrasonic cleaning to clean <u>jewellery</u> and <u>false teeth</u>.

Ultrasound Physiotherapy May be Helpful

1) Ultrasound waves <u>can</u> reach <u>inside</u> your body.
2) Some <u>physiotherapists</u> think this means ultrasound can be used to <u>treat pain</u> in parts of the body that are <u>hard to reach</u>. For example, <u>muscles</u> deep inside your <u>shoulders</u>.
3) But scientists <u>haven't</u> found much <u>evidence</u> that this actually works.

REVISION TASK

Loudspeakers do the opposite of microphones

This page is full of <u>uses</u> for the <u>energy</u> that is <u>transferred</u> by <u>sound waves</u>. Cover up the page and <u>jot down</u> each use. Then <u>write</u> as much as you know about each one.

Warm-Up and Practice Questions

Have a bash at these questions, and see how far you get.   If you can't answer some of the questions, or get an answer wrong, go back and read the relevant pages again. Then have another go at these questions until you can do them all.

Warm-Up Questions

1) What type of wave are sound waves?

2) True or false? Sound can travel through a vacuum.

3) Suggest one thing that absorbs sound well.

4) Which travels faster: light or sound?

5) Does a high-pitched sound have a low or a high frequency?

6) What is the lowest frequency of sound that humans can usually hear?

7) Which part of a microphone vibrates when it gets hit by a sound wave?

Practice Questions

1   Jim is investigating sound waves. He sets up a speaker at one end of a large school hall.
    Jim stands at the opposite end. He sets the speaker to play one loud sound.

(a) Complete the sentences below. Use words from the box.

a solid	before	the air	after

Sound usually travels faster through .... than through ....

This means that Jim may hear the sound .... he feels it through the floor.

(3 marks)

(b) After hearing the sound, Jim hears a few more sounds.
They sound similar to the one produced by the loudspeaker, but are much quieter.
Suggest what might have caused these sounds.

(1 mark)

2   Sounds are detected by the ear.
(a) (i)   What happens to the ear drum when a sound wave hits it?

(1 mark)

(ii)   What happens in the cochlea when a sound wave hits it?

(1 mark)

(b) Some physiotherapists use sound that cannot be detected by the human ear.
(i)   What name is given to this type of sound?

(1 mark)

(ii)   Explain why the sound can't be heard.

(1 mark)

(iii)   Give **one** use for this type of sound, other than in physiotherapy.

(1 mark)

Revision Summary for Section Ten

Section Ten tells you everything you need to know about waves. To really ace this section, you'll need to have a go at all these questions. If there are any answers you don't know, don't panic — just look them up. All the answers are somewhere in this section. Once you've done all the questions once, have another go. And then another. Keep going and, before you know it, you'll be a total pro at waves.

1) What type of wave is a water wave?

2) What do water waves look like? Sketch out a diagram of a water wave and label it.

3) Give three things water waves and light waves have in common.

4) Give one big difference between water waves and light waves.

5) What is the law of reflection?

6) What does the word "medium" mean in the context of light waves?

7) What is refraction?

8) What happens when light goes from a more dense medium to a less dense medium?

9) Why does light bend when it enters a glass block?

10) What does a convex lens look like?

11) Which two parts of the eye help you focus on an object?

12) Sketch a diagram of a pinhole camera.

13) Why is the image seen through a pinhole camera upside down and crossed over?

14) What happens when light hits the image sensors of a digital camera?

15) How could you show that white light is not just one colour?

16) What is the rhyme for remembering the order of colours in a spectrum?

17) What colour of light has the highest frequency?

18) What colour of light will a red filter let through?

19) What happens to all the colours in white light when they hit a black object?

20) What colour would green laces look in red light? Why?

21) In which direction are the vibrations in sound waves?

22) Why can't sound travel through space?

23) What is an echo?

24) Does sound usually travel faster in solids, liquids or gases?

25) True or false? The frequency of a sound is a measure of the number of waves per second.

26) Explain how a ruler being flicked can be heard.

27) What does auditory range mean?

28) What is the auditory range of humans?

29) How do microphones work?

30) What is ultrasound? What can it be used for?

Electrical Circuits

First up in this section, some electricity basics...

Electricity Flows Through Circuits

1) This is an electric circuit:

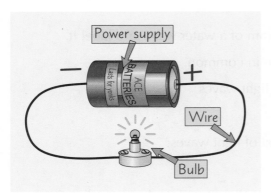

2) It has a power supply, wires, and a component (the bulb).

3) Electric current flows from the power supply in a loop around the circuit and back to the power supply.

Electric Current is the Flow of Charge

1) Current is the flow of charge around a circuit. The moving charges are negative electrons.

2) Current can only flow if a circuit is complete with no gaps.

3) CURRENT ISN'T USED UP as it flows through a circuit. The total current is always the same.

Current is a bit like Water Flowing

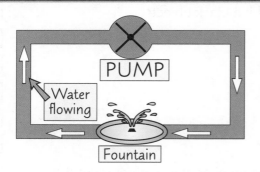

1) The pump drives the water along like a power supply.

2) The water isn't used up — all of it arrives back at the pump.

Potential Difference Pushes the Current Around

1) In a circuit, the battery provides the driving force that pushes the charge round the circuit.

2) This driving force is called the potential difference.

3) If you increase the potential difference more current will flow.

> Potential difference is sometimes called voltage.

Measuring Current and Potential Difference

Sadly you don't just need to know what <u>current</u> and <u>potential difference</u> are — you need to be able to <u>measure</u> them too. Handily, there are machines to do just that...

Ammeters Measure Current

1) <u>Ammeters</u> measure electric <u>current</u>. It's measured in <u>amperes</u>, A.

2) Remember — current <u>doesn't</u> get used up in a circuit.
   So the current through the ammeter and the bulb are the <u>same</u>.

3) You can connect the ammeter <u>anywhere</u> in the circuit.

Voltmeters Measure Potential Difference

1) <u>Voltmeters</u> measure <u>potential difference</u> in <u>volts</u>, V.

2) You measure the potential difference <u>between two points</u> in the circuit. For example, <u>either side</u> of a bulb.

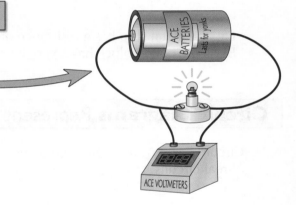

Batteries and Bulbs Have Potential Difference Ratings

1) A <u>battery</u> potential difference rating tells you the <u>potential difference</u> it will <u>supply</u>.

2) A <u>bulb rating</u> tells you the <u>maximum</u> potential difference that you can <u>safely</u> put across it.

Battery rating

1.5 V

2.5 V

Bulb rating

Ammeters measure amperes, voltmeters measure volts

The stuff on this page should be straightforward — just don't get the <u>two types</u> of <u>meter</u> mixed up.

Resistance and Circuit Diagrams

Resistance is closely linked to current and potential difference. Read on to find out more...

Resistance is How Easily Electricity Can Flow

1) Resistance slows down the flow of current. It's measured in ohms (Ω).

2) The resistance of something is equal to the POTENTIAL DIFFERENCE across it divided by the CURRENT flowing through it.

RESISTANCE = POTENTIAL DIFFERENCE ÷ CURRENT

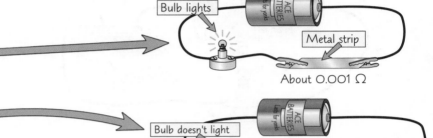

3) Conductors are materials that allow electricity to pass through them easily — such as metals.

4) Insulators are materials that don't allow electricity to pass through them easily — such as wood.

5) The lower the resistance of a component, the better it is at conducting electricity.

E.g. the metal strip has a resistance of 0.001 Ω — it's a good conductor. But the wooden block has a very high resistance — it's an insulator.

Circuit Diagrams Represent Real Circuits

1) Circuit diagrams are simplified drawings of real circuits.

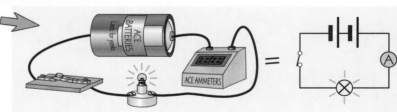

2) Here are the circuit symbols you need to know:

A cell = (a single energy source)

In everyday life we call a cell a battery.

A battery = (two or more cells put together)

An ammeter = —(A)—

A voltmeter = —(V)—

A bulb = —(X)—

A switch:

— open = ○—○

— closed = ○—○

Circuit diagrams show the setup of an electrical circuit

You'll need to get your ruler out to draw a nice, neat circuit diagram. They don't look much like the real circuits they show — but they do make it easier to see how everything is connected up. Another advantage of them is that symbols are so much easier to draw than the actual components.

Series and Parallel Circuits

The big difference between <u>series</u> and <u>parallel</u> circuits is that in parallel circuits, current can take <u>different routes</u> around the circuit. In <u>series circuits</u>, it all follows the <u>same path</u>.

Series Circuits — **Current** has **No Choice** of Route

1) In a <u>series</u> circuit the current has <u>no choice</u> of <u>route</u>. There is only <u>one way</u> it can go around the <u>circuit</u>.

2) The current gives up <u>some</u> of its <u>energy</u> to <u>each</u> of the <u>bulbs</u>.

3) But the <u>current stays the same</u> all the way around.

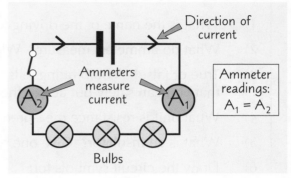

Parallel Circuits — **Current** has a **Choice**

1) In <u>parallel circuits</u>, there's <u>more than one route</u> that current could take.

2) When a circuit divides into several branches, the <u>current</u> is <u>divided</u> between each branch.

3) When the branches <u>join up</u> again, so does the <u>current</u>.

4) The current <u>after</u> the join is just the current of each branch <u>added together</u>.

5) Don't forget that current <u>isn't used up</u>. So <u>after</u> the branches join, the current is the <u>same</u> as it was <u>before</u> it split.

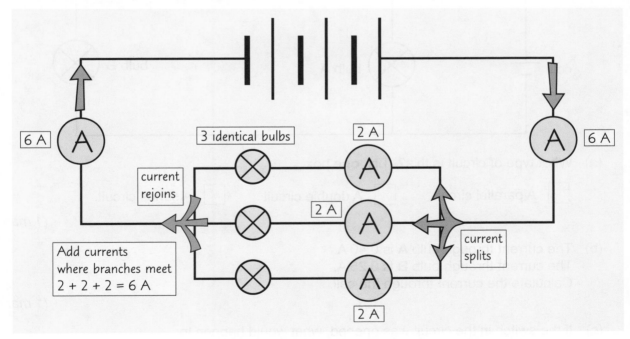

6) Parallel circuits are <u>great</u> — you can turn off <u>parts</u> of them <u>without</u> turning off the <u>whole circuit</u>. This means you can turn off <u>one</u> light without having to turn off <u>everything</u> in your house. <u>Useful</u>.

So now you know the two different types of circuits...

... make sure you know which is which — it's pretty important stuff. <u>Without looking</u> at this page, scribble down the <u>key points</u> about <u>series</u> and <u>parallel circuits</u>. And if you can't remember everything, take a sneaky peek at the page before giving it another go.

Warm-Up and Practice Questions

There's a good mix of Warm-Up Questions to get yourself started. Then you can launch yourself into the more difficult circuit diagram stuff. What a great way to spend an evening.

Warm-Up Questions

1) What is the name of the driving force that pushes current round a circuit?
2) What do ammeters measure? What do voltmeters measure?
3) True or false? A bulb rating tells you the maximum potential difference that you can safely put across the bulb.
4) What unit is resistance measured in?
5) What is an insulator? Give one example.
6) Draw the circuit symbols for: a) a cell, b) a bulb, c) an ammeter.

Practice Question

1 Look at the following circuit diagram.

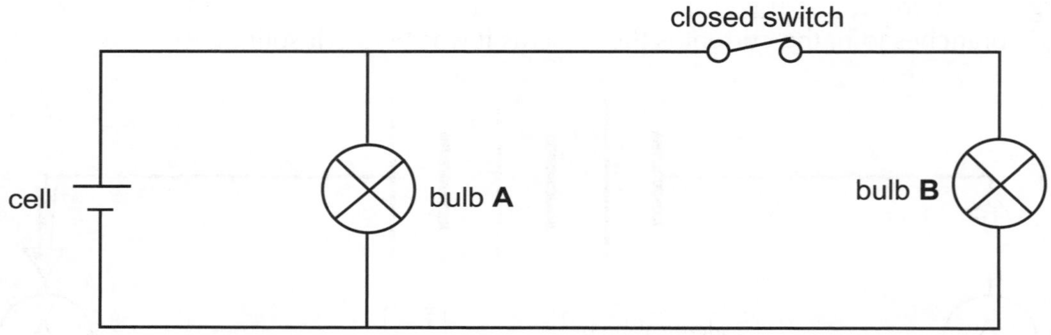

(a) What type of circuit is this? Tick **one** box.

[ ] A parallel circuit   [ ] A double circuit   [ ] A series circuit.

(1 mark)

(b) The current through bulb **A** is 0.40 A.
The current through bulb **B** is 0.25 A.
Calculate the current through the cell.

(1 mark)

(c) If the switch in the circuit was opened, what would happen to:
(i) Bulb **A**?

(1 mark)

(ii) Bulb **B**?

(1 mark)

(d) Give reasons for your answers to (c)(i) and (c)(ii).

(2 marks)

Static Electricity

Right, that's enough on charges flowing about the place. Now let's look at static charges...

Charges Can **Build Up** if **Objects** are **Rubbed Together**

1) Atoms (see page 54) contain positive and negative charges.
2) The negative charges are called electrons. Electrons can move, but positive charges can't.
3) When two insulating objects (see page 150) are rubbed together, the electrons are scraped off one object and left on the other.
4) This gives both objects a static charge:

> A static charge doesn't move.

> The object that gains electrons becomes negatively charged.
> The object that loses electrons is left with an equal but positive charge.

If you rub a plastic rod with a cloth, electrons move from the cloth to the rod.

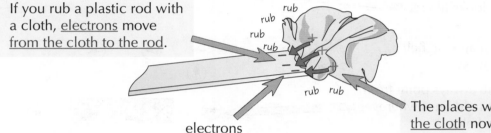

electrons

The places where the electrons left the cloth now have a positive charge.

Two Charged Objects Feel Forces **Without Touching**

1) Charged objects don't have to touch each other for them to feel a force from each other. Electric forces can act across a gap.
2) That's because charged objects have an electric field around them — an area in which other charged objects feel a force.
3) The force that charged objects feel when they come near each other depends on what type of charge they have.

Two things with OPPOSITE electric charges PULL TOWARDS each other.
Positive and negative charges ATTRACT.

positive charge   negative charge

Two things with the SAME electric charge PUSH AWAY from each other. They REPEL each other.

 Electrons move around when objects are rubbed together
When materials are rubbed together it's only ever the electrons that move — the positive charges never ever get to go anywhere. Remember that, it's super-important.

Magnets

Electric charges aren't the only things to push and pull each other without touching. Magnets do it too.

Magnets are Surrounded by Fields

1) Bar magnets are magnets that are in the shape of a bar. One end of a bar magnet is called the North (N) pole. The other end's called the South (S) pole.

2) All bar magnets have invisible magnetic fields round them.

3) A magnetic field is a region where magnetic materials experience a force.

4) You can draw a magnetic field using lines called magnetic field lines. The magnetic field lines always point from the N-pole to the S-pole.

5) This is what the magnetic field around a bar magnet looks like:

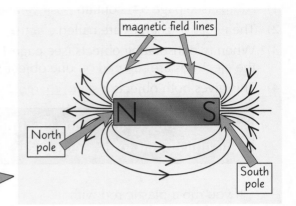

You can investigate magnetic fields using a plotting compass...

1) The compass will always point from N to S along the field lines wherever it's placed in the field.

2) Remember, the magnetic field always points from NORTH to SOUTH.

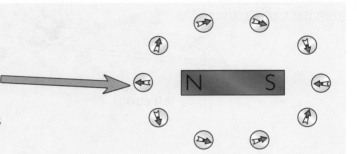
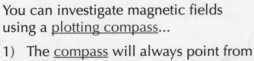

Opposite Poles Attract — Matching Poles Repel

1) Magnets don't need to touch for there to be a force between them. This is just like electric charges (see page 153).

2) North poles and South poles are attracted to each other.

3) If you try and bring two of the same type of magnetic pole together, they repel each other.

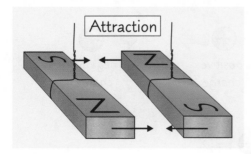
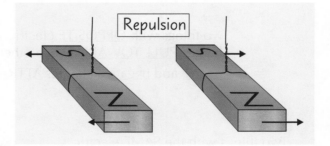

The Earth has a Magnetic Field

1) The Earth has a magnetic field. It has a North pole and a South pole, just like a bar magnet.

2) Compasses line up with magnetic fields — so unless you're stood right next to a magnet, they will point to the Earth's magnetic North pole.

3) Maps always have an arrow on them showing you which direction is North. This means you can use a map and a compass to find your way.

Electromagnets

Bar magnets stay magnetic all the time. Electromagnets are magnets which you can turn on and off.

Electric Current in Wires Causes a Magnetic Field

1) An electric current going through a wire causes a magnetic field around the wire.
2) A long coil of wire with a current flowing through it has a magnetic field just like a bar magnet's.
3) Magnets made from a current-carrying wire are called ELECTROMAGNETS.
4) They're usually made from a coil of wire wrapped around a soft iron core.
5) Because you can turn the current on and off, the magnetic field can be turned on and off.

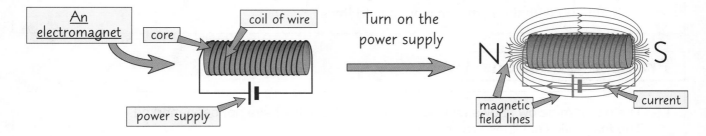

You Can Increase the Strength of an Electromagnet

There are two ways you can increase the strength of an electromagnet:

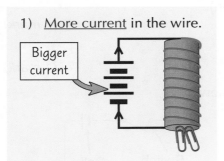

1) More current in the wire.

Bigger current

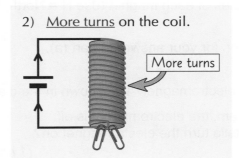

2) More turns on the coil.

More turns

Electric Motors are Made Using Electromagnets

1) A simple electric motor is made from a loop of wire in a magnetic field (between two magnets).
2) When current flows through the wire, a magnetic field forms around the wire.
3) Because the wire is already in a magnetic field, it feels a force which makes it turn.
4) Bob's your uncle, you've got a motor.

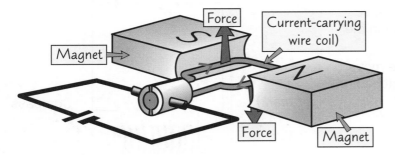

Warm-Up and Practice Questions

The end of another section, and time to test what you've learnt with another set of hand-made Warm-Up and Practice Questions. Go ahead — dive straight in and see what you can do.

Warm-Up Questions

1)   Static charges are caused by the transfer of which particles?

2)   What is an electric field?

3)   What happens if a North pole of a magnet is put next to the South pole of another magnet?

4)   True or false? If there are no magnets nearby, a compass
will line up with the Earth's magnetic field lines.

Practice Questions

1   The diagram below shows two bar magnets. The poles have not been marked.
The magnetic field lines are shown.

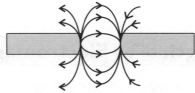

(a)   Label the poles of each magnet (use N = North, S = South).

(1 mark)

(b)   Give a reason for your answer to part (a).

(1 mark)

2   Stella makes an electromagnet. It is shown in the diagram below.

(a)   In the diagram, the electromagnet is off.
How can Stella turn the electromagnet on?

(1 mark)

(b)   How could Stella increase the strength of
the electromagnet? Tick **two** boxes.

☐   Increase the current through the wire.

☐   Increase the electrical resistance of the wire.

☐   Increase the number of turns in the coil.

☐   Remove the cell from the circuit.

(2 marks)

(c)   Stella puts a plotting compass close
to the electromagnet, as shown in the
diagram on the right.

Why does the compass needle move
when the electromagnet is switched on?

(1 mark)

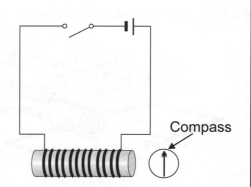

Switch (open)   Cell

Iron bar   Copper wire

Compass

Section Eleven — Electricity and Magnetism

Revision Summary for Section Eleven

Electricity and Magnetism — it's no holiday, that's for sure. There are certainly quite a few nasty bits and bobs in this section. There again, life isn't all bad — just look at all these lovely questions I've cooked up for your delight and enjoyment.

These questions test how much stuff you've taken on board. They're in the same order as the stuff appears throughout Section Eleven — so for any you can't do, just look back, find the answer, and then learn it good and proper for next time.

1) Current is the flow of what? ☑

2) Can current flow in an incomplete circuit? ☑

3) What job does a battery do in a circuit? ☑

4) What is potential difference? ☑

5) What are the units of current? ☑

6) What are the units of potential difference? ☑

7) What is resistance? ☑

8) What is the difference between an electrical conductor and an electrical insulator? ☑

9) What is a circuit diagram? ☑

10) Sketch the circuit symbol for all of these:
    a) a battery   b) a switch (open)   c) a voltmeter. ☑

11)*A series circuit contains three bulbs. A current of 3 A flows through the first bulb.
    What current flows through the third bulb? ☑

12) In a parallel circuit, what happens to current when it reached a point
    where the circuit divides into two branches? ☑

13) True or false?
    Adding the current through each branch of a parallel circuit gives you the total current. ☑

14) Which type of circuit allows part of the circuit to be switched off? ☑

15) Explain how a cloth and a plastic rod both become charged when they're rubbed together. ☑

16) Do charged objects need to touch to repel each other? ☑

17) State whether each of these pairs of charged objects will be attracted or repelled by each other.
    a) positive and positive   b) negative and positive   c) negative and negative ☑

18) What is a magnetic field? ☑

19) Sketch a diagram showing how a plotting compass points around a bar magnet. ☑

20) Name two magnetic poles that will: a) attract each other   b) repel each other. ☑

21) Explain why you can use a compass to navigate. ☑

22) What's an electromagnet? ☑

23) The wire in a simple motor feels a force when a current flows through it. Why is this? ☑

* Answer on page 197

Section Eleven — Electricity and Magnetism

Gravity

It's not magic that keeps your feet on the ground, it's gravity.

Gravity is a Force that Attracts All Masses

1) Anything with mass will attract anything else with mass.

2) The force of attraction between two objects is called GRAVITY.

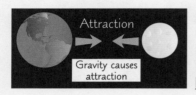

Attraction

Gravity causes attraction

The Earth and the Moon are attracted by gravity.

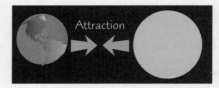

Attraction

The Earth and the Sun are attracted by an even bigger force of gravity.

3) Objects with a bigger mass attract each other with a stronger force.

4) Gravitational field strength (g) is how strong gravity is. It's different on different planets and stars.

Learn this: ⟹   On Earth g = 10 N/kg.

On Mars g = 3.7 N/kg.
Gravity is weaker on Mars than on Earth.

Learn the Difference Between Mass and Weight

MASS	WEIGHT
• Mass is the amount of 'stuff' in an object. • Mass is NOT a force.	• Weight is a FORCE. • It is caused by the pull of GRAVITY.
• The mass of an object never changes, no matter where it is in the Universe.	• The weight of an object is different on different planets and stars.
• Mass is measured in kilograms (kg) using a mass balance.	• Weight is measured in newtons (N) using a spring balance or a newton meter.

Now Learn this Formula...

weight = mass × gravitational field strength

in N   in kg   in N/kg

Example 1: An object has a mass of 5 kg. What is its weight on Earth, in newtons?

Answer: On Earth g = 10 N/kg. So the weight of the 5 kg object = 5 × 10 = 50 N.

Example 2: An object has a mass of 5 kg. What is its weight on Mars, in newtons?

Answer: On Mars g = 3.7 N/kg. So the weight of the 5 kg object = 5 × 3.7 = 18.5 N.

In these examples, the object always has a MASS of 5 kg.
But the WEIGHT of the object is different on Earth and on Mars.

MATHS TIP — ## Just make sure you appreciate the gravity of all this

If you're asked to do a calculation, make sure you write down the units of your answer. For example, weight is measured in newtons, and mass is measured in kilograms.

The Sun and Stars

Ahh. This is going to be a nice page, I can tell. Look at all those lovely pictures for a start.

The **Earth** Moves **Round** the **Sun**

1) The Sun is a star.
2) The Earth is a planet.
3) The Earth moves round the Sun in a rough circle. This circle is called an ORBIT.
4) The Sun and other stars give out light. Planets don't.

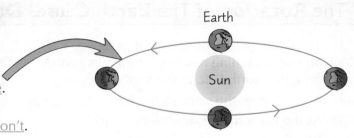

A **Galaxy** is a **Large Group** of **Stars**

1) The Universe is made up of billions of galaxies.
2) The Earth and the Sun are in a galaxy called the Milky Way.

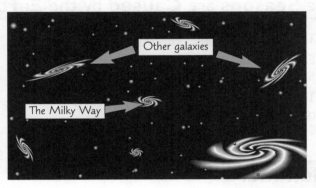

3) There are billions of stars in our galaxy.
4) The Sun is our closest star. Our next closest star is called Proxima Centauri.

A **Light Year** is a **Unit of Distance**

A light year is how far light travels in one year.

1) One light year is really far (about 9.5 trillion km).
2) Because of this, scientists use light years to measure the really big distances in space.

For example, Proxima Centauri is about 4 light years away.
This means it takes light from the star 4 years to reach Earth.

| Earth | ←——— 4 light years ———→ | Proxima Centauri |

Know the difference between a planet, a star and a galaxy

It sounds obvious, but you really need to get a feel for how these definitions all fit together.
You don't have to know the distance to every planet or star, but the more stuff you know the better.

Section Twelve — The Earth and Beyond

Day and Night and The Four Seasons

There's a fair bit to learn on this page. So let's get cracking...

The **Rotation** of The **Earth** Causes **Day** and **Night**

1) The Earth rotates (turns) about its axis — an imaginary line running through its centre, from the North Pole to the South Pole.

2) A globe does the same thing.

3) As the Earth rotates, any place on its surface will sometimes face the Sun. At other times it will face away.

4) When a place faces the Sun it gets light — so it's day time.

5) When a place faces away from the Sun it gets no light — so it's night time.

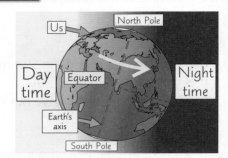

The **Seasons** are **Caused** by the **Earth's Tilt**

1) The Earth takes one year to orbit the Sun once.

2) Each year has four seasons — SPRING, SUMMER, AUTUMN and WINTER.

3) The seasons are caused by the tilt (angle) of the Earth's axis.

Summer

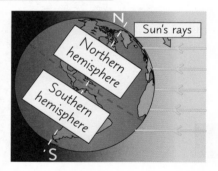

1) When it's summer in the UK, the northern hemisphere (top half of the Earth) is tilted towards the Sun.

2) This means the sunlight we get is stronger and we get more hours of it.

3) This gives us longer, warmer days — and we have summer.

Winter

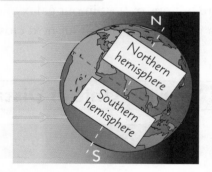

1) When it's winter in the UK, the northern hemisphere is tilted away from the Sun.

2) This means the sunlight we get is weaker and we get fewer hours of it.

3) This gives us shorter, colder days — and we have winter.

When it's summer in the northern hemisphere, it's winter in the southern hemisphere.

This page is jam-packed with fascinating facts

There's a lot to learn on this page, so you might like to try the mini-essay method. Scribble down a mini-essay that covers all the details on this page. Then check to see what you missed.

Warm-Up and Practice Questions

All this talk about the Universe — I think it's time to actually answer some questions on it.

Warm-Up Questions

1) What's the name of the force of attraction that occurs between all objects with a mass?

2) True or false? A light year is a unit of distance.

Practice Questions

1 The diagrams below show the two motions of the Earth, **A** and **B**.

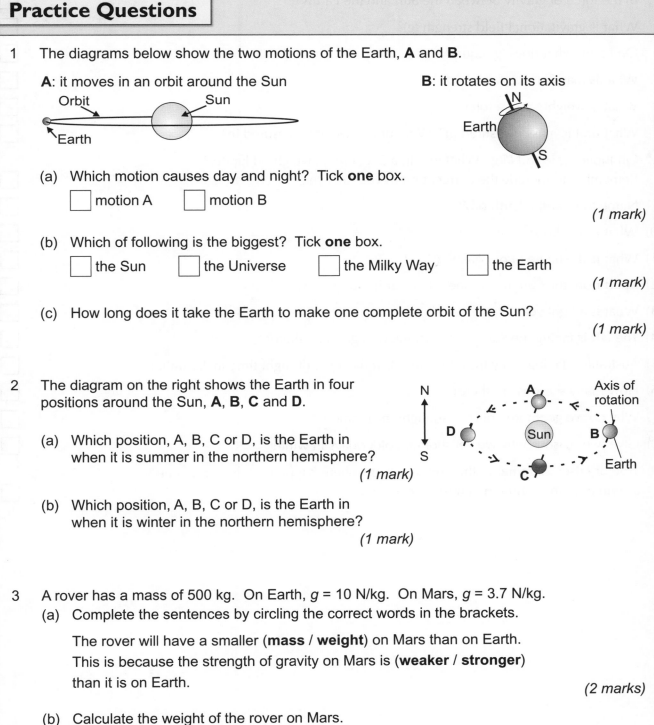

A: it moves in an orbit around the Sun

Orbit   Sun

Earth

B: it rotates on its axis

N

Earth

S

(a) Which motion causes day and night? Tick **one** box.

☐ motion A   ☐ motion B

(1 mark)

(b) Which of following is the biggest? Tick **one** box.

☐ the Sun   ☐ the Universe   ☐ the Milky Way   ☐ the Earth

(1 mark)

(c) How long does it take the Earth to make one complete orbit of the Sun?

(1 mark)

2 The diagram on the right shows the Earth in four positions around the Sun, **A**, **B**, **C** and **D**.

N

S

A

D   Sun   B

C

Axis of rotation

Earth

(a) Which position, A, B, C or D, is the Earth in when it is summer in the northern hemisphere?

(1 mark)

(b) Which position, A, B, C or D, is the Earth in when it is winter in the northern hemisphere?

(1 mark)

3 A rover has a mass of 500 kg. On Earth, g = 10 N/kg. On Mars, g = 3.7 N/kg.

(a) Complete the sentences by circling the correct words in the brackets.

The rover will have a smaller (**mass** / **weight**) on Mars than on Earth.
This is because the strength of gravity on Mars is (**weaker** / **stronger**)
than it is on Earth.

(2 marks)

(b) Calculate the weight of the rover on Mars.
(Weight = mass × gravitational field strength)

(2 marks)

Section Twelve — The Earth and Beyond

Revision Summary for Section Twelve

Section 12 only has three pages of information — and it deals with the whole Universe. It's amazing just how many people go their whole lives and never really know the answers to all those burning questions, like what is gravity? Or why are the days longer in summer than in winter? Make sure you learn all the burning answers now...

1) What is gravity?

2) Which is stronger:
   a) the force of gravity between the Moon and the Earth?   OR
   b) the force of gravity between the Sun and the Earth?

3) What is gravitational field strength (g)?

4) On Earth, what does 'g' equal?

5) What is mass? Is it a force?

6) What is weight? Is it a force?

7) What unit is mass measured in? What unit is weight measured in?

8)* On Jupiter, $g = 25$ N/kg. What would a 5 kg object weigh on Jupiter? Remember to include the correct unit in your answer.

9) Name the star the Earth orbits.

10) What is a galaxy?

11) What is the name of our galaxy?

12) Apart from the Sun, name one other star in our galaxy.

13) What is a light year?

14) The UK is facing the Sun. Is it day time or night time there?

15) Australia is facing away from the Sun. Is it day time or night time in Australia?

16) How many seasons are there?

17) Why do we get more hours of sunlight in summer?

18) Give two reasons why we get shorter, colder days in winter.

19) True or false? Summer in the northern hemisphere happens at the same time as winter in the southern hemisphere.

* Answer on page 198

Mixed Practice Tests

OK, so you've done most of the hard work — but are you ready for the big Practice Exam?
To help you decide, here are some brilliant Mixed Practice Tests for you to have a go at.

- Scribble down your answers to the questions in a test. When you've finished a test, check your answers (see pages 198-199). Tick the box next to each question you got right. Put a cross in the box if you got it wrong.
- If you're getting 7 or more out of 10 right on these tests, you should be ready for the Practice Exam on page 169.
- If you're getting less than that, go back and do some more revision. Have another go at the Revision Summaries — they're the best way to find out what you know and what you've forgotten.

Test 1

✓ / ✗

1. True or false? Work is done when a force deforms an object.

2. The Sun is...

   A ...a planet
   B ...a star
   C ...a galaxy

3. What is the pH of a neutral substance?

   A 0
   B 1
   C 7
   D 14

4. A builder climbs up a ladder. Does the energy in the builder's gravitational potential energy store increase or decrease?

5. The centre of the Earth is made from iron and nickel. What is this part of the Earth called?

6. Drugs can affect life processes. Name two of the seven life processes.

7. Give one property of ceramics.

8. What is missing from this sequence showing cell organisation: cell → .... → organ?

9. A substance changes state from a liquid to a gas. Give a reason why this is a physical change.

10. Which of the following word equations shows fermentation?

    A glucose + oxygen → carbon dioxide + water + energy
    B glucose + oxygen → lactic acid + energy
    C glucose → lactic acid + energy
    D glucose → carbon dioxide + ethanol + energy

Total (out of 10):

Mixed Practice Tests

Test 2

1. True or false? Energy can be transferred from a hot object to a cold object by conduction.

2. Sodium and water react to form sodium hydroxide and hydrogen. What are the two reactants in this reaction.

3. Give an example of a pair of antagonistic muscles.

4. Which of the following equations could you use to work out the weight of an object?

   A weight = mass × gravitational field strength
   B weight = height ÷ gravitational field strength
   C weight = pressure × mass
   D weight = gravitational field strength ÷ mass

5. Give one of the jobs of the human skeleton.

6. How did giraffes end up with very long necks?

   A Giraffes stretched their necks to reach trees.
   B Giraffes with long necks were more likely to survive and reproduce.
   C Giraffes consider long necks to be a sexually attractive characteristic.

7. How long does the menstrual cycle take?

   A 1 day
   B 4 days
   C 14 days
   D 28 days

8. Diffusion is...

   A ...when particles spread from an area where there are lots of them to areas where there aren't so many of them.
   B ...when particles move from an area where there aren't many of them to areas where there are lots of them.
   C ...when a liquid and a solid are mixed to form a solution.
   D ...when a liquid turns into a gas.

9. Give two ways that recycling is better than making an item from scratch.

10. Two bulbs are connected in parallel, as shown in the diagram below.
    The current at point Z is 15 A.
    What is the current at point Y?

    A 7.5 A
    B 10 A
    C 15 A
    D 30 A

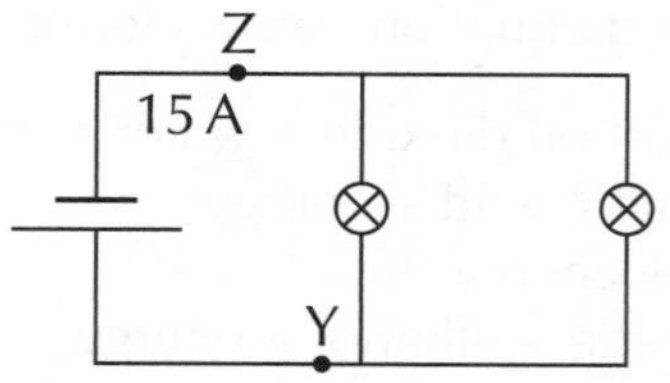

Total (out of 10):

Mixed Practice Tests

Test 3

1. True or false? The higher the resistance of a component in an electrical circuit, the better it is at conducting electricity.

2. A battery-powered fan is turned on. Energy is transferred from the battery to...

   A ...the kinetic energy store of the fan blades.
   B ...the gravitational potential energy store of the fan blades.
   C ...the electrostatic energy store of the fan blades.

3. Describe the change in state that happens when a substance evaporates.

4. A food chain is shown below:

   Waterweed ⟶ Minnow ⟶ Pike ⟶ Otter

   Which of the organisms in the food chain is the primary consumer?

   A Otter
   B Pike
   C Minnow
   D Waterweed

5. Give one example of a transverse wave.

6. A compound is heated and thermal decomposition takes place.
   What happens to the compound?

7. The main role of proteins in your diet is...

   A ...to provide energy for your body.
   B ...to grow and repair cells.
   C ...to help food move through your digestive system.
   D ...to send signals to the brain.

8. What part of a plant helps wind pollination?

   A Brightly coloured petals
   B Short filaments
   C Feathery stigma

9. What is an enzyme?

10. Two forces act on an object. The two forces are balanced.
    Which of the following statements can **not** be true?

    A The two forces have equal sizes and act in opposite directions.
    B The object is stationary.
    C The object is accelerating.

Total (out of 10):

Mixed Practice Tests

Test 4

1. True or false? When light hits a mirror, the angle of incidence is always less than the angle of reflection.

2. Do the particles in a solid have more or less energy than the particles in a gas?

3. In general, non-metals are...

    A ...good electrical conductors.
    B ...brittle.
    C ...magnetic.
    D ...strong.

4. What is the name given to a magnet made from a current-carrying wire?

5. Which of the following equations could you use to work out the speed of an object?

    A speed = distance × time
    B speed = distance ÷ time
    C speed = mass ÷ distance
    D speed = 2 × distance × time

6. Which of the following is the correct word equation for photosynthesis?

    A carbon dioxide + water → glucose + oxygen
    B glucose + water → carbon dioxide + oxygen
    C oxygen + water → glucose + carbon dioxide
    D carbon dioxide + glucose → water + oxygen

7. Some characteristics are passed down from the parents to a child. What is the name given to characteristics passed on in this way?

8. What percentage of the atmosphere is oxygen?

    A 0.04%
    B 4%
    C 21%
    D 78%

9. All the organisms in an ecosystem are interdependent. What does the word "interdependent" mean in this case?

10. Which of the following word equations correctly shows what happens when an acid and an alkali are mixed?

    A acid + alkali → salt + hydrogen
    B acid + alkali → metal oxide + water
    C acid + alkali → hydrogen + water
    D acid + alkali → salt + water

Total (out of 10):

Section Thirteen — Exam Practice

Mixed Practice Tests

Test 5

✓ / ✗

1. True or false? Body weight is an example of discontinuous variation in organisms.

2. Is copper more or less reactive than zinc?

3. What is a secondary consumer?

4. A substance contains atoms of different types, joined together. The substance is...

   A   ...an element.
   B   ...an atom.
   C   ...a compound.
   D   ...a mixture.

5. Which of these equations could you use to work out
   the daily basic energy requirement (BER) of a person?

   A   daily BER = 24 hours × body mass
   B   daily BER = 5.4 × 24 hours × body mass
   C   daily BER = body mass × gravitational field strength
   D   daily BER = 5.4 × body mass × body height

6. Name a separation method that could be used to get pure water
   from a solution of salt and water.

7. What is the highest frequency of sound that humans can usually hear?

8. The slope of a distance-time graph shows...

   A   ...the total distance travelled by the object.
   B   ...the time an object has been travelling.
   C   ...the speed the object is travelling at.
   D   ...the acceleration of the object.

9. A 40 W radio is left on for 120 seconds.
   How much energy is transferred by the radio in this time?

   A   20 J
   B   80 J
   C   480 J
   D   4800 J

10. A plastic rod is rubbed with a cloth. The plastic rod becomes negatively charged.
    Which of the following describes what has happened?

    A   Negative charges have moved from the rod to the cloth.
    B   Negative charges have moved from the cloth to the rod.
    C   Positive charges have moved from the rod to the cloth.
    D   Positive charges have moved from the cloth to the rod.

Total (out of 10):

Section Thirteen — Exam Practice

Mixed Practice Tests

Test 6

✓ / ✗

1. True or false? A 'gamete' is another word for a sex cell.

2. When universal indicator is added to an unknown solution, it turns red.
   What could the solution be?

   A a strong acid
   B a neutral solution
   C a strong alkali

3. Does photosynthesis in plants increase or decrease
   the amount of carbon dioxide in the atmosphere?

4. The mitochondria of a cell...

   A ...are filled with cell sap.
   B ...are where aerobic respiration takes place.
   C ...control what the cell does.
   D ...control what goes in and out of the cell.

5. Is energy transferred to or taken in from the surroundings
   during an endothermic reaction?

6. Which one of these equations could you use to work out pressure?

   A pressure = force × area
   B pressure = mass × area
   C pressure = force ÷ area
   D pressure = force ÷ time

7. The upthrust on an object is 100 N. The weight of the object is also 100 N.
   Will the object float?

8. Which of the following equations could you use to work
   out the moment of the force shown on the right?

   A moment = force ÷ distance
   B moment = distance ÷ force
   C moment = 2 × force × distance
   D moment = force × distance

9. Give one bad effect that alcohol has on the human body.

10. Igneous rocks...

    A ...form from cooling magma.
    B ...form from layers of sediment.
    C ...form from existing rocks that are exposed to heat and pressure.

Total (out of 10):

Key Stage 3 Science
Practice Exam

Instructions

- The test is one hour long.

- Make sure you have these things with you before you start:
  - pen,
  - pencil,
  - rubber,
  - ruler,
  - angle measurer or protractor,
  - pair of compasses,
  - a calculator.

- You may use tracing paper.

- The easier questions are at the start of the test.

- Try to answer all of the questions.

- Don't use any rough paper — write all your answers and working in this test paper.

- Check your work carefully before the end of the test.

Question	Score	Question	Score
1		9	
2		10	
3		11	
4		12	
5		13	
6		14	
7		15	
8		**Total:**	

Total score: ☐ out of 75

1. The diagram below shows the pH scale.

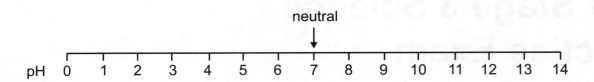

neutral

pH 0 1 2 3 4 5 6 7 8 9 10 11 12 13 14

(a) A neutral substance has a pH of 7.
Label the diagram to show the pH of the
strongest acid and the **strongest alkali**.

2 marks

(b) A student mixes together an acid and an alkali
to form a salt and one other product.

(i) What is the other product of this reaction? Tick **one** box.

☐ glucose   ☐ water   ☐ hydrogen

1 mark

The products of the reaction have a pH of 7.
The student adds universal indicator solution to the products.

(ii) What colour will the solution turn? Tick **one** box.

☐ blue   ☐ red   ☐ green

1 mark

2. The diagram below shows the food web for a lake.

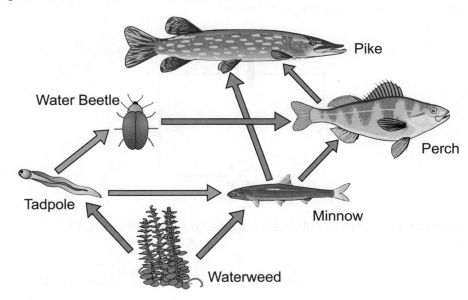

(a) Which of the following is the **producer** in the food web above?
Tick **one** box.

☐ tadpole   ☐ pike   ☐ waterweed

(b) Complete the sentences below. Use words from the box.

increase		decrease
tadpoles	perch	pike

If the number of water beetles in the lake decreases, the ....

might get hungry. This means that they may start eating more minnows,

so the number of minnows might ....

2 marks

(c) A poison has entered the food web above.
Which organism will end up with the most poison over time? Tick **one** box.

☐ tadpole   ☐ pike   ☐ waterweed

☐ minnow   ☐ perch   ☐ water beetle

1 mark

3. A student sets up an electric circuit.
The student's circuit is shown in the diagram below.

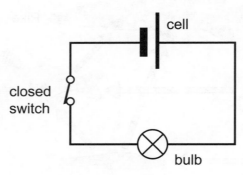

(a) Which of the components in the diagram supplies power to the circuit?
Tick **one** box.

☐ bulb   ☐ cell   ☐ closed switch   ☐

1 mark

(b) The student wants to measure the electric current in the circuit.

(i) Define what is meant by an 'electric current'.

....

☐

1 mark

(ii) What happens to the current in the circuit if the
potential difference increases?

☐ The current increases.

☐ The current decreases.

☐ The current stays the same.   ☐

1 mark

(c) Complete the sentences below. Use words from the box.

amperes	slows down
volts	speeds up	ohms

The circuit has a low resistance.

Resistance .... the flow of electrical current.

Resistance is measured in ....

☐

2 marks

4. The diagram below shows the human digestive system.

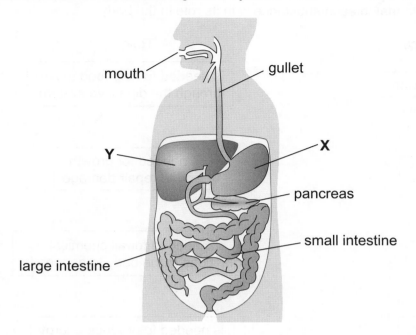

mouth

gullet

Y

X

pancreas

small intestine

large intestine

(a) (i) Name the parts of the digestive system labelled **X** and **Y**.

X is the ....

Y is the ....

2 marks

(ii) Which part of the digestive system mixes the food with saliva?

....

1 mark

(iii) What is the main job of the **large intestine**?
Tick **one** box.

☐ To absorb food.

☐ To break down carbohydrates using enzymes.

☐ To absorb water from food.

☐ To break down proteins using enzymes.

1 mark

(b) Carbohydrates, proteins, fibre and water are all needed by the body.
Draw lines to match each substance with its role in the body.

Substance   Role

| carbohydrate |

| is needed to help food move through the digestive system |

| protein |

| is needed for growth and to repair damage |

| fibre |

| is needed for all chemical reactions in the body to happen in |

| water |

| is needed to produce energy |

2 marks

(c) The table below shows the amounts of some nutrients an adult female
should eat in a day. It also shows the amounts of these nutrients that
Jane eats each day.

Nutrient	Recommended amount	Amount Jane eats
Carbohydrate	267 g	270 g
Protein	45 g	21 g
Lipids	78 g	83 g
Vitamin C	0.04 g	0.04 g

(i) Which nutrient is Jane deficient in?

....

1 mark

(ii) Nutrient deficiency can sometimes cause deficiency diseases.
Give **one** example of a deficiency disease.

....

1 mark

5. The diagram below shows an outline of the Periodic Table.
    Four of the elements have been labelled.

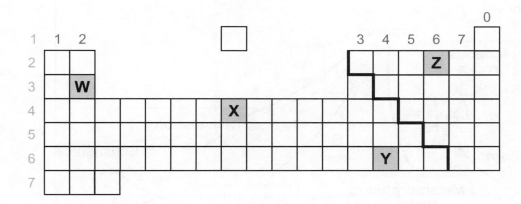

(a) Which of the labelled elements, **W**, **X**, **Y** or **Z**, is in **Group 2**?

    ....

    1 mark

(b) Elements in the Periodic Table can be metals or non-metals.

    (i)   Which of the labelled elements, **W**, **X**, **Y** or **Z**, is a **non-metal**?

        ....

        1 mark

    (ii) Verity has a sample of an element that is a metal.
          Give **two** properties that you may expect Verity's sample to have.

          1. ....

          2. ....

          2 marks

6. The diagram below shows the rock cycle.

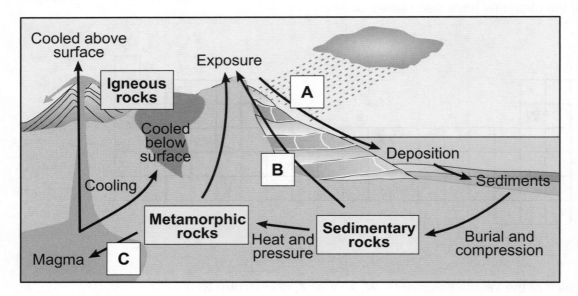

(a) Write the correct letter from the diagram next to each of the labels below.

    (i) Uplift   ....

    (ii) Melting   ....

    (iii) Weathering   ....

3 marks

(b) There are three types of rock: igneous, metamorphic and sedimentary.
Complete the sentences below. Use the names of the different types of rock.

    (i) Bits of rock and dead remains of plants and animals are deposited

    in layers. These layers form .... rocks.

    (ii) .... rocks form when rocks experience high

    temperatures and pressures. This causes their structure to change.

2 marks

7. All living organisms are made up of cells.

    (a) The diagram below shows a sketch of a typical animal cell.
         Some of the labels are missing.

         (i) Fill in the missing labels using some of the words in the box below.

         | cell membrane | chloroplast | cytoplasm |
         | vacuole | cell wall | nucleus |

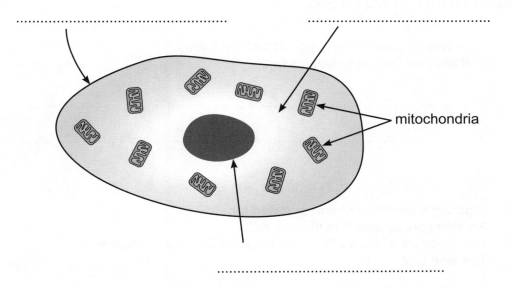

         mitochondria

         ....

         3 marks

         (ii) What happens in mitochondria?

         ....

         1 mark

    (b) A Euglena is a unicellular organism that lives in water.
         Each Euglena has a tail-like structure called a flagellum.

         Suggest why a Euglena has a flagellum.

         ....

         1 mark

8. Respiration takes place in every cell of every living organism.
    The main type of respiration that happens inside human body cells
    is aerobic respiration.

    (a) Complete the word equation below for **aerobic** respiration.

         .... + oxygen → .... + water (+ energy)

         ☐ 1 mark

    (b) When you breathe in, air fills the lungs.
         Here, the oxygen needed for aerobic respiration
         passes from the air into the blood.

         (i) Give **two** features of the lungs that make them
              well adapted for this gas exchange.

              1. ....

              2. ....

              ☐ 2 marks

         (ii) Cigarettes contain a chemical called tar.
               Smokers breathe tar into their lungs.
               How does tar make it difficult for smokers to breathe properly?
               Tick **one** box.

               ☐ The tar causes the muscles in the airways to contract.
                  This narrows the airways.

               ☐ The tar covers the cilia in the airways, which damages them.
                  This means the cilia can't clear the mucus out of the airways.

               ☐ The tar builds up in the airways and blocks them.

               ☐ 1 mark

    (c) Another type of respiration that can take place in human cells
         is **anaerobic** respiration.

         What substance is produced by anaerobic respiration in human cells?

         ....

         ☐ 1 mark

9. Amber is investigating how light is reflected.
   She shines a beam of light at a mirror.

   (a) The ray diagram below shows the beam of light hitting the mirror.
   Complete the diagram to clearly show the direction of the reflected
   beam of light. Label the angle of the reflected beam of light.

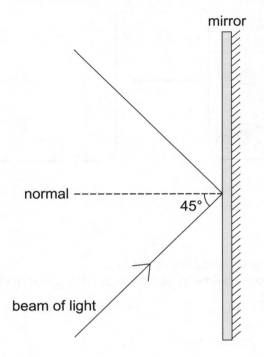

2 marks

   (b) Amber can see the beam of light because part of her eye contains cells
   that are sensitive to light. What is the name of this part of the eye?

   ....

1 mark

   (c) The beam of light is from a torch. The torch has a power of 2.5 W.
   The torch was left on for 10 minutes during the experiment.

   Work out the amount of energy transferred to the torch during this time.
   Use the formula: energy transferred = power × time.
   (1 minute = 60 seconds)

   .... J

3 marks

10. Sachin is making his own ink solution by dissolving a blue solid dye in water.

(a) Complete the diagram below to show how the arrangement of particles in the mixture changes as the dye dissolves in the water.

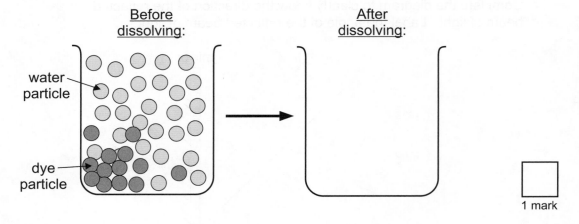

1 mark

(b) Wasim has a beaker with some of Sachin's ink in it.
He uses the equipment shown below to separate out the water from the ink.

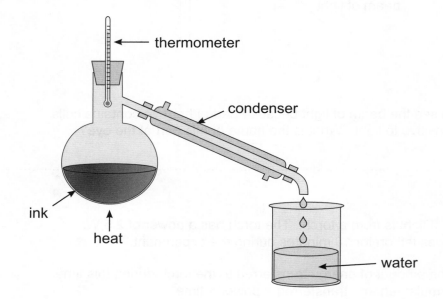

(i) Name the separation method that Wasim used.

....

1 mark

(ii) Describe how Wasim could find out whether the water he collected during the experiment is pure.

....

....

....

....

2 marks

11. Jack and Rico fill a container with smoke.
They put a lid on the container to trap the smoke.

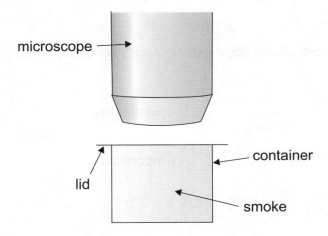

(a) Jack observes the movement of the smoke particles using the microscope. He finds that the smoke particles move around randomly.

(i) Name the type of movement shown by the smoke particles.

....

1 mark

(ii) Explain why the smoke particles move in this way.

....

....

1 mark

(b) At the end of the experiment, Rico takes the lid off the container.
Jack is standing 2 metres away from the container, as shown
in the diagram below. At first, Jack couldn't smell the smoke.
After 30 seconds pass, Jack can smell the smoke.

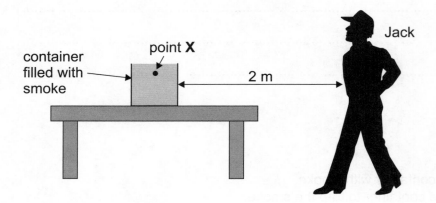

(i) Which of these processes could explain Jack's observations?
Tick **one** box.

☐ oxidation ☐ neutralisation

☐ diffusion ☐ evaporation

1 mark

(ii) Point **X** is labelled on the diagram above.
Describe how the concentration of smoke particles
at point **X** changes over time.

....

....

1 mark

12. Apple trees produce flowers.

(a) Apple flowers are pollinated by bees. Use this information to give **one** feature that you would expect apple flowers to have. Explain your answer.

Feature: ....

Explanation: ....

2 marks

(b) After an apple flower is pollinated, apples begin to grow.

The apple fruit helps the seeds travel away from the original tree.

Explain how each of the following helps the seed to move away from the tree.

(i) The apple is round and heavy.

....

....

(ii) The apple is a source of food for birds.

....

....

2 marks

(c) In one country, scientists predict that the population of bees is likely to fall by 40% over the next 10 years. This means fewer apple flowers will be pollinated.

Why might this be a problem for apple farmers in this country?

....

1 mark

13. A racing car is travelling on a track.

The horizontal forces that act on the racing car as it moves are the driving force and the drag:

driving force

drag

(a) Complete the sentences below. Use words from the box.

greater than	equal to	less than

(i) When the car is decelerating, the driving force is

.... the drag.

1 mark

(ii) When the car is accelerating, the driving force is

.... the drag.

1 mark

(iii) When the car is moving at a steady speed, the driving force

is .... the drag.

1 mark

(b) The racing car travels at a constant speed. It completes one lap of the track in 120 seconds. One lap of the track is 6.3 km long.

What speed is the racing car moving at? Give your answer in m/s.
(1 km = 1000 m)

.... m/s

3 marks

14. Hydrogen peroxide (H_2O_2) reacts to form water (H_2O) and oxygen (O_2).

(a) Hydrogen peroxide is a molecule made up of hydrogen atoms and oxygen atoms.

(i) What name is given to a substance made up of atoms of two or more different elements bonded together?

....

1 mark

(ii) Write down how many hydrogen atoms and how many oxygen atoms are present in a molecule of hydrogen peroxide.

Atoms of hydrogen: ....

Atoms of oxygen: ....

1 mark

(b) The reaction of hydrogen peroxide is exothermic.

What is an exothermic reaction?

....

....

1 mark

(c) Silver is often used as a catalyst for this reaction.

What is a catalyst?

....

....

1 mark

15. The Earth rotates about its axis, as shown in the diagram below.

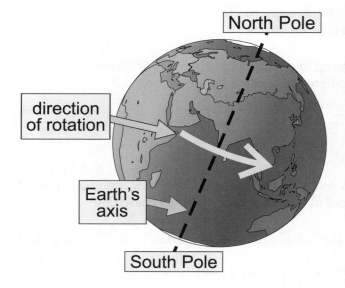

(a) Suggest how this rotation causes day and night.

....

....

....

2 marks

(b) Steve takes a plane from the northern hemisphere to the southern hemisphere. The diagram below shows the position of the Earth at that time of year.

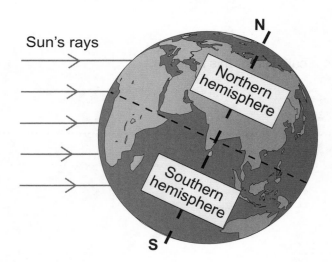

(i) The days are generally warmer in the southern hemisphere than in the northern hemisphere at that time of year.

Give an explanation for this in terms of the Earth's tilt.

....

....

....

1 mark

(ii) Steve measures the daylight hours in the northern and southern hemispheres.

What will Steve find when he compares the daylight hours?

....

....

1 mark

(c) Steve has a mass of 60 kg.
The gravitational field strength (g) on Earth is 10 N/kg.

Calculate Steve's weight on Earth.

.... N

2 marks

END OF TEST

Answers

Section One — Cells and Respiration

Page 5 (Warm-Up Questions)

1) To magnify/look at objects that are too small to see normally. (A microscope magnifies objects to make them look bigger, so they can be seen more easily.)
2) True
3) Any two from: e.g. nucleus/cytoplasm/cell membrane/ mitochondria
4) A tissue is made from a group of similar cells, while an organ is made from a group of tissues working together.
5) diffusion
6) energy
7) False
Anaerobic respiration takes place without oxygen. It's __aerobic__ respiration that uses oxygen.

Pages 5-6 (Practice Questions)

1 a) i)   nucleus *[1 mark]*
      ii) cytoplasm *[1 mark]*
      iii) mitochondria *[1 mark]*
      iv) cell membrane *[1 mark]*
   b) It gives support to the plant cell *[1 mark]*.
   c) unicellular *[1 mark]*
2 a) mitochondria *[1 mark]*
   b) i)   anaerobic respiration *[1 mark]*
      ii) glucose → **lactic acid** + energy *[1 mark]*
      iii) e.g. during (hard) exercise *[1 mark]*
3 a) **Cells** *[1 mark]* are the simplest building blocks of organisms. Several of these can come together to make up structures called **tissues** *[1 mark]* and several of these can work together to make structures called **organs** *[1 mark]*.
   b) A group of organs which work together *[1 mark]*.
4 a) 1. select the lowest powered objective lens
      2. adjust the rough focusing knob until the lens is just above the slide
      3. look down the eyepiece lens
      4. adjust the fine focusing knob
      [1 mark for each step in the correct order, up to a maximum of 3 marks]
   b) Switch the objective lens to one that is higher powered/longer *[1 mark]*, then refocus the microscope *[1 mark]*.

Section Two — Humans as Organisms

Page 13 (Warm-Up Questions)

1) carbohydrates/lipids (fats and oils)
2) e.g. vegetables/fruit/cereals
3) basic energy requirement
4) obesity
5) mechanical/chemical
6) the mouth
7) They break up the large food molecules into smaller molecules.
8) True

Page 13 (Practice Questions)

1 a)

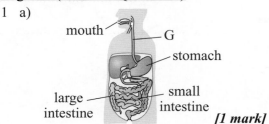

[1 mark]

   b) They have a thin outer layer of cells *[1 mark]*. They have a good blood supply *[1 mark]*.
   c) liver *[1 mark]*
   d) To kill harmful bacteria *[1 mark]*.

Page 20 (Warm-Up Questions)

1) E.g. it is rigid/tough/strong.
2) bone marrow
3) tendons
4) carbon dioxide
5) a bell jar
6) False

Pages 20-21 (Practice Questions)

1 a) To protect the lungs *[1 mark]*.
   b) Bronchus *[1 mark]*
   c) When you breathe in, the diaphragm contracts and moves **down** *[1 mark]*. The pressure inside the chest decreases, causing air to rush into the **lungs** *[1 mark]*.

2 a) e.g. supporting the rest of the body / protecting organs /making blood cells *[1 mark]*
   b) i)   True *[1 mark]*
       ii) False *[1 mark]*
       iii) True *[1 mark]*

3 a) e.g. lung disease/cancer/smoker's cough *[1 mark]*
   b) Tar from cigarette smoke covers/damages the cilia in a smoker's airways *[1 mark]*, which means they can't get rid of mucus properly *[1 mark]*. The mucus sticks in the airways and causes them to cough *[1 mark]*.

4 a) The muscles used to breathe get stronger *[1 mark]*.
       More small blood vessels are developed *[1 mark]*.
   b) i)   The amount of air you can breathe into your lungs in a single breath *[1 mark]*.
       ii) e.g. using a spirometer *[1 mark]*
       iii) E.g. there are other factors that affect the lung volume of Justin and Chris, such as their height or their age *[1 mark]*.

If you want an investigation to be a fair test, you should only change one thing, and keep all other factors the same. Otherwise you won't know what's actually affecting the results.

Page 28 (Warm-Up Questions)

1) sperm
2) Stage 1
3) a healthy mind
4) e.g. food/oxygen
5) E.g. the baby could be born early/quite small / the baby could have breathing problems.
6) True
7) e.g. lungs/brain/kidneys

Pages 28-29 (Practice Questions)

1 a) an egg *[1 mark]*
   b) the uterus/womb *[1 mark]*
   c) When the nuclei of the egg and sperm join *[1 mark]*.
   d) 39 *[1 mark]*

2 a)

name of organ	letter
sperm duct	A
foreskin	C
penis	B
scrotum	E
testes	D

[5 marks]

   b) the testes *[1 mark]*

3 a) e.g. solvents *[1 mark]*
   b) Any three from: movement/reproduction/ sensitivity/nutrition/excretion/respiration/growth *[3 marks in total — 1 mark for each correct]*
   c) E.g. the brain *[1 mark]* and the liver *[1 mark]*.
   d) Alcohol decreases brain activity *[1 mark]*.

Page 30 (Revision Summary for Section Two)

6) BER = 5.4 × 24 × 70 = 9072 kJ/day
You calculate BER like this:
5.4 × 24 hours × body mass in kg.

Section Three — Plants and Ecosystems

Page 35 (Warm-Up Questions)

1) Any two from, e.g. light / carbon dioxide / chlorophyll/chloroplasts / water.
2) E.g. they're broad and have a large surface area / they contain lots of chloroplasts / most of their chloroplasts are found in cells near the top of the leaf / the underside is covered in stomata
3) True
4) the ovule

Pages 35-36 (Practice Questions)

1 a) carbon dioxide *[1 mark]*, water *[1 mark]*, sunlight *[1 mark]*
   b) To attract insects for pollination *[1 mark]*.
   c) They would hook onto the fur of animals *[1 mark]*.

2 a) carbon dioxide + water → glucose + oxygen
       [2 marks — 1 mark for each side correct]
   b) E.g. the plants under the tree may have received
       less water/sunlight *[1 mark]*. This means they
       may not have been able to photosynthesise as
       much as the plants in the sunlight *[1 mark]*.
   c) The group in mineral-rich compost *[1 mark]*,
       because they will receive more of the minerals
       that they need in order to stay healthy *[1 mark]*.
3 a) E.g. the height the fruit is dropped from / where
       the experiment is done / the speed setting of the
       fan *[1 mark]*
   b) The sycamore fruit *[1 mark]*, because its shape
       helps it to be dispersed by wind / it has wings that
       help it to travel in the wind / it's lighter *[1 mark]*.
   c) E.g. animal dispersion/explosions/drop and roll
       dispersion *[1 mark]*
4 a) Jim is correct *[1 mark]*.
   b) A pollen tube grows out of a pollen grain into the
       ovary *[1 mark]*. The nucleus from a male sex cell
       inside the pollen grain moves down through the
       tube *[1 mark]* to the ovary, where it meets the egg
       cell *[1 mark]*.
*Don't be thrown by all the fancy names involved in
fertilisation — the process itself isn't that complicated really.*
   c) The fruit *[1 mark]*.
   d) E.g. to protect the embryo plant *[1 mark]*.

Page 39 (Top Tip Question)

Fewer pike means that fewer water beetles/minnows
get eaten. The more water beetles/minnows there are,
the more tadpoles will get eaten.

Page 40 (Warm-Up Questions)

1) True

2) Almost all energy on Earth comes from the Sun.
   Animals cannot make their own food from this
   energy. Therefore they rely on plants to capture and
   store the Sun's energy. This energy is then passed
   onto animals which eat plants and continues to be
   passed along food chains to other animals.

3) "food for" / which organisms are eaten by others / the
   direction of energy flow.

4) plankton → small fish → squid → whales

5) False
Animals are always consumers, not producers.

Page 40 (Practice Questions)

1 a) Geese
   b) E.g. the number of lemmings could decrease
       [1 mark], because there are fewer plants to feed
       them *[1 mark]*.
   c) E.g. fewer lemmings would be eaten by owls
       [1 mark], leaving more food for the jaegers
       [1 mark].
*If a species has plenty of food, then more of them will survive
and reproduce, increasing their numbers.*
   d) Toxic materials build up as they are passed along
       the food chain *[1 mark]*. The red foxes would be
       the worst affected because they are at the top of
       the longest food chain shown *[1 mark]*.
   e) Fewer lemmings would make jaegers and arctic
       foxes more dependent on geese for food, so more
       would get eaten *[1 mark]*.

Section Four — Inheritance, Variation and Survival

Page 46 (Warm-Up Questions)

1) False
Chromosomes are <u>long</u> lengths of DNA.

2) DNA

3) the environment (surroundings)

4) discontinuous variation
*Blood group can only be one of four types. You can't be
in between two types.*

5) Any two from, e.g. food/water/space

6) Scientists can store the genes of different species
   in gene banks so they might be able to create new
   members of the species if it becomes endangered or
   extinct.

Pages 46-47 (Practice Questions)

1 a)

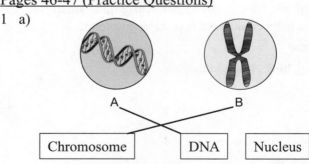

       [2 marks — one mark for each correct pair]

b) i) To provide instructions *[1 mark]* on how to build an organism *[1 mark]*.

   ii) two chains in a spiral *[1 mark]*

c) i) e.g. hair colour *[1 mark]*

   ii) e.g. hair style *[1 mark]*

   iii) heredity *[1 mark]*

2 a) i) There can be variation within a species *[1 mark]*.

   ii) Discontinuous *[1 mark]* because the ears can only be straight or floppy *[1 mark]*.

b) Rabbits with larger ears were able to hear **predators** *[1 mark]* better and avoid being eaten. This meant rabbits with larger ears were more likely to survive and reproduce and pass on their big ear gene to their **offspring** *[1 mark]*. Over time, the gene for big ears (and so the characteristic) became more **common** *[1 mark]*.

3 a) A species that is at risk of extinction *[1 mark]*

b) Any two from, e.g. food/clothing/medicines/fuel *[2 marks — 1 mark for each correct answer]*

c) Seeds from the endangered plant can be collected and stored in gene/seed banks *[1 mark]*. If the plant becomes extinct in the wild, new plants can be grown from the seeds kept in storage *[1 mark]*.

Section Five — Classifying Materials

Page 53 (Warm-Up Questions)

1) False

2) The energy of the particles increases.

3) solid

4) condensing

Pages 53 (Practice Questions)

1 a) Has a definite volume *[1 mark]*
Has a high density *[1 mark]*

b) E.g.

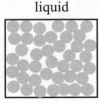
liquid

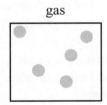
gas

[1 mark for each.]

Don't forget that there should always be more liquid particles than gas ones in diagrams like these.

c) i) The deodorant particles move from areas where there are lots of them to areas where there are less of them *[1 mark]*.

   ii) diffusion *[1 mark]*

Page 60 (Warm-Up Questions)

1) A substance that contains only one type of atom.

2) False
Periods go <u>across</u> the periodic table.

3) 4

4) B
No mass is lost or gained when a solute dissolves in a solvent, so the mass of the solution will be 10 + 200 = 210 g.

5) True

Page 60-61 (Practice Questions)

1 a) Salt will dissolve in the water because it is **soluble** *[1 mark]*. Sand will not dissolve in the water because it is **insoluble** *[1 mark]*.

b) Funnel *[1 mark]*

c) Filtration / filtering *[1 mark]*

d) E.g. by boiling the solution / by evaporating off all of the water *[1 mark]*.

2 a)

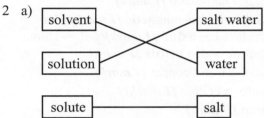

[2 marks for matching all 3 boxes correctly, otherwise 1 mark for matching at least 1 box correctly]

b) i) A — step 1, B — step 2, C — step 5, D — step 3, E — step 4
So correct order is A, B, D, E, C.
[2 marks for ordering all of the steps correctly, otherwise 1 mark for ordering any of C, D or E correctly]

   ii) E.g. she could boil the water and check that it boils at 100 °C *[1 mark]*.

3 a) B *[1 mark]*

b) A *[1 mark]*

Careful here — C is a mixture of an <u>element</u> and a compound, not a mixture of two compounds.

c) B *[1 mark]*

d) D *[1 mark]*

H_2O has two atoms of hydrogen and one atom of oxygen in each molecule. Both A and D show molecules with two of one type of atom and one of another. However, diagram A also contains another type of molecule, so it is impure.

Page 68 (Warm-Up Questions)

1) E.g. iron/nickel/cobalt.

2) a) metals
   b) non-metals
   c) metals
   d) non-metals

3) Any two from: e.g. good insulators of heat / good insulators of electricity / flexible / light/low density / easily moulded.

4) False
Concrete is made from a mixture of sand and gravel mixed in cement.

Pages 68-69 (Practice Questions)

1 a) i)   strong *[1 mark]*
       ii)   shiny when polished *[1 mark]*
       iii) good conductor of heat *[1 mark]*
   b) i)   No — you'd expect sulfur to be a poor conductor of energy by heating because it is a non-metal *[1 mark]*.
       ii)   Sulfur is **non-magnetic** *[1 mark]*. Its surface has a **dull** *[1 mark]* yellow colour. Sulfur is also **brittle** *[1 mark]*.

2 a) i)   sodium/iron/copper *[1 mark]*
       ii)   carbon/helium *[1 mark]*
       iii) iron *[1 mark]*
   b) The periodic table contains more metals than non-metals *[1 mark]*.

3 a) i)   E.g. a polymer/plastic *[1 mark]*
       ii)   E.g. metals are dense/heavy for their size. / Metals are not usually flexible *[1 mark]*.
   b) Ceramics are a good insulator of heat/don't conduct heat *[1 mark]*.
This means that it's harder for energy to be transferred from the hot drink to the hand holding the cup.
   c) i)   A material made from two or more materials stuck together *[1 mark]*.
       ii)   Strong *[1 mark]* and low density *[1 mark]*.
The low density means it will float on the water.

Page 70 (Revision Summary for Section Five)

8) a) Na   b) Mg   c) O   d) Fe   e) S
   f) Al   g) C   h) Cl   i) Ca   j) Zn

12)   hydrogen and oxygen

13)   calcium and chlorine

Section Six — Chemical Changes

Page 77 (Warm-Up Questions)

1) 92 g + 142 g = 234 g
The total mass after a reaction is always the same as the total mass before the reaction.

2) True
Catalysts aren't changed or used up in reactions, so they can be used again.

3) 14

4) True

5) a colour change

6) sulfuric acid
Sulfate salts are made from sulfuric acid and chloride salts are made from hydrochloric acid.

Pages 77-78 (Practice Questions)

1 a) In an endothermic reaction, energy is taken in from the **surroundings** *[1 mark]*. This is often shown by the temperature **decreasing** *[1 mark]*.
   b) i)   heat *[1 mark]*, fuel *[1 mark]*, oxygen *[1 mark]*
       ii)   iron + oxygen ⟶ **iron oxide** *[1 mark]*
Iron oxide is also known as rust.

2 a) thermal decomposition *[1 mark]*.
Thermal decomposition is when something breaks down when heated.
   b) E.g. the substance changed colour. / A gas was given off. / The temperature changed *[1 mark]*.

3 a) i)   lemon juice/wine/milk *[1 mark]*
       ii)   sodium hydroxide solution *[1 mark]*
       iii) water *[1 mark]*
   b) Lemon juice/wine/milk *[1 mark]*. Sodium hydroxide solution is an alkali and lemon juice/ wine/milk is an acid. Acids neutralise alkalis *[1 mark]*.

4 a) acid + alkali ⟶ **salt** + **water** *[1 mark]*
   b) E.g. he could take a small sample of the reaction mixture and add some universal indicator solution *[1 mark]*. If the indicator turns green / the pH is 7/neutral, then all of the sodium hydroxide has reacted *[1 mark]*.
If all the sodium hydroxide had reacted, the only substances in the reaction mixture would be the products (sodium chloride and water). They have a pH of 7.

5 a) There is 1 atom of nitrogen and 3 atoms of hydrogen in a molecule of ammonia *[1 mark]*.

b) $N_2 + 3H_2 \longrightarrow 2NH_3$ *[2 marks — 1 mark for each side of the equation correct]*

The question says that 2 molecules of ammonia are formed in the reaction, so you need to put a big 2 in front of the NH_3.

c) Catalysts increase the temperature of reactions *[1 mark]*.

Page 83 (Warm-Up Questions)

1) above
This means that potassium is more reactive than gold.

2) carbon/hydrogen

3) Carbon is less reactive/lower in the reactivity series than magnesium.

4) True
Iron is above hydrogen in the reactivity series, so will react with acids.

5) Zinc is less reactive / lower in the reactivity series than magnesium.

Pages 83-84 (Practice Questions)

1 a) Aluminium cannot be extracted from its ores using carbon reduction because carbon is **less** *[1 mark]* reactive than aluminium. This means carbon cannot **displace** *[1 mark]* aluminium from aluminium ores.

b) The removal of oxygen *[1 mark]*.

c) sodium *[1 mark]*, potassium *[1 mark]*
Carbon can only extract metals that are below it in the reactivity series. Sodium and potassium are both above carbon in the reactivity series, so cannot be extracted by carbon reduction.

2 a) In order, starting with the most reactive: lithium, magnesium, mercury.
[2 marks for correct order, otherwise 1 mark for one element in correct order.]

b) magnesium + hydrochloric acid
$\longrightarrow$ magnesium chloride + hydrogen
[1 mark]

3 a) E.g. he wore safety goggles/he stood the Bunsen burner on a heatproof mat *[1 mark]*.

b) i) copper oxide + zinc $\longrightarrow$ copper + zinc oxide *[1 mark]*

ii) displacement *[1 mark]*

The displacement reaction in this experiment is a bit odd because it involves solids (most of the ones you might come across tend to involve metal salts in solution). But don't be put off — it follows the same rules.

c) Zinc is less reactive / lower in the reactivity series than aluminium, so it would not displace aluminium from its oxide *[1 mark]*.

d) Yes, because metal oxides are alkaline *[1 mark]*, so will react with acids in neutralisation reactions *[1 mark]*.

Page 85 (Revision Summary for Section Six)

12) exothermic

13) endothermic

Section Seven — The Earth and The Atmosphere

Page 90 (Warm-Up Questions)

1) True

2) Element, compound, mineral, rock.

3) a metamorphic rock

4) E.g. weathering / erosion

Pages 90-91 (Practice Questions)

1 a) A — crust *[1 mark]*
B — mantle *[1 mark]*
C — core *[1 mark]*

b) The core / C *[1 mark]*

2 a) i) Igneous rocks *[1 mark]*

ii) melting *[1 mark]*

iii) When rocks are broken down into smaller parts *[1 mark]*.

b) i) (Layers of) sediment *[1 mark]*

ii) The layers of sediment are buried and compressed *[1 mark]*. The compression squeezes out the water from the sediment *[1 mark]*.

iii) The dead remains of plants and animals *[1 mark]*.

c) High heat and pressure turns a sedimentary rock into a metamorphic rock *[1 mark]*.

Page 95 (Warm-Up Questions)

1) E.g. plastic.

2) False
*Photosynthesis **removes** carbon dioxide from the air.*

3) Nitrogen

4) True

<u>Page 95 (Practice Questions)</u>

1 a) E.g. dead organisms/waste *[1 mark]*.
  b) i) respiration *[1 mark]*
    ii) carbon dioxide/CO_2 *[1 mark]*
2 a) 1. True *[1 mark]*
    2. True *[1 mark]*
    3. False *[1 mark]*
      Recycling isn't free, it just costs less than sending materials to landfill and making them again from scratch.
  b) It is important to recycle limited resources so that they don't run out *[1 mark]*.

<u>Section Eight — Energy and Matter</u>

Page 102 (Warm-Up Questions)

1) Any three from: e.g. kinetic/thermal/elastic potential/magnetic/electrostatic/chemical/gravitational potential
2) e.g. by light/heating
3) (the object's) kinetic energy store
4) it increases
5) True
Energy cannot be created or destroyed — it's only ever transferred from one store to another.

Pages 102-103 (Practice Questions)

1 a) When the torch is switched off, the energy is stored inside the **battery** *[1 mark]* in its **chemical** *[1 mark]* energy store.
  b)

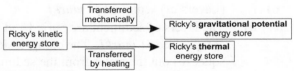

  [2 marks]
2 a) Energy in the **chemical** *[1 mark]* energy store of the coal is transferred **by heating** *[1 mark]* to the **thermal** *[1 mark]* energy stores of the room.
  b) Energy in the skydiver's gravitational potential energy store is transferred away mechanically *[1 mark]*.

3 a) electrically *[1 mark]*
  b) E.g. it was transferred to the blender's kinetic energy store/used to turn the blender's blades/given out as sound *[1 mark]*.
Remember — the seven possible energy stores are thermal, chemical, gravitational potential, kinetic, magnetic, electrostatic and elastic potential and the four ways of transferring are mechanically, electrically, by heating and by light or sound.
4 a) Her hand absorbs energy radiated by the hot cup *[1 mark]*.
  b) i) Conduction is where vibrating particles bump into other particles and transfer/pass on energy *[1 mark]*.
    ii) Plastic is an insulator *[1 mark]*. It slows down the rate at which the hot cup transfers energy to the table *[1 mark]*.

<u>Page 108 (Warm-Up Questions)</u>

1) the Sun
2) True
3) The amount of electrical energy transferred (in kWh).
4) Cost = energy transferred (kWh) × price per kWh

<u>Page 108 (Practice Questions)</u>

1 a) A non-renewable energy resource is one that will run out *[1 mark]*.
  b) Solar power *[1 mark]*
    Wave power *[1 mark]*
  c) Renewable resources won't run out but non-renewable resources will run out *[1 mark]*.
2 Cost = energy transferred (kWh) × price per kWh
    = 0.15 × 20 = 3p *[1 mark]*
3 a) The power rating of an appliance tells you how fast it transfers energy *[1 mark]*.
  b) 3000 J
The 60 W bulb transfers 60 × 60 = 3600 J
The 10 W bulb transfers 10 × 60 = 600 J
Difference = 3600 − 600 = 3000 J

<u>Page 112 (Warm-Up Questions)</u>

1) A physical change is when a substance changes from one state of matter to another.
2) False
Condensing is when a gas changes to a liquid.
When a solid changes into a gas, it is called sublimation.
3) Nothing/the mass stays the same.
When a substance changes state, its mass does not change.
4) True
5) Because the particles are constantly colliding with each other.

Page 112 (Practice Questions)

1 a) Diffusion *[1 mark]*
   b) Particles bump their way from an area of **high** *[1 mark]* concentration to an area of **low** *[1 mark]* concentration. They constantly bump into **each other** *[1 mark]* until they're evenly spread out through the gas.

2 a) The particles will move around more/speed up *[1 mark]*.
   b) There is more space between the particles of gas *[1 mark]*.

3 a) Ice is less dense than liquid water *[1 mark]*.
   b) 40 g *[1 mark]*

Remember, the mass doesn't change when a substance changes state.

Page 113 (Revision Summary for Section Eight)

4) The crane that applies the small force will lift the weight the furthest.

12) energy transferred = power (kW) × time (hours)
    = 1.5 kW × 1 hour
    = 1.5 kWh

14) cost = energy transferred in kWh × price per kWh
    = 298.2 × 15 = 4473p = £44.73

15) the 300 W device

The 300 W device has a higher power rating than the 200 W device, so it will transfer more energy.

Section Nine — Forces and Motion

Page 119 (Warm-Up Questions)

1) Speed = $\dfrac{\text{distance}}{\text{time}}$

2) e.g. m/s, mph or km/h

3) Speed = distance ÷ time = 180 ÷ 30 = 6 m/s

4) With a curve getting steeper / an increasing slope.

5) E.g. a force due to gravity/magnetism/static electricity.

6) False

The parachutist will slow down when his parachute opens, due to increased air resistance. He'll eventually reach a steady speed when air resistance becomes equal to weight.

Page 119-120 (Practice Questions)

1 a) The force due to gravity *[1 mark]*.
   b) i) The force causes the ball to change direction *[1 mark]*.
          The force makes the ball speed up *[1 mark]*.
      ii) E.g. it squashes/compresses the ball *[1 mark]*.
   c) i) Speed = distance ÷ time
          = 20 ÷ 0.4 *[1 mark]*
          = 50 m/s *[1 mark]*
      ii) air resistance/friction *[1 mark]*

2 a) The force between the engine and carriage was a **non-contact** *[1 mark]* force.
   b) E.g. the train will slow down *[1 mark]* because friction increases *[1 mark]*.
   c) i) 10 − 5 = 5 m *[1 mark]*
      ii) Time = 20 − 10 = 10 s
          speed = distance ÷ time
          5 ÷ 10 *[1 mark]* = 0.5 m/s *[1 mark]*
   d) i) 15 m *[1 mark]*

Read up from 40 seconds on the horizontal axis until you get to the line. Then read across to the time on the vertical axis. This shows that after 40 seconds the train was 15 m from the starting point.

      ii) 20 s *[1 mark]*

The model train is stationary when the graph is horizontal. So it's stationary between 40 and 60 seconds.

   e) The train is moving back towards its starting point *[1 mark]*.

Page 128 (Warm-Up Questions)

1)

Remember — the forces acting on something moving at a steady speed are balanced.

2) The forces are unbalanced (the forward force is bigger than the frictional force), so the motorbike is accelerating.

3) If the moments on an object are balanced, you know that: <u>anticlockwise</u> moments = <u>clockwise</u> moments.

You could write anticlockwise and clockwise the other way round here.

4) True

5) pressure = $\dfrac{1500}{0.3}$ = 5000 N/m² (or Pa)

6)   ↑ upthrust
     ●
     ↓ weight

The ball will sink.

<u>Page 128-129 (Practice Questions)</u>

1 a) kinetic *[1 mark]*, elastic potential *[1 mark]*

   b) 5 N *[1 mark]*

The spring is in equilibrium, so all the forces acting on it are balanced.

2 a) It will increase *[1 mark]*.

   b) upthrust *[1 mark]*

3 a) Moment = force × distance = 3 × 0.2 *[1 mark]*
      = 0.6 *[1 mark]* Nm² *[1 mark]*.

   b) Moment = force × distance = 1 × 0.6 *[1 mark]*
      = 0.6 *[1 mark]* Nm² *[1 mark]*

   c) Yes, the mobile is balanced *[1 mark]*. The clockwise moment is equal to the anticlockwise moment *[1 mark]*.

4 a) Maz and Pam apply the same force, but Maz applies it over a smaller area *[1 mark]*, so the pressure on the floor is greater *[1 mark]*.

   b) Pressure = $\frac{\text{force}}{\text{area}} = \frac{700}{0.0001}$ *[1 mark]*
      = 7 000 000 *[1 mark]* N/m² (or Pa) *[1 mark]*

<u>Page 130 (Revision Summary for Section Nine)</u>

3) Speed = $\frac{\text{distance}}{\text{time}} = \frac{5}{2} = 2.5$ m/s²

25) Pressure = $\frac{\text{force}}{\text{area}} = \frac{200}{2} = 100$ N/m² (or Pa)

27) The boat will float because weight is the same as upthrust.

Section Ten — Waves

<u>Page 140 (Warm-Up Questions)</u>

1) True

2) a) The waves join together to make a bigger crest.

   b) The waves cancel each other out.

3) False

A convex lens uses <u>refraction</u> (not reflection) to focus light.

4) dispersal

5) D

6) A blue filter lets blue light pass through it.

<u>Pages 140-141 (Practice Questions)</u>

1 a)

Tyrone's clothes	colour in red light	colour in green light
green T-shirt	black	green
blue jeans	black	black
white shoes	red	green

[4 marks — 1 mark for each correct colour]

Don't panic if you're asked about a situation you've not come across before. All you need to do is apply the rules you've learnt in this section to the question.

   b) In the white light, Tyrone's jeans appear to be **blue** *[1 mark]*. This is because the **blue** *[1 mark]* light is **reflected** *[1 mark]* by the jeans and all the other colours are **absorbed** *[1 mark]* by the jeans.

2 a) sensitive to light *[1 mark]*

   b) The cornea does most of the eye's focusing *[1 mark]*.

3 a) Paper has a rough surface *[1 mark]*. So light is reflected back in lots of different directions/ scattered *[1 mark]*.

Remember, this is called diffuse scattering.

   b) i) Specular reflection *[1 mark]*
      ii) 39° *[1 mark]*

Remember, angle of incidence = angle of reflection.

4 a) i) towards the normal *[1 mark]*
      ii) E.g.

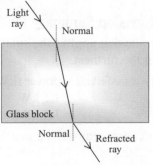

[1 mark for correctly drawing the path of the light ray.]

The light ray should bend towards the normal when entering the block, and bend away from the normal when leaving the block. To make this really clear in the ray diagram, it helps to draw the normals too.

   b) 300 000 000 m/s *[1 mark]*

<u>Page 146 (Warm-Up Questions)</u>

1) Longitudinal waves

2) False

Sounds waves can't travel without particles to vibrate, so it can't travel in a vacuum (where there are no particles).

3) E.g. carpets / curtains

4) Light

5) A high frequency

6) 20 Hz

7) The diaphragm

Page 146 (Practice Questions)

1 a) Sound usually travels faster through **a solid** *[1 mark]* than through **the air** *[1 mark]*. This means that Jim may hear the sound **after** *[1 mark]* he feels it through the floor.

  b) The sound reflected off the walls of the school hall / he's heard echoes of the sound *[1 mark]*.

2 a) i) It vibrates *[1 mark]*.

   ii) Hairs in the cochlea vibrate, sending a message to the brain *[1 mark]*.

  b) i) ultrasound *[1 mark]*

   ii) Ultrasound has a higher frequency/pitch than the normal auditory range of humans. / Ultrasound is sound with a frequency of over 20 000 Hz *[1 mark]*.

   iii) E.g. cleaning objects such as jewellery/false teeth *[1 mark]*.

Section Eleven — Electricity and Magnetism

Page 152 (Warm-Up Questions)

1) Potential difference/voltage

2) Ammeters measure current, voltmeters measure potential difference/voltage.

3) True

4) Ohms (Ω)

5) An insulator is a material that doesn't allow electricity to pass through it easily, e.g. wood (other answers possible).

6) a) 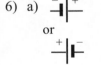 or

  b) E.g. ─⊗─   c) ─Ⓐ─

Page 152 (Practice Question)

1 a) A parallel circuit *[1 mark]*

  b) 0.40 + 0.25 = **0.65 A** *[1 mark]*

Remember the total current in a parallel circuit is the same as the current through each branch added together.

  c) i) It would stay on/nothing would happen *[1 mark]*.

   ii) It would go off *[1 mark]*.

  d) Bulb A will stay on because the electricity is still flowing through it / the circuit is still complete *[1 mark]*. Bulb B will go off because there is no electricity flowing through it / the circuit is broken *[1 mark]*.

Page 156 (Warm-Up Questions)

1) Electrons

2) The space around a charged object where other charged objects will feel a force.

3) They are attracted to/move towards each other.

4) True

Page 156 (Practice Questions)

1 a)

[1 mark]

  b) The field lines should point away from the North pole(s) and towards the South pole(s) *[1 mark]*

2 a) By closing the switch *[1 mark]*.

This completes the circuit, allowing current to flow through the copper wire.

  b) Increase the current through the wire. *[1 mark]* Increase the number of turns in the coil. *[1 mark]*

  c) E.g. the compass needle will move to align itself with the electromagnet's magnetic field. / The compass needle will experience a force due to having its own magnetic field and being in the electromagnet's magnetic field. *[1 mark]*

Page 157 (Revision Summary for Section Eleven)

11) 3 A

Section Twelve — The Earth and Beyond

Page 161 (Warm-up Questions)

1) (The force due to) gravity.

2) True

A light year is the distance that light travels in 1 year.

Page 161 (Practice Questions)

1 a) motion B *[1 mark]*.

As the Earth rotates, each place will be turned towards the Sun, then be turned away from it. While a place is facing the Sun, it experiences day, and when it is facing away from the Sun, it experiences night.

  b) the Universe *[1 mark]*

  c) one year *[1 mark]*

1 year is 365 days.

2 a) D *[1 mark]*

  b) B *[1 mark]*

3 a) The rover will have a smaller **weight** on Mars than on Earth *[1 mark]*. This is because the strength of gravity on Mars is **weaker** than it is on Earth *[1 mark]*.

   b) mass = 500 kg
   gravitational field strength = 3.7 N/kg
   500 × 3.7 *[1 mark]* = 1850 N *[1 mark]*

Page 162 (Revision Summary for Section Twelve)

8) weight = mass × gravitational field strength
   5 × 25 = 125 N

Section Thirteen — Exam Practice

Page 163 (Test 1)

1 True

2 B

3 C

4 increase

5 the core

6 Any two from: movement / reproduction / sensitivity / nutrition / excretion / respiration / growth.

7 E.g. stiff / brittle / good thermal insulators / good electrical insulators.

8 tissue

9 E.g. because no chemical reaction takes place. / Because no new substances are made.

10 D

Page 164 (Test 2)

1 True

2 sodium and water

3 E.g. the biceps and the triceps

4 A

5 E.g. protection/support/making blood cells/ movement.

6 B

7 D

8 A

9 Any two from: e.g. recycling uses fewer resources than creating a new item. / Recycling uses less energy than creating a new item. / Recycling is cheaper than creating a new item. / Recycling means less rubbish is sent to landfill.

10 C
When a circuit divides into two branches, the current will be divided between the two branches. But when the branches join up again, so does the current. So the current at point Y will be the same as the current at point Z.

Page 165 (Test 3)

1 False

2 A

3 The substance changes state from a liquid to a gas.

4 C

5 E.g. water waves/light waves.

6 It breaks down.

7 B

8 C

9 A biological catalyst
Remember, catalysts speed up the rate of chemical reactions. They are also not changed or used up in a reaction.

10 C

Page 166 (Test 4)

1 False
The law of reflection says that the angle of incidence equals the angle of reflection.

2 They have less energy.

3 B

4 An electromagnet

5 B

6 A

7 hereditary characteristics

8 C

9 The organisms need each other to survive.

10 D

Answers

Page 167 (Test 5)

1   False

Body weight can take any value, so is an example of <u>continuous</u> variation.

2   It is less reactive.

3   An animal that eats a primary consumer.

4   C

5   B

6   Simple distillation

Evaporation wouldn't work here, because the water would turn into a gas and escape. Simple distillation uses a condenser. This traps the gas and turns it back into a liquid, so that it can be collected.

7   20 000 Hz

8   C

9   D

Remember, energy transferred = power × time.

10 B

Page 168 (Test 6)

1   True

2   A

3   They decrease it.

4   B

5   Energy is taken in from the surroundings.

6   C

7   Yes

Objects float when the upthrust on them equals their weight. If the weight of an object is larger than its upthrust, the object will sink.

8   D

9   E.g. decreases brain activity/slows responses / damages the brain/liver / impairs judgement.

10 A

Pages 169-187 (Practice Exam)

1   a)

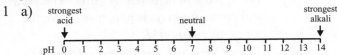

[1 mark for labelling of strongest acid at pH 0, 1 mark for labelling of strongest alkali at pH 14]

 b) i)   water *[1 mark]*

   ii)   green *[1 mark]*

2   a)   waterweed *[1 mark]*

 b)   If the number of water beetles in the lake decreases, the **perch** *[1 mark]* might get hungry. This means that they may start eating more minnows, so the number of minnows might **decrease** *[1 mark]*.

 c)   pike *[1 mark]*

Poison builds up as it's passed along the food chains. Pike are at the top of the food web, so will end up with the most poison built up in their bodies.

3   a)   cell *[1 mark]*

 b) i)   The flow of charge/electrons around a circuit *[1 mark]*.

   ii)   The current increases *[1 mark]*.

 c)   The circuit has a low resistance. Resistance **slows down** *[1 mark]* the flow of electrical current. Resistance is measured in **ohms** *[1 mark]*.

4   a) i)   X is the **stomach** *[1 mark]*.
     Y is the **liver** *[1 mark]*.

   ii)   the mouth *[1 mark]*

   iii)   To absorb water from food *[1 mark]*.

 b)

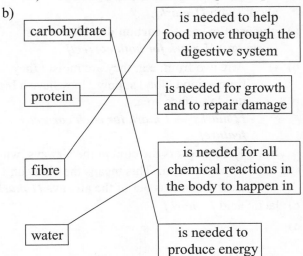

[2 marks for matching all 4 boxes correctly, otherwise 1 mark for matching at least 2 boxes correctly]

 c) i)   protein *[1 mark]*

If someone has a nutrient deficiency, it means they are not getting enough of a certain nutrient.

   ii)   e.g. scurvy *[1 mark]*

5   a)   W *[1 mark]*

 b) i)   Z *[1 mark]*

   ii)   Any two from: e.g. will conduct electricity/ an electrical conductor / a good conductor of energy by heating/a thermal conductor / strong/tough / shiny / sonorous / malleable / ductile / high melting point / high boiling point / high density / magnetic.
     [2 marks — 1 mark for each correct property]

200

6 a) i) B *[1 mark]*
    ii) C *[1 mark]*
    iii) A *[1 mark]*
  b) i) Bits of rock and dead remains of plants
         and animals are deposited in layers. These
         layers form **sedimentary** rocks *[1 mark]*.
     ii) **Metamorphic** rocks form when rocks
         experience high temperatures and pressures.
         This causes their structure to change
         [1 mark].

7 a) i)

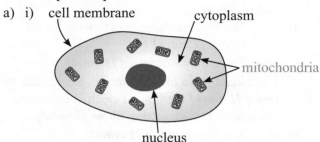

cell membrane   cytoplasm
mitochondria
nucleus
[3 marks — 1 mark for each correct label]
    ii) aerobic respiration *[1 mark]*
  b) To allow the Euglena to move
     about/swim *[1 mark]*.

8 a) **glucose** + oxygen → **carbon dioxide** + water
     (+ energy) *[1 mark for both correct]*
  b) i) Any two from: e.g. they are moist / they
         have a good blood supply / they have a big
         inside surface area.
         *[2 marks — 1 mark for each correct
         feature]*
     ii) The tar covers the cilia in the airways, which
         damages them. This means the cilia can't
         clear the mucus out of the airways *[1 mark]*.
  c) lactic acid *[1 mark]*

9 a)

mirror
normal --------- 45°
              45°
beam of light
*[1 mark for the angle between the normal and
the reflected beam labelled as 45°, 1 mark for
an arrow on the reflected beam to show that it's
moving away from the mirror.]*
*The reflected beam doesn't have to drawn at exactly 45° to
get the first mark here — you'll get the mark as long as the
angle is labelled correctly.*

b) retina *[1 mark]*
c) time = 10 minutes = 10 × 60 = 600 s *[1 mark]*
   power = 2.5 W
   energy transferred = power × time
                      = 2.5 × 600 *[1 mark]*
                      = 1500 J *[1 mark]*
   *[Or 3 marks for correct answer using another
   method]*

10 a) E.g.   After
             dissolving:

*[1 mark if the dye and water particles are spread
evenly throughout the solution]*
  b) i) simple distillation *[1 mark]*
     ii) He could measure the boiling point of the
         water *[1 mark]*. If the water boils at exactly
         100 °C, the water is pure. / If the water
         doesn't boil at 100 °C, it contains impurities
         [1 mark].

11 a) i) Brownian motion *[1 mark]*
     ii) The particles of smoke are colliding with
         each other (and air particles) *[1 mark]*.
  b) i) diffusion *[1 mark]*
     ii) The concentration of smoke particles at
         point X will decrease over time *[1 mark]*.
*This is because the smoke particles will move from an area
of higher concentration (in the container e.g. point X) to an
area of lower concentration (further from the container).*

12 a) Feature: e.g brightly coloured petals/scented
      flowers. / A sticky stigma.
      Explanation: to attract the bees. /
      To take the pollen off the bees.
      *[1 mark for any correct feature, 1 mark for a
      sensible explanation.]*
  b) i) The apple will fall from the tree and roll
         away from it *[1 mark]*.
     ii) The apple will be eaten by birds. The seeds
         will come out in their poo, away from the
         parent tree *[1 mark]*.
  c) The trees will produce fewer apples *[1 mark]*.
13 a) i) When the car is decelerating, the driving
          force is **less than** the drag *[1 mark]*.
     ii) When the car is accelerating, the driving
         force is **greater than** the drag *[1 mark]*.
     iii) When the car is moving at a steady speed,
          the driving force is **equal to** the drag
          [1 mark].

Answers

b) distance = 6.3 km = 6.3 × 1000 = 6300 m
   [1 mark]
   time = 120 s
   speed = distance ÷ time = 6300 ÷ 120 *[1 mark]*
   $\qquad\qquad\qquad$ = 52.5 m/s *[1 mark]*
   [Or 3 marks for correct answer using another method]

Your answer needs to be in m/s (metres per second). This means that distance has to be converted to metres before it's put into the speed equation.

14 a) i)   a compound *[1 mark]*
       ii)   Atoms of hydrogen: 2
              Atoms of oxygen: 2
              [1 mark for both correct]

  b) A reaction which transfers energy to the surroundings *[1 mark]*.

  c) A substance which speeds up a chemical reaction *[1 mark]*.

15 a) E.g. as the Earth rotates, any place on its surface will sometimes be facing the Sun and at other times facing away *[1 mark]*. A place experiences daytime when it faces the Sun and night time when it faces away from the Sun *[1 mark]*.

  b) i)   E.g. the northern hemisphere is tilted away from the Sun, but the southern hemisphere is tilted towards the Sun. The Sun will therefore feel warmer in the southern hemisphere *[1 mark]*.

    ii)   He will find that the daylight hours in the northern hemisphere are shorter than that in the southern hemisphere *[1 mark]*.

  c) weight = mass × gravitational field strength
            = 60 × 10 *[1 mark]*
            = 600 N *[1 mark]*
   [Or 2 marks for correct answer using another method]

Index

Index

Index